Lost Restaurants
OF
SEATTLE

Lost Restaurants
OF
SEATTLE

CHUCK FLOOD

AMERICAN PALATE

Published by American Palate
A Division of The History Press
Charleston, SC
www.historypress.net

Front cover, top, left: Fern Cafe staff. *Ballard Historical Society*; *center*: Ship-shaped with porthole windows and a lighthouse tower, everything was nautical at Skipper's. *Author's collection*; *right*: Two penguins danced atop the twin domes of the Igloo, at the corner of Aurora Avenue and Denny Way. *Seattle Public Library, spl_wl_res_00228*; *bottom*: The Twin T-P's as it looked in 1942, when it was part of Walter Clark's restaurant empire. *Museum of History and Industry, 1983.10.17115.1.*

Back cover, left: The menu for the Skillet, the successor to the Stratoplane, was naturally shaped like a skillet. *Author's collection*; *inset*: Ben Paris's location on Westlake Avenue was brightly lit with neon and a window display of sporting gear. *Author's collection.*

First published 2017

Manufactured in the United States

ISBN 9781467137041

Library of Congress Control Number: 2017940942

Notice: The information in this book is true and complete to the best of our knowledge. It is offered without guarantee on the part of the author or The History Press. The author and The History Press disclaim all liability in connection with the use of this book.

To Debbie

Contents

Acknowledgments

M any thanks to those who provided information, insight, moral support
and/or otherwise contributed to this project. They include:

Andy Yurkanin, for memories of the great restaurants and restaurateurs of
the 1950s and '60s

Phil Wong and Christina Gee, for recollections of Trader Vic's

Stephanie Graham, for describing the Polynesia in 1967

Paul Dorpat, Eric Lacitis and Jean Godden, for the use of images and
quotations

John Nicon and the Greek-American Historical Museum of Washington
State, for information about Greek restaurant owners and permission to
quote from that organization's website

Sherri King, Bartell Drugs Archives

Tony A. Johnson, chairman of the Chinook Indian Nation, for notes about
oysters and the role the Chinook and Lower Chehalis tribes played in
Washington's early oyster industry

Mary Henry, for insight into early black restaurant owners

Scott Farrar, for information about the Coon Chicken Inns

The *Seattle Times*, for permission to quote from articles

Nat Lund, John Hinterberger, Everett Boss and other culinary critics of
years gone by, for the stories they left us of meals enjoyed at restaurants
that have long since disappeared

Phil Stairs, Washington State Archives Puget Sound Regional Branch

ACKNOWLEDGEMENTS

Carolyn Marr, Museum of History and Industry
Jade D'Addario, Seattle Public Library
Julie Irick, Seattle Municipal Archives
Kris Kinsey, University of Washington Special Collections
Laura Cooper, Ballard Historical Society
Alicia Arter, Queen Anne Historical Society
Lissa Kramer, Southwest Seattle Historical Society
Vicki Stiles, Shoreline Historical Museum
Artie Crisp and Abigail Fleming, editors extraordinaire at The History Press

Images not individually credited are from my personal collection. Quotations not specifically attributed are from contemporary sources such as the *Seattle Times* and other early newspapers; business directories like Choir's Pioneer Directory of the City of Seattle and King County; and vintage advertisements and menus.

A few caveats: the term "restaurant," as used here, is purposefully broad. A restaurant can be anything from a hole-in-the-wall storefront to an upscale, elegant establishment in its own building. But restaurants weren't (and aren't) the only places to get a meal. From ancient times, inns and taverns have offered food along with lodging and drink. Over the years, a great variety of eateries—cafés, coffee houses, tearooms, grills, snack bars, lunch counters, diners, burger joints, hot dog stands, drive-ins and drive-ups—have sprung up to tempt appetites. There's not necessarily a clear distinction between these terms; in fact, individual businesses often changed their names to accord with the latest trends. For instance, Bob's Café at 101 Main Street, as it was known five years ago, might be called Jimmy's Diner today. Come back five years later, and it's the Main Street Grill.

It's not going to be possible to name all of the restaurants that have come and gone in Seattle; if they were all included, you would need a forklift to pick up this book. It's inevitable that someone's favorite restaurant will not have been mentioned. The objective is to illustrate the breadth and depth of Seattle's restaurant history with equal time given to downtown eateries and to those found in its neighborhoods and along its thoroughfares. Downtown may be the center of Seattle's universe, but that hub is surrounded by a constellation of neighborhoods. Many of them were once independent towns, and all of them have restaurant histories of their own. In fact, by the 1920s, the sheer number of neighborhood eateries outpaced what was available downtown.

Acknowledgements

Untangling the convoluted skein of Seattle restaurant ownership history, name and location changes and so on has been a challenge. The best efforts have been made to get things straight; if the intent hasn't been met, it's not for lack of trying.

Introduction

S eattle, the Emerald City: birthplace of Boeing and Bill Gates, home to Amazon, Starbucks and the Space Needle and a hotbed of innovative technology. Vibrant and alive, today, Seattle is considered one of the fastest-growing, most densely populated urban areas in the country.

It wasn't always so. In its early years, Seattle was just one of a dozen rain-swept settlements looking to become the commercial center of western Washington. Seattle wasn't the first town on Puget Sound—that claim belongs to Newmarket (today's Tumwater), the oldest permanent American settlement on the sound. Nor, for many years, was it the largest. For several decades after being settled, Seattle's population lagged far behind that of Portland, Oregon, 150 miles south and its main competitor on the west side of the Cascade Mountains. Even landlocked Walla Walla—230 miles to the southeast and from its early days benefiting from inland trade with miners, emigrants and farmers in the rich Palouse country—boasted more residents than Seattle in 1880 (3,588 and 2,533, respectively).

The original inhabitants—the Duwamish tribe and their ancestors—had occupied the region for at least four thousand years when the first Europeans arrived. Archaeologists state that as many as seventeen distinct native villages could be found in immediate vicinity of Seattle, generally close to rivers, lakes or the saltwater bays and coves.

The early European explorers of the north Pacific coast came, looked and left; they weren't interested in settling and generally spent little time in the area. In fact, the first mariners to visit the northern Washington coast—Spaniard Juan Pérez in 1774 and the renowned Englishman Captain James Cook in 1778—didn't even discover the entrance to the Strait of Juan de Fuca and the vast inland sea of Puget Sound; that was left to Captain Charles William Barkley in 1787. The Spanish established a fort named Núñez Gaona at Neah Bay in 1792 but abandoned it after four months. That same year, Captain George Vancouver thoroughly explored Puget Sound; his expedition conferred place names that persist to this day.

Though a few hardy pioneers preceded them, Seattle's birth is generally ascribed to a party of twenty-two men, women and children under the leadership of Arthur A. Denny who arrived at Alki Beach aboard the schooner *Exact* on November 13, 1851. In a short time, a village, pretentiously named New York, arose at the landing site. But the location lacked a deep-water harbor for mooring ships, so by mid-April 1852, most of the settlers had relocated to the eastern shore of Elliott Bay, about a mile away, which offered a better harbor. This new settlement was initially called Duwamps, for the local Duwamish tribe, but soon was renamed Seattle to honor Sia'hl, a Duwamish leader who had proven helpful to the early settlers. Chief Sealth, as he later became known, died in 1866.

By October 1852, Dr. David S. "Doc" Maynard had opened a store in the new town, and Henry Yesler was building a steam-powered sawmill, the first on Puget Sound, at the foot of Mill Street. The sawmill was a surefire business success given its surroundings—one early arrival observed that "the whole country around Seattle was a dense forest"—and logging rapidly became the mainstay of Seattle's economic life. Logs felled in the surrounding hills were dragged or "skidded" along the rough path leading to Yesler's mill. Legend has it that the path became known as Skid Road and eventually entered folklore as Skid Row, a term applied to the down-in-the-heels section of a city.

An 1860 description by Reverend Daniel Bagley, who arrived in Seattle with his wife, Susannah, in October that year, gives a picture of early Seattle. The town had 182 white residents. Commercial Street was four blocks long; its north end butted up against Yesler's sawmill at the foot of Mill Street, and its south end "jumped off into the bay." (Today, Mill Street is Yesler Way, and Commercial is First Avenue S.) Stores, hotels, saloons and shops clustered in a single row along Commercial between Mill and Main Streets; residences sprinkled the recently cleared hills above the shoreline. A few scattered farms could be found out in the woods. There were virtually no roads out of town—almost all travel was by water.

Seattle has the appearance of a typical raw frontier town in this 1879 view looking north along Front Street. *Seattle Public Library, spl_shp_15038.*

Seattle was incorporated in 1869; the following year, the census revealed a population of 1,107. In the 1880s, the city experienced remarkable growth and, by the end of the decade, was approaching a population of 16,000. By 1889, Seattle had shed much of its rough-and-tumble frontier town appearance. With its streets becoming lined with substantial brick and wooden buildings, its hills covered with attractive residences, its booming status as a supply point for other Puget Sound towns and a population approaching 18,000, Seattle was maturing into a sizeable city.

It took less than a day to erase most of it.

On the afternoon of June 6, 1889, a pot of glue boiled over onto the floor of a woodworking shop at the corner of Front and Madison Streets. The floor was covered with wood chips and turpentine, which immediately caught fire. Soon, the entire shop was ablaze. In a stroke of bad luck, the shop's two neighbors were saloons; once the fire spread to them, exploding bottles of alcohol added to the blaze and the entire block of Front Street between Madison and Marion was an inferno. By late afternoon, it was clear that downtown Seattle was doomed—inadequate water supply, hydrants placed too far apart and insufficient water pressure combined to make the fire unstoppable. Several buildings were dynamited in an effort to create firebreaks, but it did no good.

The fire burned until three o'clock the next morning, destroying anything combustible in its path. By the time it was over, twenty-nine city blocks—virtually all of downtown—were a smoking ruin, along with the railroad depots, most of the wharves and several nearby mills. The loss was estimated as high as $20 million (current value: about half a billion dollars). Among the casualties was the splendid Occidental Hotel, valued at $350,000 in 1889 dollars. (The year 1889, in which Washington became a state, also saw devastating fires at Cheney in April, Ellensburg in July and Spokane in August.)

By June 7, Seattle business leaders were already planning the city's recovery. Tent restaurants were set up to feed the hungry and shelters erected for the homeless. Rebuilding began almost immediately, with major changes made to the city's building code—no wooden buildings would be allowed in the burned-out area.

City engineers took advantage of the situation to fill in perpetually muddy streets to a depth of eight feet or more, with the second floors of surviving buildings becoming the new street-level entrances. The original street-level entries of businesses became buried, unintentionally creating a future tourist attraction. Half a century later, Seattle Underground began giving visitors the chance to tour some of the original storefronts.

The Southern Restaurant opened in a tent soon after the June 6, 1889 fire. *University of Washington Special Collections, SEA1201.*

Several other major events shaped Seattle's growth. Gold was discovered in Canada's Yukon Territory in 1896. The following year, when the steamship *Portland* arrived in Seattle with a ton of gold aboard, the city came down with a serious case of gold rush fever. As the gateway to the Yukon gold fields, Seattle's economy boomed; when miners returned (some successful, some not), many stayed in the city. By 1900, the city's population had reached nearly eighty-one thousand, nearly double the 1890 number.

A major earth-moving project known as the Denny Regrade saw several of Seattle's hills sluiced into Elliott Bay. The hills had been an obstacle to business growth north of the original downtown; the material filled in low areas south of the business district and created Harbor Island at the mouth of the Duwamish River. In 1909, the city hosted the Alaska-Yukon-Pacific Exposition to show itself off; people from all over the country came to visit, and many of them decided to call Seattle home. That same decade, Seattle annexed a number of neighborhoods that had once been independent towns—Ballard, Georgetown and West Seattle, among others—and by 1910, the city's geographical area had nearly doubled, with the population topping 200,000. Seattle was on its way to becoming a world-class city.

A LAND OF ABUNDANT RESOURCES

Logging may have been early Seattle's primary industrial reason for existence, but it wasn't the only one. In addition to trees, the region abounds in edible natural resources, and Seattle, sitting as it is on the edge of a great inland sea, wasn't long in exploiting them.

Fishing was important on Puget Sound as early as 1852, when salmon from the Duwamish River were being caught and packed for the San Francisco trade. Doc Maynard opened a salmon salting plant in 1853, starting a twenty-year tradition of Indians doing the fishing (mostly from local rivers) and whites doing the salting, packing and selling of the catch.

By the 1880s, river fishing was being replaced by open-water purse seining, resulting in an increased supply of fish for packers and, more importantly, justifying the need for canneries. Seattle emerged as the area fisheries center, as V.E. Tull moved his fish-pickling plant from Mukilteo to Seattle and Jackson, Myers & Company built the first local cannery in West Seattle. The Myers cannery burned in 1888 and again in 1891; reorganized as the Myers Packing Company, the firm built its own factory for manufacturing cans at the foot of Dearborn Street. Even with a capacity of making 40,000 cans per day, the cannery outstripped the supply of cans, as a crew of twenty whites, eighty Chinese and Japanese and an unstated number of women and girls packed 1,284 cases of locally caught fish per day.

Nonetheless, Seattle didn't become a leader in the salmon-canning industry. It took development of the deep-sea fisheries off Alaska and advances in refrigeration technology to catapult Seattle into the lead as a major fishing center. As early as 1888, boats laden with salmon, halibut and cod were plying the waters between Alaska and Seattle, but keeping the fish fresh in transit was an issue. By the mid-1890s, though, the problem was solved, and fresh fish were being efficiently transported not only on boats from the fishing grounds back to Seattle but also via railroad cars to markets all over the country. As is usually the case, improvements in technology led to increases in production. In 1890, 250,000 pounds of halibut were shipped; by 1896, the number had risen to 1,500,000 pounds.

Shellfish was also a major part of the seafood industry. Crabs, clams, oysters and mussels were harvested and shipped far and wide. Native oysters from Willapa Bay on the southern Washington coast were being shipped to San Francisco by 1851. In 1899, Eastern oysters were transplanted with success at Puget Sound and along the ocean. By 1910, the Puget Sound oyster beds produced five thousand sacks of oysters of excellent quality, and Washington oysters had become a regular menu item up and down the West Coast and inland as far as Denver.

Farming, however, was a different matter. Relatively little open land was available for farming when the first settlers arrived in Seattle. One such area was along the lower Duwamish River near present-day Georgetown, and by 1853, L.M. Collins's farm there was growing crops—"turnips weighing from twenty-three to thirty-five pounds each, potatoes as much as four pounds each, and onions two pounds each"—and also raising and selling apple, plum and cherry trees. By the 1880s, farms were popping up along the eastern shore of Lake Washington and other cleared areas.

Farming was key to the stable development and growth of the area; said one early writer, "Without farming there would not be large growth in other lines." But farming required timber to be removed and stumps to be pulled before crops could be grown, and in the immediate Seattle area, land was used for business and residences for the growing city as fast as it was cleared. Gradually, the rate of land clearing outpaced development, making small-scale farming possible; but then came troubles with the local tribes in 1855, which had a chilling effect on farm development. It's hard to envision today, but settlers living just outside the little settlement lived in fear of imminent attack by the Indians. The cause for the trouble was the usual: relations between white settlers and the tribes, initially friendly, deteriorated as immigrant arrivals increased and pushed the natives off their lands. The war—more like a skirmish—was part of a general uprising by the Puget Sound tribes and put down within year, with the tribes being on the losing side.

After peace was achieved, farms began to appear among the newly logged lands. But large-scale farming and ranching were almost out of the question. A search of 1860s Seattle newspapers finds scarcely a mention of the word "ranch," and virtually all early farms were small truck gardens producing enough for local needs with a bit to spare to ship to other markets. Many foodstuffs—whatever couldn't be sourced or grown locally—needed to be imported. This was particularly true for grain and livestock. Western Washington is too wet to support raising grain, and though individual farms certainly raised livestock such as cattle, pigs and chickens, not enough land was available to make it practical for large herds of cattle. Prices published in a September 1864 issue of the *Seattle Gazette* reflect the cost of living: potatoes were seventy-five cents per bushel; onions, two and a half cents per pound; cheese, twenty-five cents per pound; eggs, fifty cents per dozen; and butter, forty-five cents per pound. (One dollar in 1865 is about twenty-six dollars today.)

The coming of the railroads dramatically changed the transportation scene. By the 1890s, railroads—up and down the coast as well as transcontinental—linked Seattle to markets for its products. No longer did goods need to be moved solely by steamship, though the transpacific market soon became (and continues to be) a pillar of Seattle's economy. Then came the automobile and good roads, the federal highway system and the interstates, long-haul truckers and jetliners capable of handling huge amounts of freight. Whatever the dominant mode of transportation, Seattle has been at the center of it.

1

Pioneer Days

The idea of a restaurant as a self-contained, stand-alone business with chairs and tables, a service staff and a fixed menu is a relatively new concept. Opinions vary, but the consensus seems to be that the idea originated in late eighteenth-century France and gradually took hold in other countries. The first genuine restaurant in America, claimed to be Delmonico's in New York City, wasn't founded by John and Peter Delmonico until 1837.

Seattle's earliest eateries were often merely an adjunct to another business such as a boardinghouse, hotel or saloon. There doesn't seem to have been much difference between a boardinghouse and a hotel in the 1860s; the variations were qualitative (price and amenities) and quantitative (length of stay). In practical terms, they operated on the same principle: providing a lodging place and, optionally, meals. If offered, meals were usually on the European plan (covered in the overall cost of lodging) and almost always table d'hôte—whatever the kitchen was cooking that night, that's what you got.

It's generally agreed that the cookhouse at Henry Yesler's sawmill was the first public eating place in Seattle. Built in 1853, the cookhouse was originally intended for Yesler's millworkers but before long became the town's meeting hall, courthouse, jail, military headquarters, storehouse, hotel and church, as well as for a number of years "the only place along the east shore of the Sound where comfortable entertainment could be had."

The cookhouse, with its "weather-worn roof and smoke-blackened walls," was the domain of Yesler's wife, Sarah. It's not recorded what was on the cookhouse's menu, but if it was anything like its contemporaries in other cities, it wasn't haute cuisine. When it was demolished in 1866—the last remaining log building in downtown Seattle—the *Puget Sound Weekly* waxed nostalgic:

> *It was simply a dingy-looking hewed-log building about 25 feet square, a little more than one story high with a shed addition in the rear, and to strangers and new-comers was something of an eye-sore.....No man ever found the latch-string of the cook-house drawn in, or went away hungry from the little cabin door; and many an old Puget-Sounder remembers the happy hours, jolly nights, strange encounters, and wild scenes he has enjoyed around the broad fireplace and hospitable board of Yesler's cook-house.*

There is some disagreement about its location, but the best information places it on the west side of Commercial Street on the second lot south of Mill Street (today those streets are First Avenue S and Yesler Way). Once located nearly on Seattle's original waterfront, today the site is over six hundred feet inland.

Also dating to 1853 was Seattle's first true hotel, the Felker House, a two-story structure facing the water at the corner of Front and Jackson Streets.

Yesler's cookhouse, as it looked in 1866, the last log building in pioneer Seattle. *University of Washington Special Collections, SEA1352.*

The Felker House, Seattle's first real hotel, stood at Jackson and Front Streets. *SPL, spl_shp_22965.*

It was built by Captain Leonard Felker, a business partner of town father Doc Maynard but not a resident of Seattle. (San Francisco was his home.) Prefabricated back east and shipped around Cape Horn on Felker's brig the *Franklin Adams*, when assembled, it was hailed as "the first hard-finished house in the place…two-story, framed, and finished within in lath and plaster."

It was for a time a comfortable and respectable public house. But in the mid-1850s, one Mary Ann Conklin arrived in Seattle; the story is that she had sailed with her husband, Captain David Conklin, on his whaling ship to the waters off Alaska until he tired of her constant nagging and abandoned her in Port Townsend. Whatever the case, Mary Ann Boyer (having reverted to her original name) was soon presiding over the Felker House. Though it was said she ran an efficient hotel with clean rooms and good cooking (and a brothel upstairs), Boyer soon acquired the nickname "Mother Damnable" for her ferocious temper and ability to curse like a sailor in six languages: English, French, German, Portuguese, Chinese and Spanish. The Felker House's reputation took a downward turn, though it continued to hang on in spite of competition from newer, more sophisticated hotels until it was destroyed in the great fire of 1889.

Details of Seattle's first ten years of commercial life are sketchy (the first newspaper didn't appear until 1863), but it's believed that L.C. Harmon was operating a hotel—possibly called the Union—in 1860. Manuel Lopes, an 1852 arrival and the city's first black resident, was in charge of the kitchen. By 1864, Harmon had removed to the new, aptly named Seattle Hotel on Main Street between Commercial and Second Streets. Whether Lopes (sometimes spelled Lopez) accompanied him isn't known.

De Lin's hotel on Commercial Street also dates from this early period. Proprietor A.P. De Lin offered "comfortable rooms, good beds and a table always supplied with the best of every thing the market affords."

At the same time, the first of a series of Occidental Hotels opened on a triangular piece of ground at the junction of Mill and Commercial Streets. The original hotel, a wooden structure, was advertised as a "first class house" by proprietors M.R. Maddocks, John S. Condon and Amos Brown. "The culinary department is under the management of an experienced cook, and the table will always be supplied with the best in the market," said the same ad. By 1867, the Occidental had undergone three changes of ownership; under the management of A.S. Miller, six dollars bought room and board for a week. The wooden building was replaced by a grand brick structure in 1883; destroyed in the great fire of June 1889, it was soon rebuilt.

David Sires's What-Cheer House opened in 1865. Renamed the Sires Hotel later that same year, it was among the first Seattle hotels to operate on what it called the "restaurant principle." Though meals were at fixed hours—breakfast from 6:00 to 11:00 a.m., lunch from noon to 2:00 p.m. and dinner from 6:00 to 8:00 p.m.—persons arriving by boat were accommodated at all hours. The hotel boasted that "the table will always be supplied with the best the market affords, prepared and served up by an experienced cook." Sires didn't stay long in Seattle; in 1866, he moved to Port Townsend, a growing town forty miles to the northwest on the Olympic Peninsula, and operated the Pioneer Hotel there for many years.

By the 1870s, change was in the wind. Some hotels, such as the New England Hotel (run by the same L.C. Harmon who was in business in 1860) and the American House, continued to operate on the European plan. Newspaper ads, however, show that some hotels were starting to separate the businesses of serving meals and providing lodging. Also, by that time the idea of a restaurant as a distinct and separate business was starting to catch on. The Central Hotel, for instance, advertised lodging and meals separately: twenty-five cents per day for each.

Among the first to be billed as such was Matthias Monet's Seattle Restaurant and Coffee Saloon in 1864. Monet, an African American, arrived in Seattle from Oregon and was soon in business opposite Yesler, Denny and

Above: The elegant Italianate-style Occidental Hotel, as it looked circa 1885. *Author's collection.*

Left: An 1865 ad for Matthias Monet's Connoiseur's Retreat. *Seattle Weekly Gazette.*

CONNOISEUR'S RETREAT.

SEATTLE, W. T.

MONET & HEDGES, - - Proprietors.

The exigencies of the times induce the proprietors of this popular establishment to convert their Restaurant into a veritable

Oyster Saloon;

and having made arrangements to have a constant supply of the most choice

Olympia Bivalves

their patrons and the public generally can rest assured they will be served up in a style to suit the most fastidious.

In addition to the above, they will put up, in bottles of sizes to suit customers,

SPICED OYSTERS,

—ALSO—

constantly on hand, a supply of Fresh Oysters, opened for the immediate use of

FAMILIES AND HOTELS,

all of which will be sold at reasonable prices.

And, being as ever, grateful for past favors, the proprietors will spare no efforts to merit a continuance of patronage in their new pursuit.

Seattle, Oct. 21, 1865.   no21vo24f

Company's store on Commercial Street. In his newspaper ads, he stated, in the flowery language of the day, that due to his "long experience in the culinary art, he hopes to give general satisfaction, and to merit a share of the public patronage." By 1865, he had changed the restaurant's name to the Connoiseur's Retreat Oyster Saloon and Chop House and had taken on William Hedges as a business partner. The partnership didn't last long; by 1866, Monet was back to being the sole proprietor. He opened a hotel, the Railroad House, in 1869. It was apparently still in business at the time of the 1889 fire.

Restaurants sprang up at a rapid pace in the 1870s. The North Pacific Chop House and Coffee Saloon opened in 1872, offering chicken, ham and eggs, pig's feet, oysters and sardines at all hours—day and night—at fifteen cents and up. Owners M. Walker and A. Castro promised to always have on hand "meats and fish of every description, the best variety the market affords." Two restaurants with similar names—the Bank Exchange and the American Exchange—were in competition with each other the following year. William Rickards, who appears frequently in notices of early Seattle restaurants, had been associated with the Bank Exchange, a saloon-turned-restaurant; in 1873, he set himself up in business as the American Exchange, "a fine restaurant and oyster saloon for ladies." It's not explicitly stated but apparently understood that ladies did not venture into restaurants—let alone saloons—of that day, so Rickards's establishment of a female-friendly eating place was unusual.

William Grose (sometimes spelled Gross) opened Our House Restaurant in August 1876. Grose, an African American born in Washington, D.C., had arrived in Seattle in 1861; his wife, Sarah, and daughter Rebecca joined him soon after, becoming Seattle's first female black residents. Grose's restaurant/boardinghouse on Mill Street advertised meals and beds for twenty-five cents each. A successful businessman (he also owned a barbershop and dealt in real estate), Grose was the city's wealthiest black resident by the 1890s.

Manuel Lopes, Matthias Monet and William Grose were some of the earliest of Seattle's black restaurateurs but not the only ones. In 1889, John Randolph opened a café after the fire, and James Orr followed suit in 1890. In the 1890s, Thomas C. Collins and Allen Dean operated Collins and Dean's Restaurant, and two black women, Olivia Washington and Elizabeth Thorne, managed successful cafés on the eastern edge of the city.

The Saddle Rock Chop House and the Puget Sound Refreshment Room made their appearance in 1877. Van Wie & Knudson of the Saddle Rock Chop House ("chop house" was the common name for what we would today

Saddle Rock Restaurant

AND

OYSTER SALOON.

CHAS. KEIL, - - Proprietor.

BEST of FARE

On Short Notice.

Table Supplied with the Best
the Market affords.

Commercial Street,

SEATTLE, W. T.

Open Day and Night!

The Saddle Rock Restaurant opened in 1877 and was rebuilt after the June 6, 1889 fire. *Choir's Pioneer Directory.*

call a steakhouse or grill) promised "the best of fare on short notice." Charles Keil took over in the following year and upgraded the name to the Saddle Rock Restaurant. It was located on Commercial Street. The name is a bit of a puzzle since there's no geographic place called Saddle Rock in the vicinity of Seattle.

Trumpeted the Puget Sound Refreshment Room, "Ye Strangers! and all who feel weak and want to be restored! Know Ye! That you can have your spirits resuscitated, and the inner man satisfied" by visiting that restaurant, where "steaks, chops, and all the delicacies of the season are served in the best New York style," along with fresh candies and fine cakes.

The Maison Doree Restaurant also came along in 1877. Originally operated by Jacob Knudsen, it was sold to Horace Downs in 1879. A few years later, W.C. DeLong was running the Maison Doree lunch counter, "a first class chop house where anything desired will be cooked to order…

Spanish style cooking a specialty." By the time the restaurant took out a full-page ad in the 1890 Seattle city directory, it clearly had pretensions of being upper-crust: R.J. Stahmann, the proprietor, declared the Maison Doree "the best appointed restaurant, strictly first-class, ladies', gents' and family restaurant in the city," with catering for private dinners, receptions, weddings and a host of other special occasions a specialty. The menu featured "all kinds of fancy salads, cakes, pies, patties and ice cream," and the service staff spoke French, German and Italian.

THE ALMIGHTY OYSTER

Whether the bivalves are boiled, broiled, steamed, roasted, fried or served in pies, soups or stews, people love oysters. Apparently we always have—the ancient Greeks and Chinese, among others, were noted oyster connoisseurs. They were considered an upper-class privilege in renaissance Europe, but by the eighteenth century, the common masses had developed a taste for them, the first public oyster bar opening in England in 1738.

In America, where the oldest oyster bar is the Union Oyster House (1826) in Boston, oysters have always been a class-neutral food. Found abundantly along the Atlantic and Pacific coasts, they were commonly served in taverns; oysters were viewed as cheap food to serve with beer and liquor. By mid-century, oyster bars, cellars, parlors and saloons had become common in towns throughout the country.

In 1862, the French government sent Lieutenant P. DeBroca to the United States to study the state of the oyster fisheries. In his report, DeBroca wrote:

> *This delicious article of food has become so necessary with every class of the population that scarcely a town in the whole country can be found without its regular supply. By means of railroads and water channels, oysters in the shell, or out of the shell, preserved in ice, in pickle, or canned, are carried even to the remotest parts of the United States....It is considered one of the most common and cheap means of subsistence.*

Luckily for the hungry masses, oysters generally traveled well. Early newspapers recount shipments of oysters by the wagonload from the Atlantic coast over the Allegheny Mountains. Oysters could be prepared for shipments in a variety of ways: canned ("tinned"), "spiced" (the oysters opened; boiled with spices such as nutmeg and black pepper; vinegar and oyster liquor added; and sealed tight in earthenware or glass vessels), salted or pickled in barrels or fresh in the shell—the preferred method, though packing to prevent spoilage was always a concern.

The decade of the 1870s found America in the grips of a full-blown oyster craze. It's estimated that the total value of all U.S. fisheries in 1880 was $43 million, of which nearly a third—$13 million—was oysters. Americans were eating an average six hundred oysters a year, and the oyster beds along the Atlantic coast were being rapidly depleted.

Seattle and the West Coast weren't immune to the craze. The oyster indigenous to the Pacific coast, *Ostrea lurida* (often called the Olympia oyster), had been a significant part of the local diet and economy since earliest times. Native Americans gathered oysters, ate them fresh or dried them and used them in trade. Even before Seattle came into being, the oyster trade between the Pacific Northwest and San Francisco was well underway.

Among the early centers of the oyster industry was Shoalwater Bay, today called Willapa Bay, a broad, shallow bay with long reaches of mudflats creating ideal conditions for shellfish. (The town of Oysterville, established in 1854 and the first county seat of Pacific County, sits near the Pacific entrance to Willapa Bay.) Oysters were first shipped from Shoalwater Bay to San Francisco, a city with an insatiable appetite for the mollusks, in 1850. The first shipment spoiled en route, but the next attempt succeeded and a market was born. The gathering was done by members of the local Chinook and Lower Chehalis tribes, who were paid one dollar in gold per bushel of oysters; the same bushel sold for seven dollars in San Francisco. The trip by schooner could take up to two weeks, and since nearly all oysters from the Northwest were shipped fresh, spoilage en route was a danger.

By the 1880s, native oyster beds, including Shoalwater Bay and those at the southern end of Puget Sound near Olympia, had been over-harvested. Experiments with transplanted oysters had proven successful in Chesapeake Bay and elsewhere back east; the oyster beds had nicely rebounded, and as the supply increased, much of the West Coast trade was lost to oysters shipped from the East. It took a few years for the idea of seeding local oyster beds to catch on in the Northwest. Late 1870s efforts to introduce the larger Pacific oyster from Japan finally proved practical in 1902, and by the 1920s, the beds were well on their way to recovery.

In Seattle, oysters seemed to be associated with saloons. The very first issue of the *Seattle Gazette* in December 1863 carried ads for two such places.

The Exchange Saloon, established in 1858 on Commercial Street and run by A.G. Terry & Company, described itself as "a quiet and pleasant resort for the public" that served wines, liquors, ale and cider with fresh oysters kept on hand at all times and "served in every style." At A.B. Rabbeson's Fashion Saloon, located next to Yesler and Denny's store, W.J. Burns operated an oyster stand that sold hot coffee, cakes and oysters "in every style" (which seemed to be a popular phrase of the day). By 1866, the oyster stand had been taken over by R.R. Smith, who, besides selling prepared oysters to the saloon's customers, also sold them fresh from the boat to hotels, restaurants and private families.

In 1865, J. Summers opened an oyster stand in Thayer's Saloon on Commercial Street and promised a good supply of fresh oysters, "in readiness to serve them up in very desirable style." The Gem Saloon on Commercial Street sold oysters, as did the saloon of L.J. Keach in 1871. In 1876, the Puget Sound Confectionery Store boasted that it had served 5 million oysters the past season. Considering that Seattle's population was about 2,500 at the time, each man, woman and child in town consumed about 2,000 oysters that year if the claim were true. Piper's Saloon opened in August 1877, advertising oysters "served in a No. 1 Style" almost daily before abruptly disappearing six months later. (By 1882, the oyster saloon had morphed into Piper's Ice Cream Restaurant.)

A Period of Growth

The restaurant boom continued into the 1880s. The Wisconsin Restaurant, Daniel Pfieffer's Seattle Restaurant, Wright's Bakery and Restaurant, the Aldus Restaurant and the Dirigo Chop House, among many others, all opened early in that decade. Many were oriented toward the working class, though a few of higher refinement (basically meaning family-oriented) started to appear.

Frank Telle opened the Seattle Restaurant in 1876 at the rear of the Seattle Saloon. A few years later and with a new owner, Daniel A. Pfieffer, it relocated to Mill Street near the steamboat landing. Mrs. Pfieffer was in charge of the dining room, where meals were twenty-five cents a day; overnight lodging was the same price. J. McConville's Wisconsin Restaurant, on Mill Street near Occidental Square, also provided room and board for forty cents a day. Mrs. M.J. Wright offered both meals

The Occidental Hotel, in ruins the day after the great fire. *Seattle Public Library, spl_shp_23112.*

and baked goods (wedding cakes were a specialty) at her bakery and restaurant.

One of the relatively few high-class restaurants of the time was the Brunswick, located in the hotel of the same name. Owned by William Henry Tointon, the Brunswick served refined fare such as soups, salads and fish. By 1888, the Brunswick restaurant had been supplanted by the Delmonico, which modestly advertised itself as "the best in the city, and [having] no superior in Washington Territory. As a family restaurant it is simply perfect, having a family saloon or ladies ordinary." The Delmonico was under the management of William Rickards, who by that time had been involved in Seattle restaurants for nearly twenty years.

Sanborn's insurance maps of 1888 show thirty-nine restaurants and six hotel dining rooms downtown, along with an astonishing fifty-eight saloons. Mill, Commercial and Washington Streets were lined with restaurants and saloons; on the lower part of Mill Street alone, twelve places vied to attract hungry and thirsty workers leaving their jobs at Yesler's Wharf.

Within a year, they had all disappeared—victims of the great fire of 1889.

REBUILDING

While the city leaders looked at the fire as something of a blessing in ridding downtown of a helter-skelter growth of unplanned, unsanitary and flimsy wooden structures, it's doubtful that all the businesspeople who lost to the flames would have agreed. Only a handful of the burned-out restaurants reappeared after the fire—the Saddle Rock, Delmonico and Maison Doree among them—and almost all of them were rebuilt in new locations.

Maison Doree, previously on Commercial Street, relocated to 1403 Union Street. The Saddle Rock Restaurant, also originally on Commercial, moved to 108 Main Street. The Delmonico relocated to 116 Pike Street and, in doing so, lost its connection with the Brunswick Hotel—a void soon filled by a new restaurant run by Roderick Chisholm.

Chisholm's place, which he called the Delicate Esson Dining Palace, was one of dozens of eating establishments that had sprung up to take the places of those lost to the fire. The 1890 city directory listed over 100 restaurants (plus nearly 150 saloons). Chisholm also opened Chisholm's Dairy Lunch at 905 Front Street, the former location of the Brunswick Restaurant. Another new restaurant was the Snohomish, owned by Margaret Isaacs and open day and night with private booths for ladies. The Orth House Restaurant was in the newly built Orth House, "a first class lodging house." In his advertisements, proprietor S. Blackburn reiterated an unfortunate sentiment of the times: "None but white labor employed."

Maison Barberis, formerly known as Maison Tortoni, moved into its James Street quarters in 1900 as a fine-dining restaurant with an attached quick lunch counter. Full-course dinners were served in elegant style in the main dining hall from 5:00 until 9:00 p.m. at a price ranging from fifty cents for a four-course dinner to one dollar for a twelve-course dinner, including wine. In addition to the main hall, twenty-five small rooms were available for banquets and private parties. The lunch counter was open day and night with quick service at moderate prices. The main restaurant and lunch counter shared the same kitchen, ensuring uniform quality at both places.

Another turn-of-the-century restaurant was the Poodle Dog at 208 Washington Street. Owned by S. Bisazza, its ads repeated many of the familiar phrases of its predecessors: the table was always supplied with the best the market afforded; oysters were available in every style; everything was new, neat and first-class; and private rooms were available for ladies. With so many restaurants claiming these lofty qualities, dining out in Seattle was in good hands as the new century began.

THE ALASKA-YUKON-PACIFIC EXPOSITION

Seattle threw a party in 1909 and invited the world to visit. The nominal reason was to celebrate the Yukon gold rush. It was originally scheduled to be held on the ten-year anniversary of that event in 1907, but a competing world's fair, the Jamestown Exposition, led to it being pushed back a few years. In reality, the fair was Seattle's way of announcing to the world that it was a major city and an economic powerhouse to be reckoned with.

The fair was held on the campus of the University of Washington, at that time still a forested area rather distant from downtown. The Olmsted brothers, famed landscape architects, laid out the grounds; buildings were designed by Howard and Galloway, a San Francisco architectural firm. Unlike more recent world's fairs in which a multitude of countries erected exhibits, the A-Y-P's only significant foreign contributors were Canada and Japan; everything else highlighted the Pacific Northwest, its industries, resources and scenic beauty.

The Palm Cottage at the Alaska-Yukon-Pacific Exposition was in the Pay Streak, the entertainment section of the fair. *University of Washington Special Collections, AYP570.*

The fair's Nikko Café was an authentic replica of a Japanese temple. *University of Washington Special Collections, AYP576.*

A citywide holiday was declared on the fair's opening day, attended by at least eighty thousand people. It is claimed that William Boeing saw his first heavier-than-air flying machine while attending the fair as a teenager; his fascination with aircraft led to creation of the Boeing Airplane Company ten years later.

Of course, the fair had restaurants to serve the hungry crowds. Most were located in the fair's entertainment area, the Pay Streak (a miner's term for a rich vein of ore). There were ice cream and lemonade stands, the Vienna Café and the Washington Restaurant. Real estate dealer Corinne Simpson operated two places on the Pay Streak, the Oriental Café and the Palm Cottage Café. More elegant was the Nikko Café, a high-class restaurant designed as a replica of the famous Nikko Temple with dining rooms handsomely decorated by Japanese artists. Its proprietors were Yumeto Kushibiki and Shukich Kondo; J.R. Boldt, the manager, later went on to open Boldt's Cafeteria in downtown Seattle.

After the fair ended, the University of Washington inherited the landscaped grounds and some of the buildings; though many of the structures were intended to be temporary, a few survived and were used by the university for a number of years. Only two of them—the Fine Arts Palace and the A-Y-P Women's Building (now called Architecture Hall and Cunningham Hall, respectively)—remain today.

2
Downtown

For a city with a population of over 650,000, Seattle has a compact central business district. Definitions vary, but the area—bounded by Jackson Street at the south end, Stewart Street on the north and First Avenue and the I-5 interstate west and east, respectively—takes up a relatively small sixty blocks. On the edges of these boundaries lie residential neighborhoods and industrial areas; beyond them are districts such as Ballard or West Seattle, which once existed as separate towns, many of them still preserving their own "downtown" areas; and then start the suburbs, where the bulk of Seattle's residents live, with the attendant strip malls and shopping centers.

It's important to recognize that until the 1960s and the rise of shopping malls on the outskirts of the city, downtown Seattle was a lively and vibrant place after work hours. Stores often stayed open until 9:00 p.m. on weekdays, as shoppers either remained in town after their workday was done or came into the city from outlying areas in pursuit of goods and services that their neighborhood merchants couldn't supply. Theaters were another major draw, not to mention the nightlife of cabarets and shows and eateries of every variety—from humble take-away lunch counters to upscale, elegant dining rooms—that stayed open to attract hungry customers.

The traveling salesman stepping off the train at King Street Station circa 1910, the family cruising through the city along the new Pacific Highway in the '30s, the visiting professor checking into her downtown hotel fresh from arriving at Boeing Field in 1951—none of them would have had a problem finding a place to eat within short walking distance and at practically any hour of the day or night. Numbers are hard to come by, but a rough estimate is that in 1940, First Avenue (just to pick one street) had nearly sixty restaurants of various types between Stewart Street and Olive Way. By the 1950s, the number was down a bit to about fifty; today, it's probably less than two dozen (not including franchise take-away places). It's a certainty that in the 1940s, downtown Seattle had more restaurants open all night and day (or at least until 2:00 or 3:00 a.m.) than it does today.

Like many other cities, Seattle is experiencing a resurgence of downtown living, as previously neglected areas are rediscovered and developed to appeal to those who don't take to suburban life. Along with apartments and condos, restaurants are coming back to places they had long since left. But all things considered, Seattle has a long way to go to catch up to the multitude of cafés, restaurants, coffee shops, lunchrooms, confectioneries, soda fountains, burger joints and take-away places that downtown could boast of fifty years ago.

After the Fire and the Start of a New Century

One of the first restaurants established after the great fire was McGinty's Chop House. Originally located down on the docks, by 1902, McGinty's was on First Avenue, later moving to 224½ Pike before finally ending on the docks again by 1913. R.C. Byers was the owner, proprietor and cook. His small place—just eleven stools—drew customers from among the stevedores, truck drivers, ship hands and even captains and passengers who frequented the dock area. A bowl of stew at McGinty's cost fifteen cents; clam chowder was just ten cents. Waffles, pancakes and pastries were also available.

Peter Hallberg, a native of Sweden, set foot in Seattle as a sailor in 1888. Deciding that life at sea wasn't for him, he worked for three years at the Union Bakery on Pike Street before purchasing and running it as the Union Cafe and Bakery. By 1909, Hallberg had relocated up the block to 217 Pike, retaining the name, and in 1915, he opened a bakery under his own name at 511 Pine Street. After Hallberg passed away in 1922, the two operations were renamed Hallberg's Bakery & Restaurant. The Pike Street location closed within a few years, but Hallberg's on Pine kept serving up hearty meals for another four decades. When Hallberg's closed in 1960, it was hailed as Seattle's oldest restaurant (a claim disputed by Merchant's Lunch in Pioneer Square, established in 1890 and still going strong today).

A 1930s menu gives a glimpse of Hallberg's fare: five different cuts of steak, lamb and pork chops, prime rib, breaded veal or pork cutlets, grilled halibut and oysters served half a dozen different ways. Full dinners were available from 5:00 until 10:00 p.m. There were thirty different choices of entrée, including seafood, chicken, steaks and pork chops ranging in price from a low of $0.90 (potato pancakes with bacon and gravy) to $1.75 for a grilled top sirloin steak. Each dinner included chicken and rice, soup or clam chowder, apple perfection salad, shoestring or whipped potatoes, a vegetable and choice of dessert.

In 1899, soon after arriving in Seattle from Salt Lake City, the Manca brothers—Angelo and Victor—purchased a small storefront restaurant for $1,000. They gutted the place, completely renovated and re-equipped it and opened Manca's Cafe at 207 Cherry Street. Immediately popular, the café was packed to the doors from the day it opened. Manca's moved to 108 Columbia Street in 1903 to begin a fifty-year tenancy. After Angelo died at a relatively early age, Victor and his sons and relatives continued the business. Victor semi-retired in 1944; sons Vincent and Eugene ran the restaurant until 1955, when the building was razed.

For many years, Manca's had a national reputation for its fine cooking. The Mancas originated several specialties that have since been copied all over the country: Dutch Baby pancakes, Oysters Manca, Eggs Vienna and Combination Salad. Manca's once owned the trademark for Dutch Babies, a type of deep-dish pancake based on an old German recipe. It's told that a female visitor to Seattle from Washington, D.C., was asked by an army official to "go to Manca's and get some Dutch Babies and eat a couple for him."

With its tiled entrance, decorative oval-shaped glass panes, red leather seat cushions and fluted light fixtures, Manca's was perhaps the epitome of Seattle's old-style cafés. Victor Manca, still involved in the restaurant well into his eighties, always kept the place small so (as he said) he could have his hand on every detail. Famous visitors over the years included Sarah Bernhardt, Eleanor Roosevelt and Martha Wright, the Seattle-born star of the Broadway musical *South Pacific*.

Manca's last day of business was August 19, 1955. Even as the building was being demolished, Victor Manca was discussing plans to relocate, but it didn't happen; he passed away in 1958. Thirty-five years later, though, a new Manca's arose in Madison Park. Run by Victor's grandson Mory Manca and several great-grandchildren, it thrived for a few years before becoming a Starbucks in 1998.

For fifty years, Manca's Cafe anchored the corner of Cherry Street and Second Avenue. *MOHAI,* Seattle Post-Intelligencer *Collection, 1986.5.11377.1.*

The Manca family's recipe for Dutch Baby pancakes was and remains a secret, but this one comes close:

Dutch Baby Pancakes

3 large eggs, room temperature
⅔ cup whole milk, room temperature
⅔ cup all-purpose flour
¼ teaspoon pure vanilla extract
⅛ teaspoon cinnamon
⅛ teaspoon grated nutmeg
⅛ teaspoon salt
½ stick unsalted butter, cut into pieces (it works just fine with 2 tablespoons, but not less than that)
Powdered sugar
Juice of ½ lemon
Berries or other seasonal soft fruit

Preheat the oven to 450°. Beat eggs until pale and frothy. Beat in milk, flour, vanilla, cinnamon, nutmeg and salt and continue to beat until smooth, about 1 minute more to create a thin batter.

Heat the skillet in the oven on the middle rack for about 10 minutes; test it after 5 minutes by dropping a bit of butter in the bottom—if it sizzles, the pan is ready. Add butter to hot skillet and melt, swirling to coat. Add batter and immediately return skillet to oven. Bake until puffed and golden-brown, 18 to 25 minutes. Serve immediately, dusted with powdered sugar, lemon juice and berries.

Eggs Vienna

4 slices bacon
2 eggs
2 cups milk
2 slices white bread or English muffins
Butter

Prepare four slices of streaky American-style bacon until they are crisp. Poach two eggs in two cups of boiling milk, until they are soft. Toast two slices of white bread or English muffins, then butter them.

Place one piece of toast in each of two soup-bowls. Place two slices of bacon on top of each piece of toast, then top that with a poached egg. Pour the remaining hot milk, in which the eggs have been poached, into each bowl. Serves 2.

In 1903, Clarence Gerald, a recent arrival from Butte, Montana, started a "first class restaurant" at 824 First Avenue. Described as "one of the best appointed and equipped grill rooms on the Pacific coast," Gerald's Cafe was a long, narrow establishment; the front portion, "arranged exclusively for men," featured a long counter with mirrored back bar behind and seats (but no tables) against the opposite wall. At the rear of the restaurant was a brilliantly lighted room furnished with small tables "splendidly installed for ladies and those men who prefer to eat in this fashion." Gerald's soon became a favorite gathering place for local politicians and wheeler-dealers. A 1911 fire caused extensive damage, as did another in 1924. After Clarence Gerald's death in 1917, operation of the café passed to his widow, Clara, and cousin John. In February 1929, Gerald's relocated to 423 Seneca,

This 1914 view of Lyons' Cafe shows the typical arrangement of that time: counters and stools on one side, tables against the opposite wall. *Seattle Municipal Archives, 132.*

opposite the Olympic Hotel; the new Gerald's, "one of the finest restaurants in Seattle, with its ample space and beautiful dining compartments," would feature Puget Sound shellfish and seafood, chops, steaks and "everything that is good to eat." The café survived for only a short time at its new address; a victim of the Depression, it was gone by 1932. Wood's Cafe, which had moved into Gerald's original First Avenue location, didn't fare any better.

Lyons' Cafe on Yesler Way was another long, narrow restaurant with a long counter and stools, a line of tables against the opposite wall and a small private dining room in the rear. George Lyons was its proprietor.

Mary Schrader was running a downtown café on Second Avenue as early as 1905. Popular with the lunchtime business crowd, by 1914, she had relocated to 113 Madison, where she offered a special fifty-cent fried chicken dinner in her fifty-person café. Schrader's disappeared about the time of the Depression.

After several years of restaurant experience working at Saltair, near Salt Lake City, Frank Rippe started up his eponymous café—a few stools lining a counter and a creaking stairway leading to a balcony above where tables for ladies were available—in 1910. Within a few years, he had so prospered that he doubled his seating capacity. Rippe's was described as "just that chummy sort of a cafe where foods are carefully prepared," with an awning over the front windows and a large lighted sign bearing Rippe's name hanging above the sidewalk.

In 1923, when construction of a new building displaced Rippe's from its original location at 314 Pike Street, Frank Rippe took the opportunity to create a more elegant eatery, "one of the finest and best arranged eating places in the city." With mahogany woodwork throughout, a long lunch counter, booths on the lower floor and balcony and a separate room for ladies, Rippe's was able to handle more than two hundred guests at a time. The new Rippe's was at 1423 Fourth Avenue.

Rippe passed away in 1934, but his widow, Pearl, and son-in-law Harry Oliver continued to run the café until abruptly closing its doors in 1940. Said Pearl Rippe, "The competition of corner drugstores, quick-lunch places and one-arm tables forced us to close while still in good financial condition." Regular customers were shocked and disappointed to suddenly find Rippe's dark and shuttered after nearly thirty years of being open round-the-clock.

Later that same year, John G. von Herberg and business partner Antone J. Meyers purchased Rippe's, did a bit of upgrading (a sleek curved glass entrance replaced the earlier plate-glass windows), added new signage and reopened as Von's. They were just in time to celebrate New Year's Eve with a special $1.50 dinner for all of Rippe's old customers.

One thing the new owners pledged was to continue Frank Rippe's standards of fine food, service and atmosphere. That included Rippe's voluminous menu—claimed by some to list over seven hundred items. Whether that's an accurate number or not, it's certain that Von's offered an astonishing array of appetizers and cocktails, soups, salads and cold dishes, fish and shellfish, steaks, chops, special entrées, eggs and omelets, potatoes and vegetables, hot and cold sandwiches and desserts and cheese. For crab alone, the menu listed ten different preparations: cold, baked, deviled, curried, Creole style, à la Newberg, broiled, french fried, grilled or cracked in shell; one could also have them as a cocktail or in an omelet.

Featured were several of Von's special items, such as top sirloin steak, pan fried with gravy; browned potatoes and tomato; breast of turkey in butter crust pastry, fricassee sauce and sweet potato; chicken livers with spaghetti en casserole; and Pacific Seafood Newberg: lobster and crab (of course) simmered in butter and blended in a cream sauce with egg yolks, sherry, green and red peppers, served with choice of potatoes (whipped, french fried or baked) and a mixed green salad.

Contemporary news writers vouched that Von's was always open, always crowded and always good. A tradition added in the mid-1950s was a full-sized Easter bunny to entertain kids at Easter dinner. A 1961 facelift gave Von's a more modern appearance. Unfortunately, a few years later, Von's ran afoul of the tax man; it was closed in 1963 because of tax liens. There were hopes it would reopen—it never did. A later Von's, adjacent to the Hotel Roosevelt on Pine Street, had no connection with the original Von's except that it, too, has disappeared.

Classically trained chef Charles Joseph Blanc left his native France sometime around 1904, ostensibly dispatched by the French government to demonstrate high culinary arts at the Saint Louis Exposition. Blanc liked America, working for a time in New York City before crossing the country to become a chef in San Francisco. By 1906, he had arrived in Seattle and soon became chef at the recently opened New Washington Hotel.

Maison Blanc occupied an 1880s mansion on Marion Street. The Rathskellar later took over the more modern-looking basement. *MOHAI*, Seattle Post-Intelligencer *Collection, 1986.5.11341.1.*

In 1916, he opened Blanc's Cafe Francais in the old, elegant Martin Van Buren Stacy mansion at 308 Marion Street. He dropped "Francais" from the restaurant's name, adopted the slogan "Where Epicureans Meet" and attracted a wide and devoted following. Initially, Blanc's offered a limited menu of fixed-price dinners (family-style $1.25, dinner à la Blanc $3.00 in 1923) with a few à la carte items available such as Bengal lamb curry, Vol-au-vent chicken, braised beef à la mode de Paris and broiled reindeer steak Cumberland (not Rudolph), ranging from $0.55 to $0.85.

By the 1940s, Blanc's menu was a connoisseur's dream. The specials alone constituted a mini-menu; for October 24, 1947, they included:

baked stuffed king salmon
broiled brook trout
fried fillets of sole
tenderloin of trout à la Orly
deep fried Eastern scallops
boiled halibut in parsley sauce
pan fried oysters
barbecued fried jumbo shrimp
baked deviled crab meat in shell
baked ham
roast leg of lamb
roast duckling with dressing
roast spring chicken
prime rib
fried Louisiana frog legs
lobster thermidor
roast turkey

Blanc's was famous for its daily features of different dishes from various cuisines around the world. For Tuesday that same week, the list was:

English: steak and kidney pie
Swedish: koldolmar (spicy cabbage rolls)
Spanish: Albondigillas (meatballs)
Creole: jambalaya
Chinese: chow mein
French: tripe à la mode de Caen

Blanc encouraged adventuresome dining by offering a no-fault exchange policy. Didn't like what you ordered? You could exchange it. According to the menu, "By ordering a special dish with which you may not be familiar you are taking no chances of spoiling your meal, as the waiters will always gladly make an exchange without charge." Another encouraging menu notation: "We serve you a second helping, if you desire, of any ready-to-serve dish, without charge."

Blanc had his hand in other restaurants as well, including the Chanticleer on Third Avenue. In 1933, he opened the Rathskellar in the basement of the old mansion. Described as "a timely addition to Maison Blanc, below stairs at 306 Marion Street," it claimed to be one of the most authentic German beer cellars in the country, with a brick floor, keg on the bar, high stools, a "leaning shelf" against the wall and the finest beers and German foods.

Blanc's Cafe formally became Maison Blanc in 1935. The restaurant was almost as famous for its furnishings as its cuisine, packed top to bottom with artwork and antiques. After Charles Blanc passed away in 1955, his family kept the restaurant going; it passed to new operators in 1957 and was destroyed by fire in 1960 (the interior furnishings having been removed by then). A new Maison Blanc opened where the Rathskellar had been; unlike the original, it was a buffet and smorgasbord and didn't last long. Today, even the old Rathskellar is gone, and a modern high-rise occupies the site.

CAFÉS AND COFFEE HOUSES

The Golden Gate Cafe on Pike Street had a habit of moving around, though never far. It opened in 1921 at 411 Pike under owners Theodore (Theoharis) Vellias and Nicholas Konstantine with a seating capacity of seventy-two, serving "quality food at reasonable prices." Five years later, the Golden Gate ambled a short way up the street to 415 Pike. Well-known restaurateur Ben Paris opened a short-lived place called the Snack n' Tap at 407 Pike in 1933; when it folded after just two years, the Golden Gate packed its bags again and moved the few doors west into Paris's old location.

The new place was completely remodeled with modern fixtures and decorations, and the seating capacity was increased to 175. A glass-block façade was installed, a brilliantly lit neon sign was hung above the sidewalk and the doors reopened (as the Golden Gate Cafe & Oyster House) in June 1935. Theodore Vellias continued as manager; Nick Konstantine resumed his duties as chef; and Harry Vellias, Theodore's brother, became part of the open-all-night operation. There they remained until losing their lease in 1948 forced the Golden Gate to close down. A year or two later, Harry Vellias started up a new Golden Gate at 311 Third Avenue S; it survived into the early 1960s.

Roy Peterson and John McKeel launched the Golden Goose Cafe in 1947. Located on the first floor of the Smith Tower, its dining room and lunch counter were open twenty-four hours a day, seven days a week. The walls were decorated with murals featuring local points of interest along with a golden goose "depicted in various and amusing activities." A management change later that same year brought in Julian Venable, and the café added a cocktail lounge and new hours of operation in 1949. Twenty years later, the Golden Goose and its Submarine Room had become a typical nightclub with floor shows, dancing, cocktails and food. It went out of business in 1972.

There has been a long history of food service at 1617 Third Avenue. Back in 1908, Hans Newgard opened the Reliable Coffee Shop, running it until he retired in 1946. He served up more than coffee; hotcakes and waffles were the mainstay for the breakfast trade. In 1947, the little café was renamed the Stratoplane Luncheonette, a nod to Boeing's new airplane. Owned by Albert Lackman, the Stratoplane became a twenty-four-hours-a-day operation.

The Stratoplane was a long, narrow place with a dozen stools surrounding the horseshoe-shaped counter and six booths at the rear. On the wall, above a couple large mirrors, was a sign carrying the message "For good health eat seafoods." Apparently, the owners had plans to start a chain—the Stratoplane's menu refers to Luncheonettes—but this was the only one. By 1951, it had become the Skillet.

The Skillet's menu listed the customary short-order café food items: ham, bacon or sausage with eggs and potatoes; buckwheat cakes; hamburgers; fish and chips; and three varieties of a specialty triple-decker sandwich. For dinner, one could choose from southern fried chicken, ham steak with honey sauce or hot corned beef. Fountain treats—ice cream, milkshakes, malted milk and sundaes—were featured items. The Skillet was located across the street from the Bon Marche department store and was popular with shoppers. There's a parking garage there today.

The Home of the Green Apple Pie had humble beginnings in 1918 as a pie shop at 1409 Fifth Avenue, in the Houston Hotel building. Myrtle Smith was chief pie-maker with help from her husband, Bert, and son Floyd. By

Above: A cash register, salt and pepper shakers and sugar dispensers cluttered the counter of the Stratoplane Luncheonette in this 1945 photo. *MOHAI, PEMCO Webster & Stevens Collection, 1983.10.15911.*

Right: The menu for the Skillet, the successor to the Stratoplane, was naturally shaped like a skillet. *Author's collection.*

47

1931, they had leased space at 521 Pike Street, a spot it was to occupy for the next forty years.

By the 1950s, the Green Apple Pie had made the leap to becoming a full-service restaurant with a full menu of breakfast, lunch and dinner. Over two dozen sandwiches were listed along with roast beef, leg of veal and baked ham. Daily specials varied by day of the week and included fried king salmon and fried oysters along with less usual fare such as Spanish-style boiled ox tongue and wienerwurst with horseradish.

The main draw, though, was the green apple pie—ten cents a slice in 1947. (By 1960, they claimed to have baked and sold 2,758,000 pies.) Watching the bakers at work, fully visible through the large plate-glass front windows, was a major attraction for passersby. Anna Lauricella, one of the pie crew, remembered that "spectators watched through a front window while she and other pastrymakers turned out pies, sometimes one a minute."

Mitchell Pentell purchased the restaurant in 1953 and ran it (either as owner or manager) with his wife, Ruth, for the next thirty years. A major remodel happened in 1958 when the restaurant received a modern façade and a cocktail lounge was added. Another remodel in 1960 was celebrated

Pie makers in action at the Home of the Green Apple Pie; passersby on Pike Street could watch the goings-on through the large windows. *MOHAI, PEMCO Webster & Stevens Collection, 1983.10.15338.1.*

THE BROILER, 1918 4TH AVENUE, SEATTLE, WASHINGTON

The Broiler's neon-festooned canopy, advertising steaks and barbecued crabs, extended over Fourth Avenue. *Author's collection.*

with a grand reopening. The Home of the Green Apple Pie survived into the 1970s but closed by the end of the decade; today, even the building is gone, a victim of redevelopment.

Two places at the north end of downtown promised to bring a bit of the old South to Seattle. The Broiler was a small place at 1918 Fourth Avenue with Elvis England as its proprietor. The house specialty was southern barbecued crab, with broiled steaks, fried chicken, spareribs, seafood, beef and pork sandwiches also on the menu. Duncan Hines gave it a favorable recommendation in his book *Adventures in Good Eating*, one of only a few area restaurants to be so rated. Elvis England opened the Alaska Grill and Bowl in the Claremont Hotel. The Broiler was in business from 1938 to about 1952.

A few blocks away in Times Court, at Westlake and Pine, was the Pit. Bill Deane started the restaurant in 1942; when he died a few years later, it was purchased by Paul Johnson, who ran it until 1960. The Pit's special meal was prawns barbecued southern style and served hot with garlic bread and coleslaw. Turkey, spareribs, pork and beef—all barbecued over live oak coals—filled out the menu. The Pit was open for breakfast, lunch and dinner; cocktails were served in the Southern Room.

In 1956, the Bonanza Broiler leased space at 610 Union Street, where Vic's Grill had been ten years earlier. The new restaurant was extensively remodeled with not one but two counters and a half-dozen booths along the walls. A brick-lined charcoal rotisserie pit could broil as many as fifteen chickens at a time. By 1959, Pancake Land had moved in with "pancakes that will melt in your mouth." There was another Pancake Land on Eastlake Avenue; both were open twenty-four hours a day.

The Little Brown Jug was a breakfast and light lunch place with four locations scattered around downtown. The first branch opened in 1926 in the White-Henry-Stuart Building on Union Street. Additional Jugs appeared along Fourth Avenue a few years later—one in the Cobb Building, another at 1411 Fourth Avenue—with a final location opening in 1935 at 1023 Third Avenue. They were all found in the lobbies of important business buildings and were convenient, quick service little restaurants for office employees. Only the Cobb Building location remained by 1960.

Eighteen chickens spin on the Bonanza Broiler's rotisserie in this 1956 photo. *Seattle Municipal Archives, 67924.*

Other office buildings had on-site lunchrooms. One of the earliest was the Colman Lunch, on Post Street in the basement of the Colman Building. Open by 1905 and in business for nearly seven decades, it was recalled as a "busy little restaurant with plain cooking and great sweet rolls." For many years, it was operated by Rose Wilcox and her sister, Sarah Atkinson; Rose later opened Rose's Highway Inn on Pacific Highway S in Des Moines. A favorite of office workers, ferry commuters and laborers along the waterfront, it remained virtually unchanged over the years. It was sold in 1976 and became an upscale Cajun restaurant called Crawfish Alley.

The Civic Center Lunch was downstairs in the Vance Building at Third and Union with John Panattoni as proprietor. Opened in early 1930, it was designed for self-service, "equipped for every conceivable convenience making for maximum service and comfort to patrons," with an interior decorated in walnut and Philippine mahogany. Food items were arranged in plate-glass enclosures; steam tables kept hot dishes hot, while refrigeration kept them chilled if needed. A fountain lunch occupied a prominent place within the spacious dining room. The Yale Lunch took its place by 1940 and was still in business six years later.

Like the Vance Building, the Textile Tower at Seventh and Olive had the misfortune to open just as the effects of the 1929 stock market crash were being felt; luckily, both buildings are survivors of Seattle's ongoing redevelopment. An art deco–style structure, it played host to the Textile Tower Lunch for a few years. Over a dozen sandwiches—egg salad, minced ham, meatloaf and other favorites—were on the menu along with waffles, hot cakes and chili. Fountain treats such as fruit freezes, ice cream sodas and sundaes rounded out lunch. The cheapest item on the menu was fresh churned buttermilk at five cents a glass.

Over the years, dozens of small cafés and lunchrooms have been scattered about downtown. Among them were Brehm's Fountain Lunch at Fourth and Westlake; Elliott's Malt and Luncheonette Shop, a few blocks away at 212 Union; Irene's Fountain Lunch, in the Security Public Market at Third and Virginia; and the York Dairy Lunch, at 1510 First Avenue. The N.Y. Coney Island Cafe on Pike Street dished up homemade chili and tamales. A block west was Edouard Stalder's delicatessen. In addition to a full-service deli (one could find seven varieties of sardines, equal number types of anchovies), Stalder's sandwiches—piled high with ham or corned beef—were an inch thick, as columnist John Reddin remembered years later.

At the south end of town, Betty's Coffee Shop occupied a little triangle of land at the corner of Main Street and Second Avenue Extension S. Betty's

This little building, originally Betty's Coffee Shop, has hosted many eateries over the years. *Seattle Public Library, spl_wl_res_00106.*

was in business prior to 1938 and survived into the mid-seventies, when it became the Times Square Cafe. Later known as the Greek Villa, it was a teriyaki restaurant in the 1990s. The tiny building, complete with diminutive chimney, is now Main Street Gyros.

Back when Seattle had a working waterfront, Western and Railroad Avenues were lined for blocks with cafés and lunchrooms. The Western Coffee Shop was a hole-in-the-wall place at 911 Western Avenue known for good breakfasts and burgers. Nearby were the National Cafe (1008 Western) and Franco's Cafe, operated by Mario Franco and his son John before they moved to Lake Union and opened Franco's Hidden Harbor. Along Railroad Avenue were the Western Cafe at 833 Railroad, the B&M Lunch (559 Railroad, later relocated to 209), the M&M Coffee Shop at 207 Railroad and a café in the ferry terminal at Colman Dock. After Railroad Avenue was renamed Alaskan Way, several more restaurants opened, including the Pacific Lunch (549 Alaskan) and Hunt's Pier One Cafe at 105 S Alaskan. Construction of the Alaskan Way Viaduct in 1954 eliminated practically everything along the east side of Alaskan Way.

Confectioneries

Pig'n Whistle was a chain started by Frank Callebotta in 1908. The name, commonly used for English pubs, is thought to be based on slang for a small drinking bowl ("pig") and a corruption of wassail ("whistle"), a spiced cider drink. Its first outlet was in San Francisco, with additional locations soon opening in Oakland and Los Angeles. Eventually, there were about twenty Pig'n Whistles up and down the West Coast, arriving in Seattle in 1919 at 1009 Second Avenue.

The term "confectionery" was often used for places like Pig'n Whistle: part candy store, part restaurant (other Seattle examples included Puss'n Boots and Rogers' Confectionery). The chain's trademark image, a flute-playing pig, was used in advertising, signage and interior décor. The giant sign hanging off the Pig'n Whistle's home in the Rialto Building was used as a landmark by other businesses to steer in customers. Inside, it was decorated in whimsical fashion with family trade in mind.

Within a week of opening, the Pig'n Whistle had become so popular that the management took out newspaper space to thank the public for the

The Pig'n Whistle's sign overhanging Second Avenue was impossible not to notice. *MOHAI, PEMCO Webster & Stevens Collection, 1983.10.1900.*

Puss'n Boots rolls out pie dough while being served a milkshake in this early ad. *Seattle Daily Times.*

enthusiastic reception. Menu items included salads, soups, entrées such as lamb chops and oysters and a wide variety of hot and cold sandwiches: turkey and gravy, fried ham, club house and the house special Pig'n Whistle Three-Layer (chicken, ham, cheese, served French dip style), among others. Not surprisingly, ice cream, fountain treats and desserts (over twenty varieties) featured prominently on the menu.

Originally managed by Gilbert (also apparently known as George) Rideau, the Pig'n Whistle lasted until 1932; the next year, Dawn's Cafe occupied that address. Elsewhere, Pig'n Whistles prospered into the 1950s, when changing tastes and the popularity of drive-ins led to the chain's decline. The remaining units—except one—were sold in 1968 to an Illinois company that planned to renovate and expand the chain, but it apparently never happened. The remaining Pig'n Whistle is in Hollywood; fully restored to its 1920s glory, it still operates as a restaurant and museum.

Puss'n Boots, similar in theme to the Pig'n Whistle, was just a few blocks north at 1316 Second Avenue. Its opening-day announcement (a half-page ad in the *Seattle Times*) was done in timeless poetry:

> *Here's the house of*
> *PUSS'N BOOTS*
> *Sound the cymbals,*
> *Blow the flutes!*
> *Come ye lads*
> *And lassies all,*
> *To this wondrous*
> *Joyous hall.*

The poem continued by listing Puss'n Boot's menu items: ices, sundaes, candies ("in a box a-gleam!"), frosty drinks, oysters, fish, sugar tarts, French pastries, English muffins, tea...

> *All of these*
> *And other too,*
> *PUSS'N BOOTS*
> *Has here for you.*

Fred Hamilton was the owner of Puss'n Boots; after he and daughter Grace perished in the Lincoln Hotel fire of April 1920, his son Seaver assumed control of the company. A newspaper columnist known as Jean (we'll hear more from her shortly) praised the "refined atmosphere where daintily prepared dishes are served by courteous waitresses" at Puss'n Boots; she was particularly impressed by the variety of candies on display.

Puss'n Boots vacated its Second Avenue location in 1926 in favor of a new location in the Skinner Building next to the Fifth Avenue Theatre. Afternoon teas were added to the menu (tea along with cinnamon toast, cake or muffin for $0.25) with regular dinners priced at $1.00 and fountain and à la carte service available at all times. Orville Graves purchased the restaurant in 1927 and upgraded the menu to appeal to the theater-going crowd; Thanksgiving dinner at Puss'n Boots ($1.50 in 1929) included salad, consommé, a relish tray, a ramekin of creamed oysters, choice of entrée (grilled salmon, roast turkey, prime rib, roast duck or fricassee of chicken), vegetables, pie, fruit and a special Thanksgiving sundae. It closed in 1934.

CAFETERIAS

Jim Boldt was another of the many Seattleites who enjoyed a fifty-year career in the restaurant business. Jim's entry was a concession at the Alaska-Yukon-Pacific Exposition in 1909. That same year, he bought into the Rainier Bakery at 913 Second Avenue. Originally just a bakery, by 1914, the restaurant was "serving all kinds of meals at popular prices." Four years later, Boldt opened another location at 1414 Third Avenue; both locations were interchangeably called Boldt's Cafe, Boldt's Cafeteria or simply Boldt's. (The Second Avenue location closed sometime around 1923.)

Boldt's became a favorite downtown eatery for its roast beef, though steaks, turkey dinners and real corned beef sandwiches were also on the menu. "It's the Coffee," proclaimed the sign above his front entrance. In addition to his restaurants, Boldt developed a successful catering business; in one of his early ads, Boldt stated that, for a Shriners picnic at Woodland Park, he served up 5,400 pounds of chicken, 3,400 heads of lettuce and huge quantities of butter, ice cream and coffee. He claimed that during his years as a restaurateur, he served Presidents Taft, Wilson, Hoover, Harding and Truman. Boldt's closed after he retired circa 1960.

A.J. Meves, founder of Meves Cafeteria, went Boldt one better: his slogan was "It's the Food." The first Meves Cafeteria opened for business in 1916 at 1415 Third Avenue. Three years later, he relocated to the corner of Second and Seneca; the next year, he was to be found in the Queen City Market Building at Fourth and Pine. After six years there, he moved again, to the triangular-shaped Millard Building at 1611 Westlake. There he stayed until selling the business to Earl Kirkpatrick in 1940.

Meves took pride in offering quality meals in elegant surroundings at prices well below those of other restaurants. He did so by adopting a self-service format and, by minimizing his service staff, was able to keep prices low. But he did it in elegant surroundings. Though no photos seem to exist of the interiors of Meves's cafeterias, judging from newspaper descriptions, they weren't what we'd imagine a cafeteria to look like. In addition to a large

Right: Meves Cafeteria in its final location, the Millard Building at 1611 Westlake Avenue, 1934. *MOHAI, PEMCO Webster & Stevens Collection, 1983.10.4964.23.*

Below: A well-dressed crowd lines the counter at the Alpine Self Service Restaurant, September 14, 1960. *Seattle Municipal Archives, 67934.*

dining area, Meves's Fourth and Pine location contained a Banquet Hall, Rose Room and Blue Room for meetings and events. A 1921 ad invited the public for Easter dinner "in our big, finely appointed cafeteria…a large, light, airy dining room with the best seasoned and greatest variety of foods that expert chefs can prepare." It might have been self-serve, but it was done with style.

Meves retired after selling out to Earl Kirkpatrick. With previous restaurant business managing the Moore Hotel's coffee shop, Kirkpatrick operated Meves (keeping the name intact) for six years before it was again sold. The new owners were Madelynn Lippard and her son Rodger Benson, who had owned Rodger's Cafe at 601 N Broadway. Meves was renamed Rodger's Buffet but kept the upscale self-serve buffet motif. A Swiss steak or barbecued sparerib dinner, each with potatoes and vegetables, cost just fifty-five cents at Rodger's—about half of what the competition was charging at the time. Rodger's only lasted for about two years. It probably didn't help that during its brief existence, people continued to refer to the places as Meves.

Head's Cigar Store was a fixture at 1406 Fourth Avenue for years. In much the same mold as the Ben Paris stores, Head's was a masculine retreat with card games and an on-site restaurant and grill. Following the death of longtime owner Maurice Stoffer, Head's closed in 1960 and its space was taken over by the Alpine Restaurant. The Alpine was self-service, cafeteria-style, though a few entrées were cooked to order. The Alpine put on a yearly Christmas dinner—roast turkey or ham with candied yams and all the trimmings for $2.90 in 1968. By then, the Seattle location was part of a chain of three Alpine restaurants, the others being in Everett and Bellingham and all owned by Denver Burtenshaw. The Alpine on Union closed by 1976; the other two locations kept going for a few more years before disappearing.

Fine Dining

Webster's dictionary defines a café as "a usually small and informal establishment serving various refreshments (as coffee)." In that case, George's Cafe was a café in name only—its menu gives it away as a full-scale restaurant with dozens of items to choose from.

When George's opened in 1922, it was a three-stool, four-booth lunch counter operation that could barely accommodate one dozen people. In a

A huge assortment of edibles lurked behind the rather plain menu cover of George's Cafe. *Author's collection.*

newspaper interview on the café's seventeenth anniversary, soon after enlarging, remodeling and redecorating, owner George Diafos stated he could comfortably seat one hundred patrons and had a service staff of twenty. "We have always served the finest of food at moderate prices, to which we attribute our success," he said. George's was located on Sixth Avenue, at the eastern edge of the business district but only a block away from the famous Olympic Hotel, from which he derived much of his trade.

Breakfast was an important part of George's menu: twenty different egg dishes and omelets were listed along with cereals, hot cakes, waffles, fresh fruits in season, juices, jellies and preserves. George's special luncheon offered four different choices of entrée (grilled halibut or tuna, corned beef, hot beef sandwich) plus a vegetable, dessert and beverage for forty cents. Two dinners were available. One, called the complete dinner (sixty cents), included clam chowder, salad, entrée (halibut, corned beef, oysters or leg of lamb), vegetable, dessert and beverage. The full course dinner (ten cents more) offered a different choice of entrée (turkey, half a chicken, pork tenderloin, finnan haddie or scallops) along with the usual chowder, vegetable and such.

If the special dinners didn't fit one's taste, there was always the à la carte menu: nearly forty different types of steaks and chops, ten different fish dishes, nineteen different oyster preparations and another ten of shellfish, plus soups (six different), seafood cocktails (six listed), potatoes and vegetables (choice of twelve), sauces and gravies (four different) and fifteen varieties of salads and dressings—do the math, and that's well over a million combinations to choose from. It's probably certain no one could claim they didn't find anything appealing to eat at George's.

George's stayed open all hours, a fairly common thing in those days. A cocktail lounge, the Spartan Room, was added in the 1950s. Then came construction of the Interstate 5 freeway. George's was threatened with destruction in 1961, though he managed to hold on for another two years. When the end came in 1963, George Diafos stated he intended to purchase property along Sixth Avenue and rebuild. Sadly, it never happened; he passed away a few years later. Today, motorists exiting Interstate 5 at Seneca Street drive right through where George's once was.

The Richelieu Cafe opened for business in 1929. Located at 703 Union Street in the Wilhard Hotel, its proprietor was Gus Pappas, formerly associated with the Oxford Cafe and the Argonaut Cafe (both on Pike Street). The Richelieu offered a merchants' lunch for forty cents and special dinners ("cook[ed] as only our chefs know how") for fifty-five cents and seventy-five cents. In 1939, Pappas moved to Head's Grill, and the Richelieu was taken over by Paul Chapas. By 1947, the price of special dinner (choice of six different entrées including grilled fillet of halibut and chopped veal steak) had risen to eighty-five cents. The menu had an appealing array of steaks and chops, seafood and oysters; sandwiches; and eggs and omelets. It was open all night, but the Richelieu closed around 1970.

Smorgasbord was practically unknown in Seattle until John Utterstrom opened John's Rendezvous in 1934. A 1934 ad listed nine different entrées, including halibut with parsley and butter, grilled salmon, fried oysters, New York and sirloin cuts of steak, lamb chops and turkey—along with several dozen side dishes, many of them traditional Scandinavian delicacies like *gaffelbitar* (preserved herring) and *pressylta* (head cheese). John's Rendezvous became A Little Bit of Sweden in 1936 and continued the smorgasbord tradition into the 1950s when it became the Home Plate, a conventional steakhouse. Another Little Bit of Sweden—no connection with the original—was on Broadway in the 1960s. (There was also A Little Bit of Norway at 900 Elliott.) Once, Seattle could claim a number of fine Scandinavian-style buffet restaurants—King Oscar's, Selandia and the Vasa Sea Grill, to name but a few—but today the city is practically devoid of authentic smorgasbord.

Kirkpatrick's was at 416 Union. Earl Kirkpatrick had previous restaurant experience, having managed the Moore Hotel Coffee Shop, and purchased Meves Cafeteria in 1940. His new restaurant opened in 1945 with the usual fanfare and added a cocktail lounge, the Blarney Room, in 1949. St. Patrick's Day—complete with pretty colleens and smiling Irishmen—was always a party at Kirkpatrick's. Murals on the walls, painted by E.P. Ziegler, depicted the Battle of the Factions, an Irish fishing village, a thoroughbred horse and a castle. For all the Irish atmosphere, Kirkpatrick's menu listed nothing Irish—just typical American fare such as grilled halibut, pork chops, veal cutlets and sirloin steak. At the same time Earl Kirkpatrick was running his downtown restaurant, he also owned Kirkpatrick's Coach Inn (previously the My Pal Tavern) on Aurora Avenue. Possibly he overextended; in 1954, Kirkpatrick's ran into tax problems, and the equipment was auctioned off.

Back in the waning days of Prohibition, there was a roadhouse called the Ranch on the Seattle-Everett Highway (Highway 99) about eight miles north of downtown. It had a shady reputation for drinking, gambling and all sorts of other nefarious stuff. When World War II began and gas was rationed, its owners temporarily closed it down and opened a new place named the Town Ranch at 1421 Eighth Avenue, a building that had previously been the Olympic Theatre. It was billed as Seattle's "swank new theatre-cafe," with dance music provided by Wyatt Howard's orchestra, entertainment (vaudeville shows) and fine food: steak, chicken and turkey dinners served "before theatre" (5:00 to 8:00 p.m.) and supper-dancing until 1:00 a.m. When the war ended, so did the Town Ranch. The owners reopened the Ranch out on the highway, and the Town Ranch became the Town and Country Club, finally closing in 1970. Fire destroyed the Ranch roadhouse in 1959, and freeway construction took the Town Ranch's building.

A few years after the Town Ranch left downtown, a new, similarly named restaurant—The Ranch—appeared at 1424 Sixth Avenue. The Ranch did it in style: a full-on cowboy motif of brick and rough board walls, rodeo photos, fence rails, saddles, bridles, spurs, horseshoes and wagon wheels. Waitresses wore gingham dresses; checkered tablecloths covered the tables. Steaks from the chuck-wagon broiler and country-fried chicken were specialties, along with baked beans and beef cooked using the JucyRay method. (JucyRay was a trade name for rare beef turning on a spit in the restaurant's front window.) The Ranch was a hit with families but only lasted for about ten years.

Don Ehle ran several downtown restaurants over the years. First up was Don's Oyster House, opened in 1899 with his father Frank at 207½ Yesler. A few years later, Don bought out his father's interests and moved into larger quarters at 203 Yesler, previously occupied by a competing oyster house called Wright's. Ehle sold (or leased—it's not clear which) Don's Oyster House in 1924 and opened Don's Seafood, somewhat inaccurately billed as "the only real sea food restaurant in Seattle," at 515 Pike Street.

The new proprietors of 203 Yesler kept the original name and stayed open for an additional thirty-five years. Seafood, particularly oysters, dominated the menu, though a variety of steaks and chops were also available. Everything was à la carte. The place was open day and night and had an extensive list of breakfast items on the menu.

In 1933, another Don—Don Andrews—entered the picture when he opened Don's Alaskan Log Cabin immediately adjacent to the Oyster House. A façade of logs was applied around the entrance to the otherwise modern building; inside, murals depicting Alaskan scenes decorating the walls played up the Klondike gold rush theme. A convenient pass-through connected the Log Cabin to the Oyster House. The Alaskan Log Cabin apparently didn't last for long, but Don's Oyster House was still going strong into the 1950s.

Meanwhile, Don's Seafood prospered. Of course, seafood (as many as ninety-seven varieties, it was claimed) featured heavily on the menu alongside the typical steaks, roasts and chops. Don Ehle retired in 1941, but his restaurant continued without him. In 1956, Don's Seafood was purchased by Ivar Haglund of "Acres of Clams" fame and became Ivar's Captain's Table, which it remained until relocating to the shores of Elliott Bay in 1965.

The San Francisco Oyster House, a close neighbor of Don's on Yesler Way, dated to about 1890. Lars Peterson was the proprietor. A contemporary newspaper writer described it as "inconspicuous as to its outward appearances, modest as to its arrangements and lacking entirely in display," but none of that mattered—the food was what counted. It moved to 216 James Street in 1914 and disappeared when the L.C. Smith Tower was built, though Peterson went on to operate another restaurant, the Lion Oyster House, at 714 First Avenue.

The American Oyster House, uptown at 1512 Westlake Avenue, was owned by J.L. Hatfield and A. Henry Suddreth. Hatfield departed the scene in 1911, but Suddreth, who had worked at the San Francisco Oyster House, carried on until his retirement in 1954. Its interior was finished in teakwood and was the first Seattle restaurant to contain an aquarium. The California Oyster House opened in 1908 at 513 Third Avenue, near the Seward Hotel and Arctic Club. J. Mihich and A. Marinovich operated it along with another place, the Golden Gate Oyster House on Cherry Street. It was still in business in 1936.

The Lowell Dining Room, at 1102 Eighth Avenue, took its name from the building it was housed in: the Lowell Apartments, which opened in 1928 with 154 two-room units and all the contemporary amenities, including a dining room "for the convenience of those who make their home at the Lowell"—which might mean that originally the dining room wasn't open to the public. It definitely was by 1930, though, since the Lowell Dining Room, under management of Ruth Holland, advertised a forty-cent luncheon and dinners priced at fifty cents and seventy-five cents

When it opened, the dining room featured two hundred feet of tube neon lighting—the first installation of its kind in Seattle—which "threw against the dome-like ceiling of the dining room the tones of blue and orange-red characteristic of neon lighting." Thirty years later, the décor had become more subdued; it had transformed into what one writer described as a "quiet Old English tearoom atmosphere" with elaborate plaster decorations, mirrored panels on the walls and lace tablecloths laden with gleaming candlesticks and silverware. A relatively small place, for years, the Lowell was considered one of Seattle's best-kept restaurant secrets. It attracted a steady and loyal clientele but wasn't well known beyond its local area.

After Herb and Cathie Pryor took over the Lowell Dining Room in 1953, the restaurant's fame began to grow. Herb was well known for made-from-scratch soups and salad dressings, Cathie for her pies—often as many as ten varieties available, with special favorites being pecan and banana cream. Their son Jack presided over the kitchen. Daily specials included lamb, baked ham and pot roast. Open only for dinner, no liquor was served.

Restaurant reviewer Tom Stockley recorded a visit to the Lowell in 1974:

> *Nobody goes hungry at the Lowell, as my family and I found out on a recent Saturday evening. On that particular occasion the menu featured a steak at $6.50, which we ignored because we were on a budget evening. There were five items, at $4.50 each: fresh salmon, Swiss steak (farm style), breaded veal cutlet and two daily specials which were fresh sole and oven-baked chicken. Finally, there was a ground sirloin steak for $3.95. If the prices don't seem particularly budget conscious, remember they include EVERYTHING: soup, salad, main course and dessert.*

On the day the Stockley family visited, the soup was a creamy clam bisque; salads were fresh; and the choice of pies included lemon meringue, cherry, custard, banana cream, fresh rhubarb and pecan. Everything was homemade. Stockley noted that complimenting the food—the soup, mashed potatoes with gravy or hot biscuits—got rewarded with an additional helping. Said Stockley, "Our total bill (for a party of four) was $20. It was a sum gladly spent for a satisfying and happy experience."

Unfortunately, the Lowell experience didn't last much longer. Just three months after Tom Stockley's review, Jack Pryor died suddenly at age forty-one. Perhaps his passing took something out of the place; despite its steady patronage, quality home-cooked food and refined atmosphere, the Lowell Dining Room had closed by the early 1980s. An upscale pizzeria has taken its place.

It wouldn't be politically correct these days: Pancho's "mascot" was a heavily mustachioed, obviously Latino caricature with a sombrero the size of a mattress on his head. Opened in 1949, Pancho's was the creation of Jim Ward, who had his hand in several other restaurants of the day, including

Herb and Cathie Pryor display a variety of desserts to a happy patron at the Lowell Dining Room in 1962. *MOHAI,* Seattle Post-Intelligencer *Collection, 1986.5.11392.*

the still-thriving 13 Coins on Boren Avenue. Despite its name and interior decor, Pancho's wasn't a Mexican restaurant. Its forte was charcoal-broiled steaks, done on what was claimed as the first open-pit broiler in Seattle. Other specialties included prime rib, hickory barbecued spareribs, double loin lamb chops, shish kabobs and a house special baked potato. Pancho's was at 1901 Fourth Avenue, in premises earlier occupied by one of Nick Jorgensen's Finer Food Shops. (Jim Ward worked for Jorgensen in the late 1940s; we'll meet Jorgensen later on.)

Another Jim Ward restaurant, El Gaucho, appeared in 1953. Like Pancho's, it took over a previous Jorgensen location (624 Olive Way); like Pancho's, it was often taken for a Mexican place but wasn't. Its theme was the Argentine pampa. Considered an expensive place at the time, El Gaucho was a small, L-shaped place, dimly lighted and full almost any hour of the day. The restaurant's slogan was *"Barriga llena corazon contento"* (A full belly makes a happy heart), building its reputation on steaks (prepared over hot coals as at Pancho's), though beef tenderloin en brochette, lobster, steaks and prime rib also made the menu. All entrées came with garlic bread, a baked potato and fresh fruit. Desserts included cherries jubilee with vanilla ice cream and pineapple cheesecake.

Shish kabob was a main feature: large hunks of marinated lamb, green pepper and a whole green tomato were cooked on a skewer in a rotisserie, brought to the table doused with vodka and set aflame—a spectacular show that delighted patrons. (To make the point, in 1961, the restaurant installed a huge flaming shish kabob outside its front door.) Another draw was the Hunt Breakfast, served from midnight until 4:00 a.m. A fruit tray came first, followed by a chicken liver omelet, a steak, a lamb chop, spicy sausage and hash browns—all you could eat for $6.50.

Paul Mackay assumed management of El Gaucho soon after it opened, later moving on to 13 Coins. Most of Jim Ward's restaurants were sold off after his death, though the Ward family retained El Gaucho and continued running it until 1985. Today there's a new El Gaucho in a different spot but with Paul Mackay, from the original restaurant, in charge.

In the late 1920s, Victor Rossellini's family moved from Tacoma to San Francisco, where his widowed mother started a small eatery called the Tunnel Restaurant. Victor gained his early restaurant experience there as busboy and waiter. He briefly moved to Seattle in 1932 to work at his brother's restaurant but went back to San Francisco and the famous Bimbo's 365 Club a few years later. He learned every facet of the restaurant business while at Bimbo's, and when he returned to Seattle, his timing was perfect.

In 1949, Seattle voted to allow sales of liquor by the drink, ushering in a new era of posh restaurants. In short order, Peter Canlis opened his eponymous restaurant on Aurora Avenue; John Franco's Hidden Harbor arose along Lake Union; and downtown at 610 Pine Street was Rosellini's 610, a partnership between Victor and John Pogetti, his brother-in-law and head chef. While Pogetti presided over the kitchen, Rosellini took on the role of host, making all patrons feel comfortable—even members of the so-called carriage trade visiting a high-end restaurant for the first time. The menu expressed Rosellini's philosophy: "It is our intent to give the public a restaurant where one may go in full confidence that his most exacting demands will receive the attention they deserve."

Dinner De Luxe at the 610 offered a choice of two dozen entrées, including the traditional chicken, steak and seafood dishes and a few surprises, such as abalone (in season), squab and pheasant in casserole with wild rice and currant jelly. All dinners came with assorted hors d'oeuvres, soup, a pasta dish, a tossed green salad, dessert (choice of ice cream, sherbet, fried cream or cheese) and a beverage. Prices ranged from $2.75 (for fried prawns) to $4.25 (whole boneless stuffed squab). Many of the entrées (even steaks) were priced for two. Almost all of the dinner entrées were also available à la carte along with sandwiches and standbys like ham and eggs.

In 1956, Rosellini left John Poggetti and Al Bredice to manage the 610 while he created Victor's Four-10 at 410 University in the White-Henry-Stuart Building, an even more upscale place described as "a landmark in the recent trend of fine restaurants…combining the elegant atmosphere and superlative food of fine, old-time restaurants with the best in modern service and equipment…the finest in continental cuisine, superbly prepared.…The list of delicacies is as complete as any this side of Europe." Waiters in tuxedos patrolled tables draped in white linen and laden with heavy silverware. As with the 610, the Four-10 emerged as a place where Seattle's movers and shakers gathered to discuss politics and city affairs. Though Rosellini's brother Albert was the Democratic governor of Washington at the time, Victor remained determinedly apolitical.

Victor Rosellini pays personal attention to two fortunate guests in this 1959 photo. *MOHAI, Seattle Post-Intelligencer Collection, 1986.5.11398.1.*

Rosellini and Poggetti sold the 610 in 1972, though most of the staff, including Poggetti, remained with the new owners. In 1975, with the White-Henry-Stuart Building to be demolished for construction of the Rainier Square development, the Four-10 moved to Fourth Avenue and Wall Street in the Denny Regrade. Rosellini brought many of his old staff with him to the new, larger location, and his clientele followed. The relocated Four-10 prospered until 1989, when the building was sold to make room for an apartment complex. Victor Rosellini, one of the legends among Seattle's restaurateurs, passed away in 2003.

In the Stores

Most longtime residents remember Frederick & Nelson and the Bon Marche as being Seattle's premier department stores. Frederick's and the Bon, as they were affectionately known, followed similar paths during their lifetimes: from humble beginnings through several relocations, opening grand new stores within a few years of each other, expanding with branch stores in various cities and finally encountering financial issues in the 1990s. One was forced into bankruptcy, the other subsumed into a national chain and its name changed.

Over the years, Frederick's and the Bon each offered a variety of dining opportunities—everything from grab-on-the-go lunch counters to formal dining rooms. Another downtown department store, Rhodes, competed for the lunchtime crowd's business, as did the large five-and-dime chains Woolworth's and Kress. Local pharmacies, including Bartell Drugs, G.O. Guy and Barney O'Connor, had lunch counters in most of their stores both downtown and in the rapidly growing suburbs.

In 1891, Frederick & Nelson was a new- and used-furniture store owned by partners Donald E. Frederick and Nels Nelson in the 1200 block of Second Avenue. By the beginning of the century, they had expanded their line to include furniture, carpets, stoves, ranges, crockery and household goods; a few years later, they began selling ready-to-wear men's and women's fashions. They also opened a tearoom, the first of many in-store restaurants Frederick's hosted over the years.

Frederick assumed full control after Nelson died in 1907, and in 1916, he made a bold move. Purchasing a parcel of land on Pine Street at Fifth Avenue—a location considered outside the city's retail core at the time—he erected a new building at a cost of over $1 million. The new store opened in September 1918 with six stories and a full basement for displaying and selling goods, as well as amenities such as a candy factory, hairdressing salons (including one for children, complete with kid-sized chairs), a kindergarten and a ladies' lounge. Frederick's immediately became the centerpiece of Seattle's Times Square District.

Restaurants weren't overlooked. The Tea Room, which had opened in the original location in 1903, found a home on the fifth floor. Afternoon tea at Frederick's became a long-standing tradition for Seattle mothers and daughters. The menu offered tea and other beverages as well as sandwiches (orange marmalade, toasted nut and cheese and lettuce with mayonnaise for light appetites) and a variety of desserts and cakes. A complete fountain service with over one dozen types of sundaes and ice cream treats was available. In later years, the Tea Room expanded its menu to include full lunches and dinners; in 1932, the fifty-cent lunch offered a choice of baked salmon with egg sauce, creamed chicken on toast with buttered carrots or roast leg of lamb with mint jelly, potatoes and green beans.

Soon after the new store opened, an additional restaurant joined the Tea Room on the fifth floor: the Men's Grill. When Frederick's expanded the store by adding an additional four stories in 1954, both the Tea Room and the Men's Grill moved upstairs to the eighth floor. The grill's name said it all; even as late as 1969, the *Seattle Daily Times* felt it necessary to explain that the Men's Grill was "a 'men only' sanctum with a men-oriented menu." A year later, Frederick's tried to clarify its policy—the name was only meant to inhibit women from entering; they weren't actually prohibited. Whatever the case, by then, the same menu was provided to guests in either restaurant. The name was changed to the Grill circa 1970, and by 1973, women had become frequent diners there.

The Fountain Lunch occupied a portion of the store's basement (Frederick's called it "The Downstairs Store") by 1921. The menu was oriented toward the lunch crowd with sandwiches, salads and pastries. In the 1960s, the Paul Bunyan Room took the Fountain Lunch's place and quickly became a favorite among shoppers, particularly those with children. Murals depicting Paul and his sidekick Babe the Blue Ox decorated the walls along with forest scenes celebrating Seattle's logging heritage. The room itself was long and narrow, with a center counter surrounded by over forty stools and a soda fountain built into its side. The menu, overall not much of a change from the Fountain Lunch, was updated to include crisp salads and a few hot dishes such as beef or chicken potpies (also available for takeout).

By 1939, yet another restaurant—the Continental Buffet—had joined the Frederick's family. Advertised as "a new luncheon service for busy men and women" and located next to the Tea Room on the fifth floor, the buffet included Continental coffee cakes (fifteen cents); salads "with tempting garden-fresh vegetables, seafood and meat concoctions" and Frederick's own dressings; a sandwich platter called the "Byte-a-Board Plate"; and various casseroles, "piping hot and delicious," for thirty cents à la carte or fifty cents with vegetables, rolls and butter, a beverage and dessert. When the building was expanded in 1954, the Continental Buffet apparently disappeared. The other restaurants, though, remained in place until Frederick's final days in 1992.

No coverage of Frederick & Nelson is complete without mentioning Frangos, their signature chocolate mint truffle creation. What began as a frozen dessert—offered on Tea Room menus as early as 1918—evolved into a full line of pies, ice cream sodas and milkshakes. Debate persists about the origin of the name—one guess is that it is a combination of "Fran" (Frederick and Nelson) and "go" from tango, a popular dance at the time Frangos first appeared. Flavors in addition to the original mint were offered, among them Jamaican rum, mocha and almond. Frangos survived Frederick & Nelson's demise, and they're still available today at the downtown Macy's (formerly Frederick's competitor, the Bon Marche) and other locations.

Edward Nordhoff founded the Bon Marche in a humble storefront at First Avenue and Cedar Street in Belltown in 1890. The name ("good deal" in French) was inspired by Le Bon Marché of Paris. In 1896, the Bon relocated to a one-story L-shaped building on Second Avenue between Pike and Union. Nordhoff died in 1899; after his wife remarried in 1901, she and new husband Frank McDermott joined forces with Edward's brother Rudolph Nordhoff in operating the store. In 1929, the Bon moved to Third Avenue and Pine Street—$10 million worth of luxurious floor space, four stories tall plus basement and boasting the largest copper marquee of any building on the Pacific coast. Even competitor Frederick & Nelson, two blocks farther east on Pine Street, took out an ad in the *Seattle Daily Times* congratulating the Bon on its grand opening.

The Bon was in the restaurant business as early as 1912, with a café on the fourth floor of the old Second Avenue building. A large, high-ceilinged room with dark polished wood tables and chairs, the café took pride in being a no-frills place to enjoy lunch: "No orchestra din, no extras, no extravagances in the service. Yet the service is ideal. A sensible place to dine," claimed the advertisements. In 1915, a lunch of cream of corn soup, roast spring lamb, new green peas, potatoes, raspberry cobbler and a beverage (tea, coffee or milk) cost just thirty cents. By the 1920s, the café had been replaced by the Food Shop and Men's Grill on the sixth floor, and a lunch counter and soda fountain lunch had opened on the main floor.

In the years after moving to the new building, the soda fountain lunch was reestablished on the main (street) floor and renamed the Soda Grill. Sandwiches, salads and ice cream desserts were its main fare, though the menu also offered several entrées such as broiled filet of salmon with parsley butter, whipped potatoes and a vegetable for sixty cents. At some point in time, the Soda Grill was moved to the basement. In 1940, the Crystal Tea Room opened on the main floor; as with Frederick's tearoom, the Crystal Room was a notch up from the lunch-counter atmosphere of the Soda Grill. The entrance was surrounded by glass blocks; inside, fine linen tablecloths and silverware greeted guests.

The Bon's restaurant scene was revamped in 1955, the same year that two additional floors were added to the building. The Crystal Tea Room and Soda Grill were replaced by two new venues: the Cascade Room on the top floor and the Jet Room in the basement. Ads describe the Cascade Room: "A high-style room, beautifully accented in flamingo and brown tones and inviting the relaxed dining of those who have time to listen to soft music and watch pretty models…flamingo-and-brown block-printed draperies… white-linen napkins on chocolate-brown tablecloths and dishes to match." The entrance was flanked by two totem poles carved by local artist Dudley Carter; murals painted by Mrs. Wellwood Beale covered the walls. A Men's Grill, separated by a movable partition, was part of the Cascade Room.

The Jet Room, "so named for its speedy service and with a nod to the city's largest industry," was billed as a radical departure for the Bon's food service. Speed and low cost were emphasized: "The customer will be able to get a complete meal and leave within 15 minutes of the time he enters. And it will cost just 85¢, tax included." A customer would enter, pay up front and then be escorted to a table by a hostess. A waitress costumed like an airline stewardess offered a choice of four entrée items, dessert and beverage. The order, with the entrée apparently already prepared, was picked up from a service counter and promptly delivered to the customer. The entire operation was based on then-current standards of airline service; even the utensils, salt and pepper shakers and sugar service were "disposable airplane type." With three hundred seats, the Jet Room's management counted on rapid turnover to make it profitable. The model must have worked—the Jet Room lasted for twenty years before being replaced by the Market Place in 1974.

In 1992, the Bon, which had been purchased by the Allied Stores chain in 1934, became part of Federated Department Stores, which also owned the Macy's and Bloomingdale's chains. The Bon retained its original name until 2003, when the inevitable rebranding happened—first, it was changed to the Bon-Macy's, then finally Macy's. With the demise of the old familiar Bon Marche name, the store dropped out of the food service business.

The story of Rhodes Department Store is a bit of a tangle. The four Rhodes brothers—Albert, William, Henry and Charles—opened a coffee shop in downtown Tacoma in 1892 and made the leap into the department store business a decade later with stores in Tacoma and Seattle. In 1924, they opened a second Seattle location, Rhodes Brothers Company Ten Cent Store No. 2, at the corner of Fourth Avenue and Pike Street. In the basement was a fountain and lunch counter called Burr Oaks, done in Italian marble and mosaic tile, with a "novel seating arrangement" and special ventilating system to carry away the odor of food. A turkey lunch—creamed turkey on toast with mashed potatoes, green peas and a choice of pie or ice cream—cost thirty-five cents at the lunch counter in 1935.

Meanwhile, Albert Rhodes, apparently having moved to Seattle, started his own business in the Arcade Building on Second Avenue in 1907. After his death in 1921, his widow, Harriett, continued operations. Having outgrown its original space, Rhodes commissioned a new building in 1927, six stories in height, on a portion of the land occupied by the Arcade Building at Second and Union. Bridging the gap between five-and-dime stores and upscale places like Frederick's and the Bon, Rhodes Department Store and the Rhodes Brothers Ten Cent Stores apparently remained in friendly competition for a few years, though by 1937, Rhodes Brothers had apparently vanished from the Seattle scene.

A Fountain Lunch opened on the Second Avenue side of Rhodes in 1929 with a menu that included soups; entrées such as chicken à la king; sandwiches, including hot roast beef and Rhodes house-specialty chicken sandwich; and various desserts. The Fountain Lunch, later relocated to Rhodes's basement, was still going strong in 1943.

Helen Malloy, who had previously operated a tearoom at 721 Virginia Street, moved into Rhodes in 1931 and remained there for five years until relocating yet again to the City Light building. Rhodes kept the tearoom going after Helen's departure, and in 1947, a completely remodeled Mezzanine Tea Room reopened. Obviously intended to compete with the tearooms at the Bon and Frederick's, Rhodes's version presented music from an Aeolian pipe organ, smorgasbord-style dinners on Monday evenings and a child's menu with meals such as "The Farmer in the Dell" (two vegetables with potatoes and gravy) and the "Jack Spratt" (a hamburger with potato chips and chocolate milk).

The Jay Bird Cafeteria made its appearance in Rhodes's Bargain Basement in 1962 with a seventy-five-cent lunch aimed at office workers, shoppers and commuters. Unfortunately, Rhodes fell on hard times a few years later, and the magnificent downtown store was closed. The building was demolished in 2003, and the Seattle Art Museum took its place.

Mention "lunch counter" to any American over the age of sixty, and the first word that springs to mind is probably "Woolworth's." Picture it: a gleaming counter along one wall (usually adjacent to the main entrance) stretching as far as the eye could see; the countertop laden with salt, pepper and sugar shakers; small signs advertising the daily special spaced every few feet; and swivel stools with bright chrome backs. Against the wall, a back counter featured soft drink dispensers (both Coke and Pepsi), a fountain service, milkshake stirrers and coffee urns; display cards listing the menu items; and small boxes of cereal neatly stacked. Between the two counters, a bevy of waitresses patrolled the narrow corridor taking orders and delivering meals.

Woolworth stores could be found in the center of practically any city in America in the 1930 and '40s, and almost all of them had lunch counters. Frank Woolworth, pioneer of low-cost mass marketing, started selling candy in his stores as early as 1886, soon expanding to soda fountains and "refreshment rooms"—in-store cafés with fine china and linen tablecloths. By the 1920s, refreshment rooms were being phased out in favor of lunch counters; they occupied too much space, and customers tended to dawdle at their meals instead of being out on the floor shopping.

The first Woolworth's in Seattle (apparently without any food service) opened in 1912 at 1305 Second Avenue. Six years later, a second Woolworth's appeared at 503–5 Pine, opposite the new Frederick & Nelson building, and this one did have a lunch counter. (A 1940 *Seattle Daily Times* article claimed it was the "first service of its type" in Woolworth stores.) When the Second Avenue location was remodeled in 1924, it featured "the finest and best equipped Woolworth Fountain and Lunch Counter on the Pacific Coast, 230 feet long, seating capacity 100." Every item on the menu—whether roast turkey and dressing or a side dish of creamed peas—was fifteen cents.

Yet another downtown Woolworth's opened at 1612 Third Avenue in 1933, and it, too, boasted "the most up-to-date lunch counter of any Woolworth store in the country." Said one of the newspapers:

A feature of the new store, which will be incorporated in many of the Woolworth units to be built in the future, is the up-to-date lunch counter and soda fountain....The counter is located directly inside and to the right of the south entrance to the Woolworth store. Food served across the counter will be prepared on the premises in large daylight kitchens situated on the upper floors of the building. From these kitchens, the food will be transferred, piping hot, for the taste of the patrons who will fill the many seats surrounding the counter.....Nothing has been overlooked to make the lunch counter the most efficient and sanitary of any Woolworth store in the country....Modern electric sterilizers and a new refrigeration plant have been installed in order that the customers may secure the best foods at all times.

The fourth and final downtown Woolworth's arrived in September 1940—a three-story, million-dollar art deco edifice at the corner of Third Avenue at Pike Street—the largest Woolworth's in the country at the time. The new store had two lunch counters—on the main floor and in the basement—with modern chromium counter chairs and counter-backs of Oriental yellow field tiles. Both counters were served by a kitchen located on the second floor.

Contrary to the name, Woolworth's lunch counter also served breakfast and dinner items. In 1962, a breakfast of two buttermilk pancakes, an egg and two strips of bacon cost sixty cents. The usual burgers, sandwiches and ice cream fountain treats made up the lunch menu. Dinner items included turkey, country fried steak and liver with onions. Woolworth stores across the country generally standardized on what the lunch counters served, though regional specialties occasionally crept onto the menu.

The company even developed its own cookbook—*Woolworth's Bakery and Lunch Counter* recipe book—to make sure that individual store kitchens prepared food in a uniform manner. Recipes included diner standards like chicken croquettes, egg salad, baked canned ham and German chocolate cake, along with a few Woolworth's specialties, such as Frito pie.

Though Woolworth's was one of the world's largest retail chains in its day, market dynamics were shifting toward discount stores like Target, K-Mart and Wal-Mart by the 1970s, and the struggling company closed the last of its lunch counters in 1997. It was the end of an era for thousands of loyal lunchtime customers.

Woolworth's Coconut Pie

15 ounces sugar
1 dozen eggs
1 ounce salt
½ teaspoon nutmeg
1½ ounces cornstarch
1 pint milk
1 ounce vanilla
2½ quarts milk
9 ounces long shred coconut
6 unbaked pie shells

Mix together sugar, eggs, salt and nutmeg. Do not beat. Stir until thoroughly incorporated. Suspend cornstarch in 1 pint milk. Heat to 155 degrees, but do not boil. Add slowly to above mixture, stirring thoroughly.

Add vanilla and mix into 2½ quarts milk, stirring easily. Place in refrigerator and allow to stand 2 to 4 hours. Do not stir. Skim foam from top, if any has formed. Place coconut in each pie shell and fill unbaked shells with refrigerated mixture. There may be sediment in bottom of bowl. Do not use, as this will settle to bottom of crust when baking and form a thin film, making crust soggy. Bake at 450 degrees for 30 minutes. Makes six pies.

Woolworth's Lunch Casserole

1 pound pork sausage links
2 (16-ounce) cans sweet potatoes
1 (8¾-ounce) can drained pineapple tidbits
¼ cup raisins
¼ cup firmly packed brown sugar
1 teaspoon grated orange zest
½ teaspoon salt

Brown sausage links in a skillet, drain and set aside. Mash sweet potatoes. Combine with remaining ingredients. Turn into a 1½-quart buttered casserole. Arrange sausage on top. Bake at 350 degrees for 20–25 minutes.

Another nationwide retailer, S.H. Kress, arrived in Seattle in 1924 with a store at Third Avenue and Pike Street, just across Third from the 1940 location of Woolworth's. Founder Samuel Henry Kress got into the five-and-dime business at about the same time as Frank Woolworth, and their careers charted similar paths. Kress's Seattle store (160th in the national chain) included a lunch counter located in the basement and "fitted throughout with white tile and porcelain and equipped with every modern device for the rapid serving of food and refreshments." The kitchen, under the direction of C.M. May, took pride in emphasizing Seattle-area products in its cooking.

The lunch counter was enlarged and remodeled in 1934; a modernized version reopened in 1942 offering a twenty-five-cent breakfast (available until 11:00 a.m.) and complete plate lunches from 11:00 a.m. until 6:00 p.m. The entire store was remodeled in 1967 and a lunchette installed on the main floor, with a 122-seat cafeteria in the basement. A hot dog at the Whirly-Q Lunchette was just nineteen cents that year. The lunchette was still going strong—serving breakfast, macaroni and cheese, country-style steak and spaghetti to hungry shoppers and office workers—right up until Kress closed the store in 1974.

Pharmacies didn't miss out on the lunch counter business. Bartell Drugs, the nation's oldest family-owned drugstore chain, began when George Bartell purchased a drugstore on Jackson Street in 1890. Details are fuzzy as to when Bartell's began serving food, but it's known that in 1901, five cents could buy an ice cream soda at its 506 Second Avenue store. Additional stores were opened as the Bartell chain grew, and nearly all of them had soda fountains. By 1925, the Second Avenue and Pike Street location had become home to the Balcony Tea Room ("the only tearoom of its kind in the Northwest"), and a 1928 newspaper ad listed thirteen Bartell locations, with fountain lunches available at all of them. (Apparently, the terms "tearoom" and "fountain lunch" were used interchangeably.) By 1940, Bartell's was serving more than ten thousand meals a day.

Bartell's turned sixty-five in 1955, and the occasion prompted several longtime employees to look back and recall how food tastes and styles had changed over the years. Bill Brown recalled a few of the most popular food items—Bartell's specialty chipped ham sandwich served sizzling hot on a bun and their famous homemade soups, chili con carne and forty-nine-cent lunch specials—while others fondly remembered fancy sundaes like the Lover's Delight (strawberry and vanilla ice cream, fresh strawberries and pineapple, crushed walnuts and whipped cream with a cherry on top) and the Brown-Eyed Susan (vanilla ice cream, chocolate sauce, marshmallow sauce, whipped cream, toasted almonds and chocolate drops).

By this time, the Bartell chain was up to twenty-two stores and boasted the largest fountain lunch business in the Northwest. O.J. Allen ran the Bartell Food Department commissary building on Minor Avenue and oversaw menu planning and food purchasing for all the Bartell fountains. In the early days, individual stores prepared food in their own kitchens, but this became impractical. By the 1930s, short orders such as sandwiches were still put together at the stores, but hot foods like soup and chili were made daily at the commissary's kitchen and sent out to the stores.

Food service was a big part of Bartell's business, accounting for a quarter of sales during the 1930s and early 1940s. The company bought only nationally recognized food products but emphasized that local produce was brought daily to the kitchens. While stores adhered to a standard menu, some allowances were made for local variations. The Madison Street store, being located near several hospitals, catered to nurses who preferred soup and sandwiches over the usual lunch specials. A few fountains even served breakfast. But with the 1960s came the rise of fast-food franchises, and the popularity of in-store lunch counters began to fade. Bartell's closed its last remaining soda fountain in 1982.

G.O. Guy, another home-grown drugstore chain, was founded in 1888 by George Omar Guy. A 1930 newspaper article claimed that Guy invented the ice cream soda—accidentally—while working part time at a Philadelphia pharmacy's soda fountain in 1872. ("Soda" at that time meant soda water, usually flavored.) As the story goes, Guy dropped the ice cream ordered by one customer into the soda water ordered by another. Guy was about to throw it all out when one of the customers asked to have a taste and liked it so much he recommended it to his friend. A new taste sensation had been born. The chain celebrated the event with a special Anniversary Ice Cream Soda in 1954.

Throughout much of the twentieth century, G.O. Guy's was the second-largest drugstore chain in Seattle, trailing Bartell Drugs. In 1928, the year after Guy died, the chain consisted of three stores, all with fountains lunches. "The best lunch in town" was thirty-five cents, with a special fifty-cent dinner served from 5:00 until 8:00 p.m. Breakfast at Guy's—two eggs, bacon, toast and coffee—set you back just twenty-five cents in 1931. The chain eventually grew to eight locations: four downtown, with others in West Seattle, the University district and Ballard. Guy's food service lasted well into the 1950s but, like Bartell's, was eventually phased out. G.O. Guy became

Lunch was a busy time at Bartell's Pine Street store—all the stools are occupied and there are six waitresses behind the counter. *Bartell Drugs Archives.*

part of Pay 'n Save in 1987. Today, the flagship store at Third and Union is the Wild Ginger Restaurant.

Another small chain, Hallmark Pharmacies, opened three locations in the late 1920s: the Fifth Avenue Drug Company at Fifth Avenue and Union Street, the Stolle Drug Company in the Olympic Hotel and the Sorrento Pharmacy at Terry Avenue and Madison Street. The Sorrento fountain was designed by Vern Hogenson, head of the soda fountain department of Western Dairy Products, and featured a twenty-four-stool counter with a color tile base, hardwood top and "a gleaming array of fruit flavor fixtures." By 1936, the chain had become Barney O'Connor's, and the soda fountains had been upgraded to lunch counters. That year, a special twenty-five-cent plate lunch, such as hamburger steak Spanish or Boston baked beans, scalloped potatoes, Waldorf salad and coffee or milk, was available at all Barney O'Connor's locations. For ten cents more, a customer could have a lunch that included baked ham with raisin sauce, sweet potatoes, buttered beets, a hot buttered roll, orange bisque, ice cream and a beverage.

Various other downtown Seattle drugstores also had lunch counters. Star Drugs at 1001 Second Avenue advertised its fountain lunch in 1925, as did the Warren Drug Company at Fourth and Olive. The small Owl Drug chain operated soda fountains in its stores in the 1940s.

At the Hotels

As with restaurants, many Seattle hotels (at least a dozen) were destroyed in the 1889 fire. However, like the restaurants, the hotel business quickly rebounded, with over sixty operating by 1895. Many of those were the simple boardinghouse-like structures that had proliferated during pioneer times, but a number of hostelries with aspirations of elegance began to appear. In 1901, the *Seattle Times* pointed to four of them as being the best in the city: the Hotel Butler, the Seattle Hotel, the Northern and the Rainier Grand. Unfortunately, said the paper, all four fell far behind their competition in other cities regarding their grandness, and of Seattle's top four, only one had a first-class restaurant.

Only the Butler Grill, in the Hotel Butler at Second and James, met the newspaper's standards of restaurant quality, and even then, huffed the *Times*, the Grill "is located in a cellar, where it is absolutely impossible…to deceive anyone into the notion that it could possibly be part of a grand hotel." Despite its location, the Butler Grill was good enough that James J. Hill, president of the Great Northern Railway and a famous epicurean, was a frequent patron; whenever he was in Seattle, he made a point of visiting the Grill to enjoy one of several special dishes that the restaurant would prepare for him. One of the first Seattle restaurants to specialize in seafood, the grill's menu featured broiled Alaska black cod with hazelnut butter, halibut, sand dabs, smelt, sole, flounder, sea bass, deep sea crabs, shrimp, oysters (both native and Eastern Toke Point oysters from Maryland) and clams served in a variety of ways. The Butler Grill celebrated its thirtieth anniversary in 1926 and was still going strong when, done in by the Great Depression, the hotel closed in 1933.

The Rainier Grand Hotel's dining facilities included tables, cozy nooks and a coffee shop, with quality service and modest prices. The hotel was located at First Avenue and Marion Street; opened in 1889, it was demolished in 1930 to make way for a new federal building. The Northern Hotel, on First Avenue S between Yesler and Washington, hosted a café from its opening until the 1930s, by which time it had become a Chinese restaurant operated by Sen Yic. The Seattle Hotel—successor to the Occidental, which had burned in the great fire—also had a café, though it didn't compare with the Occidental's famous dining salon. In the 1960s, the Seattle Hotel became the focus of a historic preservation effort. The preservationists lost, though a movement was born that eventually resulted in saving the famous Pike Place Market, among other historic buildings, from demolition. The site of the Seattle Hotel is now occupied by what Seattleites call the Sinking Ship Parking Garage.

These four weren't the only hotel eateries in turn-of-the-century Seattle, of course. The Hotel Diller, one of the first to be built after the great fire, had a dining room that lasted as long as the hotel did. A 1901 menu from the Diller's dining room presented quite a list of options: chicken gumbo; shrimp salad; a relish tray (celery, sliced tomatoes, pickles and olives); several seafood entrées, including baked sea bass, boiled salmon and Olympia oyster patties; roast turkey; prime rib; vegetables (boiled and mashed potatoes, corn and cauliflower); and a variety of desserts. The Diller is long gone, though the building that housed it still stands at the corner of First Avenue and University Street.

Another early hotel famous for its dining room was the Washington Hotel. It was located on Denny Hill, between Stewart and Virginia Streets along what is Third Avenue today, and was named for city father Arthur Denny, one of the investors. Construction began in 1889 (it was out of the fire zone) and was partially completed when the 1893 depression halted work. The building sat empty and unfinished, brooding over the city below, until it was purchased by James Moore in 1903. Renamed the Washington Hotel, it opened that year just in time to greet President Theodore Roosevelt on his visit to the city. Roosevelt, an avid outdoorsman, surely admired the animal heads mounted on the lobby walls and the elk at the foot of the massive stairway to the second floor. Every guest admired the views of the Olympic Mountains to the west, Mount Rainier to the south and Mount Adams on the east; the first decision facing patrons when entering the dining room was to choose which window to sit by. Unfortunately, the Washington Hotel and the hill it perched on stood in the way of urban growth; the Denny Regrade project, the massive reshaping of Seattle's landscape, completely eliminated Denny Hill.

Almost from Seattle's beginning, any self-respecting hotel had to include a dining room, café, grill or coffee shop. The Lincoln Hotel, opened in 1899 at Madison Street and Fourth Avenue, claimed a dining room seating four hundred with à la carte service in separate gentlemen's and ladies' cafés, plus a tearoom and banquet rooms. The Lincoln Hotel was destroyed in a spectacular fire in 1920 with the loss of four lives and never rebuilt. The 1906 Waldorf Hotel waited until 1915 to open its dining room. For awhile, the Waldorf was home to one of Chauncey Wright's restaurants, though management reverted to the hotel after Wright's restaurant empire crumbled. The dining room seems to have been discontinued during World War II but reopened shortly thereafter and was still in business when the hotel was converted to apartments in 1970.

The Savoy Hotel, at 1216 Second Avenue, included a kitchen and grill from the time it opened in 1906. The Savoy dining room was completely renovated in 1926, and a new coffee shop was installed just off the lobby; that year, the Savoy dining room hosted a dinner for world heavyweight boxing champion Jack Dempsey. Remodeled again in the 1930s and renamed the Savoy Grill, by the 1960s, it was serving up Italian food "with spaghetti a specialty." The restaurant was in business into the 1980s, when the site was cleared to make way for the Washington Mutual Tower.

Several new hotels arose in 1907, possibly in anticipation of the upcoming Alaska-Yukon-Pacific Exposition. James Moore, who had previously owned the Washington Hotel and planned to add a theater annex to it until it was removed by the Denny Regrade, opened the Moore Hotel and Theatre at Second and Virginia. It wasn't until 1925 that the Moore Hotel Coffee Shop appeared, but once it did, it became a prominent part of Seattle's nightlife. Open twenty-four hours a day, it appealed to night owls and theatergoers. After the city approved liquor by the drink in 1949, the Moore opened the Firelite Room, a cocktail lounge with curved chairs, a huge stone fireplace and mirrors hung on the black walls. A dining room, the Flame Room, opened later the same year with a full-course New Year's dinner for two dollars—shrimp cocktail, chicken barley soup, relish tray, fruit salad, entrée (roast turkey, baked ham, filet mignon or prime rib) and dessert. Today, both the hotel and theater are still in business, and the Nitelite Lounge occupies part of the premises.

The New Washington Hotel, built in 1907 but not opened until October 1908, was intended to fill the gap literally and figuratively left by the old hotel on Denny Hill. Dining rooms, a Japanese tearoom and a rathskeller (German-style bar) were in place within a few years. The menu offered an extensive selection of soups, oyster dishes, chicken and beef. A specialty of the house was lemon custard pie, only fifteen cents a slice. (A dish of cauliflower was forty cents.) A 1949 remodel replaced the original dining facilities with the Regency Dining Room, described in a contemporary ad as "a happy blend of historic beauty and modern practicality…ultra modern kitchen serving a regal dining room highlighted with antiqued mirrors, white statuettes and a display of our original gold service which has served many of Seattle's pioneers in the early 1900s." A cocktail lounge called the Colonel's Corner opened at the same time (who the colonel was is a mystery). The New Washington was converted to a retirement living facility in 1963.

Directly south across Stewart Street from the New Washington Hotel was the Washington Hotel Annex, which paradoxically opened for business earlier than its "parent." By December 1907, the Annex had added a café and grill with à la carte service (club breakfast; table d'hôte lunch and dinner) from 6:00 a.m. to 1:00 a.m. In 1922, longtime manager T. Harry Gowman purchased the Annex and renamed it Hotel Gowman after himself. As with other Seattle hotels, the Hotel Gowman had the tradition of offering a full dinner on Thanksgiving; the 1929 menu, in addition to the customary roast turkey, also featured king salmon, stuffed goose with baked apples and prime rib. The Gowman became a favorite among Alaskans doing business in Seattle (or over-wintering here to avoid the cold weather back home), and in 1949, the hotel opened the Alaskan Room in recognition of their patronage. By 1951, the Gowman had become the Hotel Stewart; the dining room was open twenty-four hours a day and continued a full menu along with a fried chicken buffet and salad bar. The Hotel Stewart closed in 1968 to make way for a big development that apparently never happened.

The Hotel Sorrento, a seven-story building in the Italian Renaissance style, was built in 1909 on a site at the corner of Madison and Terry with sweeping views of the city, the harbor, Puget Sound and the distant Olympic Mountains. Dining rooms—a large public room and several smaller private rooms, eight thousand square feet in total and accommodating three hundred persons—occupied the top floor along with an orchestra balcony, a Japanese tearoom ("for the ladies") and a rooftop garden. In the 1930s, the dining room was known as the Marine View Room, with a reputation for excellent cuisine and luxurious atmosphere. During World War II, the top floor was converted to a private club so as to allow liquor to be served, and the dining facilities were moved to the first-floor lobby.

Dining resumed on the top floor when the Top O' the Town, renowned for its prime rib, opened in 1954. For many years, the Top O' the Town Choice Prime Rib Dinner was the only entrée on the menu, priced at $4.75 and served with creamed horseradish, fresh vegetables and a baked Idaho potato with sour cream, butter, chopped bacon, green onions and cheese. A

Above: A cable car transported an array of customers to the Top O' the Town, as its menu pretends to show. *Author's collection.*

Opposite, top: This 1941 picture shows the smiling kitchen workforce of the Hotel Gowman. *Seattle Municipal Archives, 18915.*

Opposite, bottom: Linen-draped tables and straight-backed chairs line the fancy dining room of the Sorrento Hotel, circa 1921. *MOHAI, PEMCO Webster & Stevens Collection, 1983.10.2195.3.*

loaf of garlic bread and dessert (vanilla ice cream, fig-rum parfait, coconut sundae or assorted cheese) topped off the meal. Starters—crab, shrimp or oyster cocktails—added another $1.50 to the total. The Top O' the Town closed in the 1980s; its space is now a private banquet room.

The first-floor Fireside Dining Room and Grill opened in 1947. Its main attraction was the open fireplace with tiles from the Rookwood Pottery Company of Cincinnati. In the early 1960s, a portion of the Fireside Room became the Dunbar Room, later yet to be called the Hunt Club and, even later, the Dunbar Room again. Today, a renovated Hunt Club and Dunbar Room coexist adjacent to the Sorrento's elegant lobby.

For many years, the Frye Hotel and the New Richmond Hotel anchored the southern edge of Seattle's business district. Both were built in 1911 and emphasized convenient adjacency to the city's two railroad depots. (The golden age of the automobile was still a few decades in the future.) When it was constructed, the Frye was the tallest building in the city—eleven stories with a brick and terra-cotta façade wrapped around a steel-frame core—but there wasn't a dining room until 1920. A 1929 remodel added a coffee shop. Both the dining room and coffee shop closed during World War II when the hotel was taken over to house wartime personnel, but after the war, the facilities reopened, completely remodeled and redecorated, "with improved dining room and coffee shop facilities, serving the finest of foods; banquet rooms available upon request." Thanksgiving turkey dinner in the Frye Hotel Coffee Shop—cocktail, relish, salad, vegetables, beverage and dessert—cost $2.50 in 1952. Ten years later, Stuart Anderson of Black Angus fame opened the Gold Quarter in the Frye; renamed the Gold Coast in 1969, it was gone by the end of the decade.

Like the Frye, the New Richmond Hotel lacked dining facilities when it opened; it made amends in 1919 with the New Richmond Cafe. A 1940 remodel added a coffee shop; designed by Seattle architect Bjarne Moe in what was called a "bohemian ultra-modern design," it featured colorful decorations and special lighting effects. In the 1950s, a series of restaurants occupied the New Richmond's first floor: the New Orleans Room, with murals and watercolors of New Orleans on the walls and white wrought-iron tables with glass tops, was joined by the King Rex Room, a smorgasbord offering eighty American and Scandinavian dishes plus several hot entrées.

Unfortunately for both the Frye and the New Richmond, Seattle's business district had gradually been growing to the northeast in the 1920s as the Metropolitan Tract and Times Square districts were developed. Travel by rail declined, and by the mid-1960s, both hotels had fallen on hard times. At the New Richmond, one employee murdered another in 1964, and the next year, the place was closed after having been labeled a public nuisance by the police. Luckily, both buildings survive. The Frye was converted to federally subsidized low-income rentals in 1970 and is today called the Frye Apartments. The New Richmond Hotel has been renovated into apartment homes and renamed the Addison on Fourth. There are no public dining facilities in either of them, but Seattle is fortunate that these two classic hotel buildings remain standing.

The city experienced a hotel-building boom in the 1920s as the commercial district pushed northeast. The Metropolitan Tract, original location of the University of Washington, became home to the Olympic Hotel. Nearby were the Exeter and Hungerford Hotels. A few blocks north, the Times Square district, already hosting several of the city's largest department stores, including the Bon Marche and Frederick & Nelson, found itself surrounded by new luxury hotels. All of them provided fine dining experiences; several still do.

Since it opened in 1924, the Olympic has been Seattle's most elegant hotel. Built on the original site of the University of Washington, it was part of the massive Metropolitan Center development and was financed by a public bond subscription. Bond sales were so successful that the initial design of the Olympic was modified and enlarged to take advantage of all the money raised. Several thousand people turned up to celebrate its opening as searchlights raked the night sky.

Five kitchens serviced myriad public and private dining rooms and banquet halls. Best known and longest lasting were the Georgian and Marine Rooms. The Georgian Room was probably best remembered for its high ceilings, ornate trim, chandeliers and refined service. Though the menu differed over the years to keep pace with changing tastes, it was always the epitome of fine dining: a Sunday brunch in 1983 featured omelets along with roast baron of beef, roast lamb and various other hot entrées along with pâtés, terrines and cold poached salmon. After ninety years of eighteenth-century elegance, the Georgian Room discontinued dinner service in 2016.

The Marine Room, also there from the beginning, was the Olympic's music venue, always keeping up with the times. Dancing to orchestral music in the '20s gave way to a nightclub scene in the '40s. It was later called the Downstairs, then became Casey's, a sports bar. Another nightclub, the Olympic Bowl, came along in 1935. In those early days, when practically every establishment with class had to have a tearoom, the Olympic offered the Palm Room.

Many other eating places came and went within the Olympic Hotel over the years. The East Indian–themed Golden Lion opened in 1960. Shucker's, a seafood-oriented bar/café, took over the spot that Piccadilly Corner, a faux old English-style pub, had occupied; it's still there. The Garden Court was a place with multiple personalities: a conventional café for breakfast and lunch, it changed into a sushi bar after lunch and an English tearoom in the late afternoon before becoming a Viennese coffee house in the evening.

A few blocks east of the Olympic on Seneca Street, the Exeter Hotel opened in 1926 with a coffee shop on the premises. Gilbert's Restaurant found a home there in the mid-1940s. A celebration marked the remodeling of the Exeter in 1959 with a redecorated dining room open for lunch and dinner, several private banquet rooms and a coffee shop open for breakfast and snacks. Purchased by Presbyterian Retirement Communities Northwest in 1962 for retirement living, the dining room remained open for residents. It has since been turned into condominiums.

The Hungerford Hotel was located at the corner of Fourth and Spring, a block south of the Olympic. The hotel, built by and named for Earl Hungerford, contained 180 rooms (a mixture of accommodations for overnight guests and semi-permanent residents), a ballroom and an "attractive coffee shop, under the personal direction of Mrs. Earl Hungerford, where excellent foods, served at reasonable prices, is a feature." A.L. Pellon took over the coffee shop in 1929, and for a time it was known as Pellon's Hotel Hungerford Coffee Shop and Grill—"home cooking plus cuisine experience"—and served club breakfasts, merchants' lunches and steak dinners. The Hungerford renamed itself the New Hungerford in 1935. Today, the building is the Pacific Plaza Hotel, and modern restaurants have replaced the old coffee shop and dining room.

In 1916, the *Seattle Times* moved into new offices at 414 Olive Way. Even though the building was flatiron-shaped (triangular), it became known as the Times Square Building, and the surrounding area was called the Times Square district. Often referred to as the uptown shopping district, it rapidly became a focus of new development. Frederick & Nelson relocated there in 1916, and the Bon Marche followed in 1929. Many other businesses gravitated to the area, and hotels sprang up to handle visitors.

Among the earliest was the Claremont Hotel on Fourth Avenue. Opened in 1926, it had a coffee shop a few years later, and the Brittany Tea Room lodged there for a few years. Well-known Seattle restaurateur Les Teagle managed the coffee shop for awhile before pursuing his own enterprises. The Three Crowns Cafe and Dining Room occupied space in the Claremont in the mid-1940s. Mori's Clef Restaurant, operated by orchestra leader Mori Simon, took over in the 1950s, and later that decade, it became the Colony, a nightclub offering music and entertainment along with food service. Today, the Claremont is called the Hotel Andra.

The Camlin Hotel opened its doors the same year as the Claremont. It stood at the eastern end of the district and, at eleven stories, was the most prominent structure in the vicinity. The Camlin introduced the Cloud Room in 1947—"a room with a view…a steak with a sauce…a salad with a flourish…service with a smile"—located on the top floor under management of chef Victor Bruzzi. The Cloud Room became celebrated for its fine fare—appetizers (hot crab and cheese, marinated herring in sour cream, Olympia oyster cocktails), salads (Caesar and a special Cloud Room salad) and entrées such as sesame fried breast of chicken, beef stroganoff, Hawaiian chicken en brochette flambé, charcoal-broiled filet mignon, medallions of beef tenderloin with sauce béarnaise and roast rack of lamb diablo—as well as for the spectacular view. A culinary competition at the Cloud Room in 1967 featured such dishes as beef consommé with quenelles (force meat of veal filled with egg white), lobster thermidor and chateaubriand. Over time, the Cloud Room became part fine dining, part smoky nightclub; it's said that visiting musicians, including Miles Davis, Frank Sinatra and Sammy Davis Jr., put on impromptu performances there. The Cloud Room closed in 2003 when the Camlin was converted to timeshare condos.

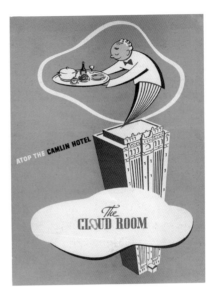

A stylized waiter hovered above the Camlin Hotel to serve Cloud Room guests, as this menu cover shows. *University of Washington Special Collections, MEN004.*

Another 1926 hotel was the Vance, at 620 Stewart Street. The Vance threw open its doors just in time for a New Year's Eve party to welcome 1927. A coffee shop was on site from the beginning; two years later, it had been upgraded to a café. Another restaurant arrived in 1941; part of an overall hotel modernization, it was called the Vance Grill, a finely appointed dining room featuring warm-colored, deep-pile carpeting and Spanish leather upholstery with individual lamp-lit booths in addition to regular dining tables. The grill's decorative motif was centered on a series of hand-painted murals of Northwest scenes, the work of local landscape artist Franz Zollinger. By 1949, the Cedar Room and the Mill Room had joined the Vance Hotel's restaurant family—the Cedar Room for dinners, the Mill Room for cocktails and light entrées such as New Orleans Creole sandwiches, Welsh rarebit en casserole and chicken tamales. These days, the Hotel Max occupies the Vance Hotel's location.

The Bergonian Hotel was another 1927 arrival. It opened in July that year and was built by and named for Stephen Berg, who operated it until 1933. Unlike certain other hotels in the vicinity that appealed to a mix of overnighters and permanent guests, the Bergonian was explicitly tourist-oriented, with 240 rooms, a large dining salon in the basement level, a club

The Vance Grill occupied a prominent ground-floor location next to the Vance Hotel entrance, as this 1940 photo shows. *Seattle Municipal Archives, 18868.*

Streamlined art deco styling dominated the Benjamin Franklin Coffee Shop in 1940. *MOHAI, PEMCO Webster & Stevens Collection, 1983.10.13673.3.*

dining room off the mezzanine lobby and a coffee shop. The year 1933 saw the opening of two new eateries: the Jack and Jill Grill and the Terrace Dining Room. The Jack and Jill Grill featured small tables to ensure prompt service amid an array of scenes from Mother Goose rhymes painted on the walls. The Terrace Room, larger and with group, family and individual tables, was more elaborately decorated with a built-in fireplace at one end of the room and sea-green Tiffany glass windows hung with henna-colored drapes. Both were open for breakfast, lunch and dinner, with the dining room staying open until 1:00 a.m. on weekends.

The Depression hit the Bergonian hard, and it was sold and renamed the Mayflower Hotel in 1934. A new cocktail lounge, the Carousel Room, was introduced in 1949. It became Oliver's in 1976. Today, the hotel is called the Mayflower Park Hotel; the venerable Oliver's is still going strong and has been joined by an upscale restaurant called Andaluca. It is located at 405 Olive Way.

The Benjamin Franklin Hotel, unfortunately, did not survive. Built in 1928, its site is now part of the Westin Hotel, the two circular towers that dominate the northern end of the business district. The Benjamin Franklin had the usual dining room facilities—the full-course Thanksgiving turkey dinner was priced at $1.25 in 1941—but is best remembered for being home to one of the Trader Vic's Polynesian-themed restaurants. The Franklin-themed Key 'n' Kite Restaurant made a brief appearance in the 1960s with breakfast, lunch and dinner served in "typical Benjamin Franklin décor."

Built in 1929 and named for former president Theodore Roosevelt, the three-hundred-room, twenty-one-story Roosevelt Hotel was among the last of the classic hotels to rise in downtown Seattle. Its coffee shop, just off the modernistic lobby, was "futuristic to the nth degree….[I]ts decorative motif is known as 'Off the earth'…[and] every month of the year is represented in correct astronomical figures." There were also one large and several smaller dining rooms. In 1960, the coffee shop gave way to the Bib'n Tucker, where "polished paneled walls, soft lights, music, leather, gold murals create the perfect setting for the delicious foods"; breakfast, lunch and dinner were served, with cocktails available in the Rough Rider and Lanai Rooms. For those not in the know, "bib 'n tucker" means "best set of clothes," as reflected in the restaurant's fine dining and linen tablecloths. In later years, Von's Grand City Café occupied a portion of the Roosevelt's first floor; it disappeared in the early 2000s. (It's not to be confused with the earlier Von's Café, formerly Rippe's, of Fourth Avenue.) The Roosevelt Hotel continues in business at 1531 Seventh Avenue.

TEAROOMS

Tea has been part of human culture for at least 4,000 years. The custom of cultivating and drinking tea originated in southeast Asia. The world's oldest cultivated tea tree, some 3,200 years old, is said to be still extant in Yunnan Province, China. At first considered a medicinal drink for its restorative properties, tea-taking became a recreational pastime among the elite and eventually found its way to the lower classes.

Portuguese merchants and missionaries returning from China introduced Europe to tea in the 1500s. In the minds of many, England is most closely identified with the tradition of taking tea, though it was popular throughout Europe within one hundred years of its arrival. Drinking tea was certainly common in seventeenth-century England, though the high cost restricted consumption to the richer classes. After the British broke the Chinese monopoly on exports by introducing tea cultivation to India, the price declined and tea became an everyday beverage. It was also advocated as a solution to the growing problem of public drunkenness.

Taking tea came to be associated with refinement, gentility and well-mannered society. By 1850, afternoon tea had become a firmly fixed part of British culture. Afternoon tea consisted of more than just drinking tea—scones, jams, pastries and small portions of other foods were an accompaniment. Public tearooms opened as the custom outgrew the confines of the private home, and teas turned into looked-forward-to social gatherings.

According to various dictionaries, a tearoom is a small restaurant of refined, subdued atmosphere where beverages and light meals are served. Tearooms began to appear in finer American hotels in the 1880s. Seattle's Lincoln Hotel had one by 1904, and other hotels followed suit. A 1907 newspaper article mentioned a Japanese tearoom operated by M. Furuya Company, 806 Second Avenue, with carved teak wood furniture, Japanese maidens in silk kimonos and "tea, cakes and candy as the Japanese serve it."

Department store tearooms began opening at about the same time, often doubling as luncheon spots. As early as 1907, the Bon Marche's tearoom was serving lunches—cream of chicken soup, roast beef hash with green peppers, hot chicken pies and hot oyster patties—for twenty to thirty cents each. Frederick & Nelson's tearoom opened the following year, as did one in the Garvey-Buchanan Company department store on Second Avenue. Advertisements boasted, "The lunches are dainty, the service excellent." Even organizations like the YWCA had public tearooms.

The YWCA Tea Room was pleasantly furnished with wicker tables and chairs, hanging plants and coffered ceilings. *Author's collection.*

Tearooms as stand-alone businesses (not within a larger store such as Frederick's) made their appearance in the early 1920s. Mostly operated by women, they were characterized, somewhat stereotypically, as feminine retreats—a place where women could gather apart from male-dominated restaurants and saloons—with small, cozy, elegant furnishings, usually tables/chairs but occasionally done up soda fountain style with a counter and glass display cases. A contemporary newspaper article suggested that opening a tearoom was one of the few options for a college-educated woman to go into business for herself. Ralph Nelson Elliott, in his 1927 book *Tea Room and Cafeteria Management*, laid out some of the basics for a successful tearoom: "The ideal size and type of tea room is one which provides seating accommodation for some seventy people....The food problem may be succinctly stated thus: everything of superior quality with ingenious variety, skillfully cooked, served promptly and in a pleasing way."

Seattle experienced an explosion of tearooms in the 1920s. As with hotels, the epicenter seems to have been the rapidly developing north end of the business district: Times Square and the Metropolitan Tract. Within a few short years, nearly a dozen tearooms were clustered near the big department stores, with another group within easy walking distance of the elegant

Three well-dressed ladies give their orders to the waitress in this idealized tearoom vignette. *Seattle Post-Intelligencer.*

Olympic Hotel. The Metropolitan Tea Room was one of the earliest, opening in the White-Henry-Stuart Building. In 1923, it claimed to serve "a daily average of 400 girls and women from all parts of the city" and was still in business in 1946.

Many of the tearooms went through numerous name, ownership and location changes over the years. The Pine Tree Tea Room is a good example. A March 1923 newspaper article announced its opening in the

McDermott Building at Fourth and Pine: "All decorated in blue, black and orange, with the daintiest service you ever saw!...Miss Emily L. Taggart and Mrs. Darsie Bard are the hostesses." Within a few months, the Pine Tree was serving dinners in addition to light lunches. Tuesday night was baked ham with candied sweet potatoes, and turkey dinners were a Sunday regular. A specialty of the house was lemon sponge pie. When the building that housed it was demolished to make way for the new Bon Marche store, the Pine Tree relocated to 1610 Times Court, an alley running between Pine and Westlake.

A second Pine Tree Tea Room opened in the Shopping Tower, at Third and Pine, in 1929, with Emily Taggart in charge. The original location stayed in business, becoming the Paraquette Tea Room in 1932. The Pine Tree in the Shopping Tower was sold in 1932 to Ruth Holland, who moved it into the Republic Building in 1939. It closed its doors in 1953, one of the longest-lasting tearooms in downtown Seattle.

After selling her interest in the Pine Tree, Emily Taggart opened a new tearoom named for herself in 1934 in the Ranke Building at Fifth Avenue and Pike Street. She served luncheons from 11:30 a.m. to 2:30 p.m. and dinners from 5:00 p.m. to 8:00 p.m., with butterscotch rolls being a crowd pleaser. By 1937, she had moved away from Seattle and was running a tearoom at Gravelly Lake south of Tacoma; 1941 found her doing the same in the San Francisco Bay area.

The Paraquette Tea Room, done in a color scheme of black and platinum and featuring parakeets in cages, began in 1931 at 1519 Fifth Avenue under the management of Gertrude Burwell and Marjorie Reiner. Within a year, it found itself displaced; after a short stint at the old Pine Tree location in Times Court Alley, the Paraquette found a new home at 1616 Fourth Avenue. Like several other tearooms and many businesses, it didn't survive the Depression.

Another early tearoom, the Dixie, started up in the White-Henry-Stuart Building in 1923. According to the *Seattle Times*, "When ladies wish tea they call at the Dixie Tea Room, where their afternoon tea service includes such delicious meals." The room was furnished with old Colonial furniture, cool green and yellow tables and even a grandfather clock. The Dixie started dinner service in 1925, with fried spring chicken dinners a specialty.

Betsy Jarvis took over the Dixie in 1929, renaming it the Betsy Jarvis Tea Room. Betsy's place was a favorite of a *Seattle Times* columnist known only as Jean, who frequently mentioned it in her weekly part advertisement–part gossip column "Jean a' Shopping Goes." Jean recommended it in 1938: "The Betsy Jarvis Tea Room—For delicious foods! Salads supreme! Hot biscuits of a melting quality and for desserts—do order that angel food ice cream sandwich with butterscotch sauce and roasted almonds on top!" Betsy sold out in 1939, and her tearoom became the Hearthstone; she moved south to join Emily Taggart in the tearoom business in Oakland, California.

Jean apparently found the Hearthstone much to her liking; that year, she favorably commented on a lunch she had at the Hearthstone: Crab Newburg in pastry shell, green peas, grapefruit-avocado-tomato salad, hot orange rolls, coffee and baked ice cream meringue with sliced strawberries and whipped cream—all for seventy-five cents. The Hearthstone stayed in business for another fifteen years before finally fading from the Seattle restaurant scene.

The Green Gate Tea Room made its appearance in 1926 at 1526 Westlake Avenue. Owner Mrs. J.R. Moore modeled it after a Greenwich Village type of tearoom and drew a large clientele with a menu offering baked ham with fruit salad, homemade chocolate cake with bombe glaze and creamed crab. Within a year, the Green Gate had outgrown its space. The aforementioned Jean wrote in March 1927, "The Green Gate Tea Room has moved into its spacious new quarters at 614–16 Pine. Delightfully appointed, exquisite in color scheme—it is one of the smartest of tea rooms!"

Rose Jacobs purchased the original Green Gate on Westlake and reopened it as the Rose Garden Tea Room on Thanksgiving Day 1928. To celebrate, she advertised a full-course turkey dinner for $1.25. Betsy Jarvis, mentioned earlier, gained her tearoom work experience at the Rose Garden for a few years before going off on her own. The Rose Garden was well known for its cream pecan nut waffles and pastries and lasted into the 1940s.

In 1931, Rose Jacobs purchased the other Green Gate location at 614 Pine and renamed it the Red Candle. By this time, many tearooms had pushed the boundaries beyond simply afternoon tea service and were increasingly featuring lunches and dinners. (Lunch at the Red Candle was thirty-five cents; dinner cost fifty cents.) Male customers were also on the increase, whether businessmen hunting a good lunch or accompanying their spouses. The ubiquitous Jean commented on "cleverly planned menus and cheerful background" at the Red Candle and the "man sized portions" of food at "women's purse sized" prices. The Red Candle survived into the 1950s.

Yet another tearoom pioneer was Louise Dumbleton and her Fleur-de-Lys Tea Room, opening in March 1923 at 1536 Westlake, a close neighbor to the Green Gate. The Fleur-de-Lys's menu featured eighty-five-cent steak and chicken dinners and a chef's special three-course dinner with salad for sixty-five cents. In 1929, Arthur Gabler bought the Fleur-de-Lys as an adjunct to his Dolly Madison Antiques store and renamed it the Dolly Madison

Tea Room. Gabler, one of only a handful of male tea shop proprietors in Seattle, moved his tearoom to the Ranke Building in 1936—probably into the space left vacant by the departure of Emily Taggart—and it became the Dolly Madison Dining Room, decorated in Colonial style in keeping with the traditional southern-style cooking served. A 1939 article described the Dolly Madison decorated for Christmas with holly, old European Christmas plaques and other adornments and its windows bearing hand-painted scenes from rural old England and Switzerland. In honor of the season, a daily shoppers' lunch (thirty-five cents) included a salad, grilled lamb steak, a vegetable, hot rolls, coffee and dessert. The Dolly Madison closed in 1946, and the Restaurant Stockholm took its place; it apparently didn't last a year—the contents of the former Dolly Madison Tea Room were sold at auction that September.

Helen Swope was among the earliest tearoom operators; she and her sister Alice had one in the White-Henry-Stuart Building prior to 1922. They sold it and acquired the dining room at the Wilsonian Hotel and Apartments in the University District. Alice dropped out of the business, but Helen returned downtown in 1928 and leased half of the second floor of the new Republic Building, where she opened "a delightful restaurant and tea room with appointments and cuisine of the same high standard to be found at The Wilsonian Dining Room and Via Fontana, which have made Miss Swope's name notable among discriminating Seattleites." Within a year, her Helen Swope Tea Room had nearly doubled in size; furnished in the Early American manner, it seated 350 for lunch, afternoon tea and dinner. Meanwhile, Helen was continuing to manage the Wilsonian Dining Room. When the Edmond Meany Hotel opened in 1931, she took over food service operation there, dropping the Wilsonian but keeping her Republic Building tearoom. It finally closed in 1938.

Erna Brown acquired the early Swope Tea Shop in the White-Henry-Stuart Building in 1923, renaming it the Brownie Tea Room. Columnist Jean complimented the reasonably priced home-cooked dinners, describing the Brownie as a place where "food is daintily served," a retreat for those who "enjoy going to a place where there is nothing commercial." Unfortunately, the Brownie seems to have vanished within a year, and Martha's Tea Room and Sandwich Shop took its place. Jean, who seems to have been a fan of tea shops, had praise for Martha's: conveniently located, with excellent service, fountain specials and "piquant salads."

The Parrot Tea Room (not to be confused with the Paraquette) briefly occupied part of the McDermott Building at Fourth and Pine in the mid-

1920s. Described as a quiet and restful place with good food and reasonable prices, its lunch menu listed several varieties of hot and cold sandwiches (toasted chicken, cold baked ham, minced green olives and bacon and olive pimiento, among others), apple and butterscotch pies and lemon nut cake. Zoe Benstead and Belle Kern had charge of the Piccadilly Tea Room on the second floor of the Shafer Building at 523 Pine Street (many of the tearooms were so situated, on the second floor of the buildings that housed them). In 1929, Gertrude Hale, previously at the College Center Tea Room in the University District, was serving luncheons, teas and dinners at the Bob-O-Link Tea Room, 1619 Westlake. The Green Cupboard Tea Room was in the Medical and Dental Building in 1931. A latecomer to the Times Square District was the Anna Kurtz Tea Room, in the Old Times Building at 414 Olive Way. It appeared in 1941 and only lasted a few years.

Carolyn's Brittany Tea Room was a bit of provincial France within the Liggett Building at Fourth and Pike. A popular place for lunches and candlelit dinners (baked ham and steak dinners topped the menu), it was famous for desserts. The Brittany opened at an inopportune time in 1929, just as the Depression hit, but managed to stay in business for at least five years. Not far away was the Gypsy Tea Room in the McKelvey Building at Third and Pike, where "real Italian dishes are features of the lunches and dinners." A block or two farther along was the English Tea Room at 1508 First Avenue, which, strangely, advertised Rainier beer on draught in 1924, the height of Prohibition.

Helen Malloy's first tearoom, the Banquet, was located at 721 Virginia Street in 1929. The following year, she moved into the new Security Public Market at Third and Virginia and reopened as the Helen Malloy Tea Room. A year later, she took over tearoom operations at the Rhodes department store, and by 1935, she was also managing the Rhodes lunch room. Tafney's Tea Room was farther downtown on Marion Street and was a favorite for club and group meetings for the short time it was in business. The Pickwick Tavern, 522 Seneca Street, was described as "an excellent little tearoom where delicious home-cooked meals are served at moderate prices." Rideau's Tea Room made a brief appearance on Second Avenue in 1928.

On the fringes of downtown, the Peter Puget Tea Room at 918 Boren Avenue—"a tea house with a tower"—was open for lunch, tea, dinner and "waffles any time." The Pollyanna Tea Room was at 619 E Pine Street, and farther up the hill was the Blue Lantern Tea Room at Broadway and Roy Street.

3
Restaurant Empires

The term brings up visions of nationally franchised chains or large corporations that own huge numbers of restaurants across the country (or, for that matter, the world). These days we're accustomed to restaurant conglomerates and national franchises (think McDonald's, Wendy's, Applebee's, the Olive Garden) whose main claim, other than their presence everywhere, is their standardized appearance and menus. With a few exceptions, the Burger King you eat at in Seattle—the food choices, the general layout of the place—is likely identical to one you would visit in Portland, Maine. The chains count on that; uniformity breeds familiarity, and familiarity makes customers comfortable.

It was a different world, though, up into the mid-1950s when the franchises and chain restaurants began dominating the restaurant scene. Prior to that time, the majority of restaurants were stand-alone, owner-operated businesses. They changed names frequently and locations occasionally, but rarely were multiple restaurants under the control of a single individual. Seattle had a few exceptions to the rule, though; as early as the 1910s, several restaurateurs were putting together local chains whose names became household words in the city.

Chauncey Wright and the Seattle Restaurant Company

Chauncey Wright's restaurant roots ran deep. Even as a young boy, he was helping out in his father's lunch counter in Los Angeles. After the Wrights moved to Seattle in the 1880s and his father opened a restaurant on Front Street where the Colman Building is now, Chauncey would fish off the back porch of his father's restaurant. (The tidelands had not yet been filled in, and Elliott Bay lapped up against the rear of the building.) Whatever he caught often appeared on the menu that same evening. Chauncey opened his first restaurant while still in his early twenties but soon caught gold fever and took off for the Klondike. Up there, he soon realized that toiling in waist-high freezing water wasn't his path to riches, so he started up a small café. Selling a cup of coffee for fifty cents, a sandwich for one dollar or a meal for four to eight dollars soon earned him the grubstake he sought.

Returning to Seattle, he reentered the restaurant business in 1900 at 1205 First Avenue. By 1908, he had sold that location and was operating a restaurant at 164 Washington Street in partnership with his wife, Annie. His new place was typical of the day: a storefront restaurant with large plate-glass windows bearing signs advertising oysters, fish, steak and chops. Chauncey Wright's soon became famous about town for its fine steaks and chops, cooked to perfection; its reputation was such that one day ten men lodged in the city jail for disorderly conduct temporarily busted out of confinement in protest of the food they were getting and headed straight to Chauncey's place for a good meal.

In 1910, the Wrights sold the Washington Street location, incorporated as the Seattle Restaurant Company and opened restaurants at 108 Madison Avenue and 110 Occidental Avenue. Uproar ensued when the new owners of the old Washington Street location kept Chauncey's name on their signboard while Chauncey himself opened a new restaurant under his own name a short distance away. Legal matters ensued and turned a bit ugly before the parties reconciled a few years later. Chauncey's Madison Avenue restaurant apparently didn't last long, but 110 Occidental became a well-known destination for knowledgeable Seattle diners.

A 1912 newspaper article gives a description of 110 Occidental Avenue: a $40,000 restaurant, open twenty-four hours a day, providing "lightning service" to three thousand persons daily. It had a massive range and charcoal broiler for hot items, a refrigeration unit to "keep things cold that should be kept cold" and rolls kept warm and fresh in a warmer specially built for the

A sidewalk stroller stops to examine the giant lighted CW in the window of Chauncey Wright's restaurant on Occidental Avenue in 1913. *University of Washington Special Collections, SEA0209.*

purpose. The menu was extensive for its time. Oysters (either Olympia or Eastern) were available raw, stewed, pan roasted, fried or as a cocktail. Six types of fish, including smelt, flounder, sole, halibut and salmon, were listed along with seventeen types of steaks, chops and roasts prepared various ways. Breakfast—buckwheat cakes with maple syrup for fifteen cents (add three rashers of bacon for another ten cents)—was available all day. Lunch offerings included a hot roast beef sandwich for fifteen cents, various cold sandwiches at ten cents apiece, corned beef hash for twenty cents and oyster stew at thirty cents a bowl. Dinner options included broiled chicken, sirloin steak and lamb or pork chops. A customer favorite was hamburger steak smothered with onions.

Chauncey Wright's next restaurant opened at 1420 Third Avenue in 1914 with "the same high-class food and service that has made his restaurant at 110 Occidental Avenue famous." Shortly after the L.C. Smith Building opened in 1914 (at thirty-eight stories and 484 feet, it was for many years the tallest building west of the Mississippi River), he opened a tearoom on the top floor, a small café on the ground floor and an elegant restaurant, air-conditioned and "finished in Old English tile in brown, tan and green," to seat seven hundred people in the basement. The three Wright restaurants in the building were connected by a special service elevator.

By 1917, Chauncey had opened another location, his "latest restaurant and bakery," at 1209 Second Avenue, with fourteen tables, eighty chairs and a one-hundred-foot-long lunch counter. Large plate-glass display windows with the restaurant's CW logo outlined by frosted neon tube lighting faced the street; inside, long counter tables lined tiled walls with the kitchen at the rear. By now, Wright's was selling products under its own brand, such as French vanilla ice cream ("the biggest plate in the city for 10 cents, served in a glass dish set in a silver bowl of cracked ice") and Chauncey Wright's own chocolate eclairs, made by a French pastry expert and served and sold retail at all four Chauncey Wright locations.

After several months of illness, Chauncey Wright died in December 1917. Annie remarried and continued the business as the Chauncey Wright Restaurants Company. Hazen J. Titus, who made the "big baked potato" famous throughout the nation as a feature of the Northern Pacific Railroad dining car service, became president while Annie, styling herself as Mrs. Chauncey Wright Johnston, stayed on as vice president and assistant general manager.

A new Chauncey Wright's opened in 1919 in the Colman Building at the corner of First Avenue and Marion Street, bringing to eight the number of Wright's restaurants then open. Mahogany-finished woodwork created an artistic contrast to the buff tint of the walls. A distinctive feature of the new restaurant was the height of the dining tables; they were specifically scaled to accommodate "the trade of women." The front half of the restaurant's south wall was equipped with elaborate showcases displaying the pastries and confections produced daily by the Chauncey Wright bakeries, which were playing an increasingly important part in the business.

Another Wright's opened in the Waldorf Hotel, at Seventh Avenue and Pine Street, in 1920. That same year, Annie Wright Johnston sold most of her interest in the Chauncey Wright Restaurants Company to Abe Frank, who became equal partner with Hazen Titus. A new bakery opened the following year in North Seattle. Baked goods, particularly mince meat and fruitcakes, were available by mail order as well as at retail outlets in other cities. But by 1922, the Chauncey Wright empire was starting to crumble. Hazen Titus spun off the fruitcake business under his own name. The Second Avenue location was sold off, renamed the Peacock Restaurant and promptly went into foreclosure. The following year, all equipment of the Chauncey Wright Restaurants Company was sold at auction. Hazen Titus moved to Southern California, where he unsuccessfully tried to convince the town of Puente to change its name to Fruitcake. By 1926, he was managing a hotel in Sarasota, Florida.

After a brief hiatus, Annie Wright plunged back into the restaurant business, and in 1921, she was operating two locations in the Smith Building, doing business under the ungainly company name of 42-Story L.C. Smith Bldg. Restaurants Inc. She operated two dining rooms on the upper floor with capacity for 250 seats. Saturday Supper Dances—9:00 p.m. until midnight with à la carte meal service—became a weekly staple. By 1926, Annie had removed from the Seattle restaurant scene and was operating the Friendly Inn on the road to Mount Rainier south of Eatonville. She passed away in 1932.

After legendary Seattle restaurateur Ivar Haglund purchased the Smith Tower in 1976, plans were announced for the Chauncey Wright Cafe on the ground floor. A café was eventually opened, but it did not bear Chauncey's name; it vanished, and the lofty Smith Tower building was left without an eatery.

BEN PARIS RECREATION CENTERS

Billiards tables, a cigar stand, a barbershop, a shoeshine stand, hunting and fishing gear and a lunch counter: Ben Paris Sporting Goods & Recreation Centers had it all for the 1930s man-about-town. Shortly after arriving in Seattle in 1906, Alabama native Benjamin M. Paris opened a five-table pool parlor in West Seattle; within a few years, he and his brother Jack were running four billiard saloons in Seattle, Auburn, Bremerton and Mount Vernon. When the new Eitel Building arose on Pike Street in downtown Seattle in 1923, Ben went in with Bartell Drugs on a long-term lease and opened the first of his recreation centers at 120 Pike. Ben advertised his place as the perfect spot for downtown businessmen to relax on their noon hour. The lunch counter was nothing special—entrée, soup, dessert and coffee for forty-five cents—but the appeal of one-stop shopping (why not get a haircut and a shoeshine while there?) made it a popular destination.

In 1930, Ben moved uptown to the rapidly developing Times Square district near the big Bon Marche and Frederick & Nelson department stores

Ben Paris's 120 Pike Street restaurant was a modest affair, as this 1940 photo attests. *Seattle Municipal Archives, 18617.*

and opened a new recreation center at 1609 Westlake Avenue; another followed in 1932, just a stone's throw away at 1608 Fourth Avenue. For many years, the 1609 Westlake location was Ben's flagship store. Upstairs was a full-service sporting goods store selling everything from baseballs to outboard motors. Down a flight of stairs was a restaurant (two counters with stools, tables set against the wall), barbershop, shoeshine stand, cigar store and a booth selling tickets to boxing matches and other sporting events. Women weren't excluded, but the place definitely had the feel of what these days we would call a man cave, with animal heads adorning the walls and a feeling of rugged manliness.

Within a few years, though, Paris realized that the restaurant side of his business was rapidly overtaking the sporting-goods component. He also realized that the overly masculine atmosphere discouraged women from patronizing the restaurants. The old Pike Street location received a makeover. (Al Hendrix, Jimi's father, worked there in the early 1940s.) The cafés in the 1609 Westlake and 1608 Fourth Avenue stores were enlarged. To attract women shoppers and families, tables and booths outnumbered counter stools. A new menu was featured with an emphasis on quality and family-oriented meals. Plate luncheons were just twenty-five cents, and full-course dinners started at fifty cents. To attract moviegoers (several theaters were within walking distance), Ben Paris stayed open nightly until 1:30 a.m.

In 1934, Paris, along with Leonard Hesse, opened a "luncheon rendezvous" called the Snack 'n Tap at 407 Pike Street. It didn't last long; within a year, it was replaced by the Golden Gate Cafe. More successful was a new restaurant at 2424 Fourth Avenue, which opened in 1948. It's claimed that Ben Paris obtained the first beer license in Seattle after Prohibition ended, and by 1941, his annual sales of draft beer reached 167,000 gallons (plus another 150,000 bottles).

Ben Paris passed away in 1950; his recreation centers lived on, though their reputation started declining. Today, only memories remain of Ben's restaurants. The 2424 Fourth location became Danny Sprout's in the late 1950s. The Hard Rock Café occupies the original 120 Pike site. In 1978, 1609 Westlake was transformed into a cabaret theater and later demolished (along with 1608 Fourth) to make way for the Westlake Center.

By contrast, Paris's location on Westlake Avenue was brightly lit with neon and a window display of sporting gear. *Author's collection.*

CLARE COLEGROVE, THE NOTHOLD INN
AND THE PURPLE PUP

December 1914 saw the opening of an elegant new restaurant in downtown Seattle: the Northold Inn, at 214 University Street. It was the creation of Clare Colegrove, a gentleman farmer living on Vashon Island and at that time manager of the tearoom in the Fraser-Paterson department store. At three stories (plus basement and subbasement), with an exterior of red tapestry brick and cream-colored stucco and copper hinges on the doors, the Northold was an imposing building projecting an old English inn feeling that, as Colegrove stated, would "perpetuate the old-fashioned hospitality for which England became famous three centuries ago."

The main dining room on the ground floor, paneled in Early English style, was light and airy with walls of beautiful Washington fir stained a rich warm brown, highlighted along the top by a frieze of soft tan. Hand-hammered copper plates of medieval pattern were set into the walls; bowls of hammered copper were suspended from the ceiling. The room was illuminated by indirect lighting that brought out the tan color of the ceiling, the gleam of the copper and the shine of the polished oak floor. A huge fireplace of Oriental brick dominated one side of the room. Linen-draped dining tables bore crystal glassware and fine Syracuse china bearing the inn's own crest. A private dining room for parties of twelve or fewer was off to one side. In the basement was the more informal English Grill; apartments occupied the second and third floors.

The Northold Inn was fine dining at its best. A menu describes Sunday dinner: crab cocktail, cream of tomato soup, a choice of entrée (filet of salmon, half a fried spring chicken or filet mignon), new potatoes browned in butter, asparagus in cream, pineapple salad, hot rolls, dessert (Neapolitan ice cream, loaf cake or strawberry meringue pie) and a beverage—all for $1.25. Much of the produce came from Colegrove's own Northold Farm on Vashon Island.

Happy with the success of the Northold Inn, Colegrove opened three more restaurants in rapid succession: Colegrove's Specialty Food Shop, at 110 Pike Street, in 1919; Colegrove's Auto Kitchen (820 E Pike Street at Broadway); and Colegove's Egyptian Kitchen (1524 Third Avenue) the following year. The Auto Kitchen was so named for its location on what at the time was Seattle's "auto row." How the Egyptian Kitchen got its name isn't known.

Clearly, the Northold Inn was a cut above Colegrove's other restaurants, which were more along the lines of neighborhood cafés. Unfortunately, the Northold Inn closed in 1924. It later became the Hollywood Tavern and, in the 1970s, was resurrected as the Medieval Inn. Its site is now occupied by Benaroya Hall, home of the Seattle Symphony.

Shortly after losing the Northold Inn, Colegrove also closed the Egyptian Kitchen. Undaunted, he soon opened another restaurant, the Purple Pup, in the Medical-Dental Building at 1628 Fifth Avenue. Its décor was Spanish with mahogany counters, wainscoting and seats. On the menu were Swiss steak, baked chicken and noodles, breaded pork steak and filet of halibut plus a table d'hôte service with daily specials. Twenty different luncheons were listed ranging from twenty-five to fifty cents; the regular dinner special was fifty cents (seventy-five cents on Sunday). For a quick lunch, a patron could choose "sandwiches of dozens of combinations of meats, fowl, vegetables and preserves."

Colegrove undertook his most ambitious project in 1928: the Spanish Buffet and Coffee Shop. When it opened at 511 Pike Street, he took out newspaper ads describing it as "Seattle's most beautiful restaurant…an eating place of distinction." Two dining areas held seventy-five tables, a forty-four-foot counter and a separate soda fountain for quick snacks and lunches. Colegrove

implemented a concept he called "instant service" based on ideas he had seen on trips to California: food was displayed in glass cases and a menu posted on the wall. The patrons would choose, order, proceed to a "service station," pay, pick up the order, find a seat and enjoy their meals—rather like a glorified cafeteria. After 5:00 p.m., regular coffee shop service took over—orders were taken at tables and food was brought by waitresses in Spanish costumes. The restaurant was open nineteen hours a day. By 1929, the "instant service" idea had been abandoned. Now called the Spanish Buffet-Grill, a more traditional bill of fare ("a New York menu with Seattle prices") featured steaks, chops, seafood and casserole and chafing dish specialties.

A dollar bought three meals a day at Colegrove's Spanish Buffet, announces this newspaper ad from 1928. *Seattle Times.*

The 1929 crash hit Colegrove hard. The Spanish Grill succumbed first; the Cafe Sorrento took its place. The Purple Pup closed and was soon taken over by Walter Clark, remodeled and renamed Clark's Coffee Tavern. The Specialty Food Shop and the Auto Kitchen lasted until about 1931, but they, too, eventually disappeared. Clare Colegrove didn't give up, though. He and his wife, Blanche, relocated north of Seattle and opened Colegrove's Fine Foods at 23628 Highway 99 in 1935, operating it until retiring in 1945. He did the cooking; she did the waitressing. Once a restaurateur, always a restaurateur. Colegrove died in 1971 at the rich old age of 101.

WALTER CLARK AND CLARK'S RESTAURANT ENTERPRISES INC.

For over forty years, Walter Clark was Seattle's "Mr. Restaurant." In his roles as a clerk in a Manning's Coffee outlet to enterprising owner of his first restaurant; his innovations in managing expenses while ensuring quality; and his personal code of conduct and leadership role in the food service industry, as friendly competitor Victor Rosellini said, "[Clark] represents the epitome of the great restaurateur who believes in serving the industry and the community. He's always been a perfect gentleman and an idol for all of us. He commands great respect throughout the industry. Hell, he's the father of the restaurant industry in Seattle."

Clark's career began inauspiciously as a box boy at a department store in Portland, Oregon. At that time, many department stores had full-service food sections, and Clark soon became a "clerk on the floor," taking food orders from customers and relaying them to the workers behind counters where the orders were filled. His work ethic didn't go unnoticed, and he was hired away by the coffee roaster at the local Manning's. After duty in the army during World War I, he relocated to Manning's Pacific Northwest supervisor in Seattle until a falling out led to his leaving the company in 1929, just as the Depression was starting.

Unfazed, Clark saw the opportunities that came with owning his own restaurant, and in 1930, he purchased Marie's Bar-B-Q, a three-booths-with-a-counter operation in the University District. Small though it was, Marie's was doing a booming business with students from the university as well as neighborhood locals. Wisely, Clark kept almost everything about Marie's intact after he took over—same name, same recipes, same cook. His improvements were to add a few additional waitresses and to keep prices low so as to continue attracting customers. It worked, and Marie's thrived.

It wasn't long before he gave thought to other opportunities, and after taking on a business partner, another Manning's alum named Karl Monson, Clark purchased two more small food operations in downtown Seattle. One of them was disposed of quickly, but the other, the Clark & Monson Fountain Lunch, on Fourth Avenue, proved to be a success. Emboldened, they expanded again with the purchase of the White Spot (soon renamed Clark's Top Notch) on Second Avenue. They also took space in the White-Henry-Stuart Building previously occupied by the Red Robin Inn (no relation to the later chain of Red Robin burger outlets). After remodeling, it opened in 1931 as the Salad Bowl, a restaurant intended to appeal to women with a menu that featured salads and lighter fare as well as sandwiches and compete dinners.

Clark expanded his empire in 1933 by leasing Colegrove's Purple Pup in the Medical-Dental Building, renaming it Clark's Coffee Tavern and opening another location, Clark's Third Avenue, at 1426 Third. This latter restaurant didn't work out as planned, apparently. In 1934, it was renamed the Pretzel Tree, a "highly modernistic version of a combined bar [and] restaurant," and occupied the entire ground floor, with steam tables and serving facilities, a balcony along the entire south wall and commodious booths "lighted with novel 'pretzel tree' shaded individual lamps." The Pretzel Tree didn't succeed either and was gone within a year.

In 1937, after the dust had settled from selling off a few locations and recouping losses from others, Walter Clark found himself owner of three restaurants: the Salad Bowl, the Coffee Tavern and the Top Notch. But the Clark-Monson team was just getting started. Clark's Round the Clock opened in 1939 on Olive Way at Terry Avenue; the same year saw Clark's Fountain Lunch move into the Seattle Bowling Recreation at Sixth Avenue and Pine Street.

As its name implies, the Round the Clock was open twenty-four hours a day; a newspaper writer commented that the "Round the Clock, Clark's all-nitery at 1001 Olive Way, is another fine spot for post-dinner, pre-breakfast dining. Perhaps you won't go for the ice-cream covered waffles, as the teenagers do, but there are other things to stave off starvation." The "other things" listed on the menu included half a dozen different salads; hot sandwiches, including roast pork, beef and a chickenburger; a dozen types of cold sandwiches; a few seafood items (pan-fried salmon, grilled oysters and oyster stew); and fountain treats. The Fountain Lunch, located on the

Clark's Round the Clock was an all-day/all-night operation at 1001 Olive Way. *MOHAI, PEMCO Webster & Stevens Collection, 1983.10.17115.3.*

bowling alley's third and fourth floors, was more down-scale, "serving good food at low prices; also your favorite wines and beer."

Walter Clark took over and resuscitated the faltering Twin T-P's on Aurora Avenue in 1943, bringing his restaurant total to six. Growth over the next twenty years included:

> *1948: the Totem Restaurant (later called the Westerner), 423 Pike Street*
> *1951: Clark's Fifth Avenue (formerly the Coffee Tavern, later the Red Carpet), 628 Fifth Avenue, and Clark's Continental, 2230 Seventh Avenue*
> *1952: Clark's Northgate, in the Northgate shopping center*
> *1956: Clark's Crabapple (in Bellevue) and Clark's Minute Chef, 1316 Fourth Avenue*
> *1960: Clark's Pancake Chef, on Highway 99 south of the city; Clark's Little Chef, on Market Street in Ballard; Clark's Village Chef, in the University District; and Dublin House, downtown at 319 Union Street*

And that's not even a complete list. Along the way, Walter Clark also found time to operate restaurants in Yakima and Olympia, start a catering service and an industrial food operation to handle Boeing's plants and serve as president of the National Restaurant Association.

Walter Clark stands in front of the Dublin House in 1960, shortly after it opened. *Museum of History and Industry, 2002.46.14.*

The Clark restaurants ran the gamut from short-order eateries to elegant dining salons. With just a few exceptions, each Clark restaurant was unique to itself, with different appearances inside and out, different menus and different target audiences. His masterpiece was Dublin House, located in the ground floor of the recently completed (1959) Washington Building at 319 Union Street and the forty-seventh unit in his chain. Inside and out, the setting was evocative of an Irish townhouse: outside, marble panels and green-tinted copper trim, and inside, dark mahogany walls stretching to the nineteen-foot-high ceiling, woven carpet incorporating traditional Irish colors and myriad antiques imported from Ireland.

In 1961, the Dublin House's menu won honor from the National Restaurant Association as the country's most remarkable menu of the month. Not only was it elegantly designed, the entrées were all listed in Gaelic (with English translations for those who didn't understand the language), *Rointt Mairt-Fheoil* (beef strips in sour cream) and *Fillean Bhrsadain* (filet of sole Tullamore) among them. In later years, the Gaelic names were phased out, and the entrées became more ordinary—prime rib, chicken Kiev, veal Cordon Bleu, broiled shrimp, broiled oysters—along with a few specialties such as chicken Dublin House (chicken breast stuffed with seasoned rice) and filet of salmon River Boyne. Only a few vaguely Irish dishes, including Irish stew and corned beef and cabbage, made the list.

In 1970, Walter Clark sold the bulk of his holding in Clark's Restaurant Enterprises to the Campbell Soup Company. Even though several of Clark's children made the jump to the new owners, it was soon evident that a company whose main focus was putting soup in cans had no idea how to successfully run a string of restaurants. Though a few new places opened under Campbell's tenure, by the mid-1970s, the sell-off was well underway. The Dublin House closed in 1974; in 1976 alone, seven restaurants were sold. Eugene Clark purchased the Red Carpet from Campbell and kept it running for a few more years; it closed in 1983.

Walter Clark passed away in 1990 at the age of ninety-three, and with him ended the era of the grand restaurateur in Seattle. None of his restaurants survive today.

Rogers' Confectioneries

Sometime around 1915, candy maker William Rogers, who had been in business since 1907, decided he needed his own outlets for his products in addition to selling them through local stores. His first unit was located right within the Rogers Candy & Ice Cream company plant at 4339 Fourteenth Street NE (later renamed University Way). By 1916, two additional outlets had opened in downtown Seattle, at Ninth Avenue and Union Street and at 1302 Third Avenue in the Pantages Building. After Homer Soules became company president in 1919, the chain expanded with a new store at 409 Pike Street (later relocated to 326 Pike) and another at 1408 Second Avenue. Yet another downtown store appeared at 1533 Fourth Avenue in 1931.

The Rogers stores were known by different names over the years—Rogers' Confectionery being the most common—and originally sold only candy and ice cream treats but were offering fountain service and short-order lunches by 1916. The University Way location had been upgraded by 1930 and renamed Rogers' Community Center with a coffee shop, cafeteria, dining room, soda parlor, pastry shop, fountain lunch counter and seating for 350 people all under one roof. That year, a complete Thanksgiving Day turkey dinner cost just one dollar.

By the mid-1930s, the Rogers stores were beginning to disappear, as the company refocused on wholesale candy production. The Community Center, largest of the restaurants and the last to remain open, lost its space to Nordstrom's (at that time merely an upscale shoe store) in 1935. Rogers Candy remained in business for another fifty years, finally being purchased by Hazel's Candies of Tukwila. By then, the lights had long since gone out in the Rogers lunchrooms.

HORLUCK'S MALTED MILK SHOPS

Horluck's Malted Milk appeared on the Seattle restaurant scene just as the Rogers shops were fading away. In the early 1920s, George Horluck, son of Danish immigrants, decided to take a break from the family business (the Horluck Transportation Company, operators of a small fleet of Puget Sound ferries) and undertake a tour of Europe. While visiting Copenhagen and other northern European cities, he became intrigued by the idea of the *conditore*, which he described as a "shop where people gathered for a social hour over their pastries, coffee and ice cream." On returning from Europe, he resolved to create similar shops in Seattle and opened a small store on Second Avenue where he sold "malted milks, ice cream and kindred foods" in 1928.

The idea caught on almost immediately, and additional stores were opened under the company name of Horluck's Malted Milk Shops. Horluck built his own ice cream plant at 600 Westlake Avenue N in 1929, producing a brand called Danish Ice Cream (claimed to be based on a traditional recipe he found while touring Denmark). Within a year, the ice cream plant was producing one thousand gallons a day, and Horluck's had over twenty retail outlets for its products. The same year, the company name was changed to simply Horluck's to resolve a trademark impingement claim made by the Horlick Malted Milk Corporation.

Horluck's adopted a consistent design scheme: black- and white-tiled counters and bars, stools with black seats atop white pedestals and a malted milk machine at each stool and walls of white tile with wainscoting bordered at the top with black. Even the menus and advertising cards conformed to this distinctive color theme. The shops sold only dairy products—ice cream and malted milk (no gum or cigars, as many competitors did)—as well as a line of sandwiches called "Tasty Tenners": chicken, ham and spicy condiments, made at a central location and delivered to individual stores daily.

In the early days, Horluck's called its outlets "Naborhood shops" and offered a hostess service for those who needed help planning parties. (Horluck's products were sure to top the list of suggestions.) Eighteen shops were listed in 1930, most of them in downtown Seattle, with a few others located in the University and Madrona neighborhoods and even in other cities (two in Tacoma, one each in Bellingham and Bremerton). A second round of expansion in the mid-1930s added another half dozen outlets. Only two of the shops were actually called conditores: one at the ice cream

White-coated waiters and a gleaming white counter gave Horluck's Malted Milk Shops an air of cleanliness. *University of Washington Special Collections, SEA2939.*

plant on Westlake and another in 1930 in the newly opened Shopping Tower Building at 217 Pine Street.

In a 1929 newspaper article ascribing near-mystical powers to malted milk, George Horluck said the "experience of [his] company has demonstrated, while highly popular as a beverage, malted milk serves another and far more important service as 'the food of the metropolitan citizen.'…People in the larger cities desire a lunch that will not be too heavy, and malted milk, backed by a sandwich or a piece of tasty cake, just about fills the bill."

The malt mystique didn't last long, though. In 1933, with the end of Prohibition in sight, Horluck turned his attention to brewing beer. He built a brewery adjacent to the ice cream plant at Westlake and Mercer and by the following year was supplying Seattle's taverns with a high-quality Vienna-style fire-brewed beer. The ice creamery—renamed Horluck Creameries and relocated to Airport Way S—still operated as a separate business but refocused on wholesale production. The individual Horluck locations were either closed or sold off, and by the late 1930s, Horluck's was out of the malted milk shop business.

Thirty years after Horluck's sold its last malted milk and Tasty Tenner sandwich, columnist John J. Reddin fondly recalled them: "As a young teen-ager, my favorite eating spot was the Horluck's shop at Third and Union that served the thickest milk shakes and malted milk, plus sandwiches on real fresh bread and sliced chicken or turkey white meat almost an inch thick. In my humble opinion, there never has been a better sandwich or chocolate milk shake made by anybody anywhere in the United States. They had both quality and quantity."

Jorgensen's Fountain Restaurants

When George Horluck began selling off his retail outlets, one of his store managers, Nick Jorgensen, leaped at the opportunity to own his own place. He purchased the 600 Westlake shop in 1937, renamed it Jorgensen's Finer Foods and, a year later, opened another location downtown at 529 Pine Street opposite the Frederick & Nelson department store. Jorgensen's flagship store opened in 1941 at Fourth Avenue and Stewart Street, and in celebration, patrons received free dishes of ice cream. At the same time, the interiors of the other stores were thoroughly remodeled with new booths, counters and display space. New stores opened annually for the next few years, and by its tenth anniversary, Jorgensen's (now called Jorgensen's Fountain Restaurants) had ten locations—five of them downtown, the others on the edges of the city—plus an additional three Danish Bakeries (like Horluck, Jorgensen was of Danish descent).

In its early years, Jorgensen's continued the Horluck custom of a limited bill of fare, offering Danish ice cream (up to forty flavors) and fountain drinks. By 1944, Jorgensen's shops had transformed from ice cream fountains to full-scale lunch and dinner restaurants. The menu featured a fine array of food items, including Danish-style beef burgers, farm steak and chopped round steak; chicken à la king on biscuits; baked beans; spaghetti; and special sandwiches (roast beef and tomato club, baked ham and egg salad and grilled ham and cheese) along with the usual sandwich standbys, such as tuna, chicken and cheese. Fountain treats—ice cream sodas and floats and malted milks—were still on the menu. Except for items that were best prepared within each shop, food items were prepared in a central commissary for efficiency and to ensure consistent quality.

Baked goods played an important role in Jorgensen's food offerings. Devil's food, angel's food and sponge cakes; bear paws, honey nut pasties and butterhorns; and donuts—plain, sugared, glazed and cinnamon—all tempted Jorgensen's customers. In addition to being featured on the menu, several of the restaurants had a display case of bakery items strategically located near the cash register so customers could pick up some sweets to take home. All baked goods came from Jorgensen's own central bakery located at 214 James Street. By the 1950s, as the baked goods began playing a larger part in Jorgensen's sales, the bakery business was spun off as Jorgensen's Danish Bakeries Inc. Several varieties of Jorgensen's Danish cookies—chocolate wafers, butterscotch, mixed fruit and butter cookies—were sold in traditional grocery outlets up and down the West Coast.

Meanwhile, the number of fountain restaurants began to shrink, and in 1954, only three were listed in the city directory. Nick Jorgensen himself moved on to bigger things. In 1960, he was named as manager of food and beverage concessions for the upcoming Century 21 Exposition. After the fair ended in October 1962 and the site became the Seattle Center, he was involved in setting up operations for two major restaurants that had been constructed especially for the fair but had become permanent residents. He was also involved in setting up a food court at the Seattle Center, a concourse with room for forty-five to fifty shops. Jorgensen resigned his position with the center in 1964 and moved to California to take on a similar job with that state's world's fair, scheduled for 1967–68. By that time, all of the Jorgensen's Fountain Restaurants and Danish Bakeries had vanished from the Seattle food scene.

Sander's Fountain Lunches

At the same time Nick Jorgensen was planning his malted milk shop empire, brothers Donald and William Sander launched their own foray into the business. By 1938, there were Sander's Malted Milk Stores in operation at 321 Pine, 325 Pike and 1424 Fifth Avenue. The chain grew quickly; by the time Donald Sander entered military service in 1942, seven shops were in operation and the company name had changed to Sander's Fountain Lunches. An apparent downturn in 1948 led to the selling off of a few shops, but Sander's bounced right back with eleven Fountain Lunches open in 1951.

The Sanders' strategy seemed to be: (1) blanket downtown with their shops and (2) change locations for underperforming stores. As many as eighteen Sander's Fountain Lunches were scattered around downtown Seattle, though not all were in business at the same time. The main concentration was along and adjacent to the busy Pike-Pine corridor, where it seemed that a person was never more than one hundred yards away from a Sander's Fountain Lunch. A few shops were located farther downtown on Second and Third Avenues, and the company offices and commissary were located at 1508 Seventh Avenue. Several Sander's shops had previously been Horluck's outlets; one went in at 110 Pike, where Colegrove's Specialty Foods had been. Even a Jorgensen's shop became a Sander's after Nick Jorgensen began shedding some of his stores.

Sander's menu features a full page of fountain treats: malts and shakes, sodas and floats, freezes and ades (lemonade, orangeade), sundaes, parfaits and fruit juices. An old-fashioned banana spit—a meal in itself—cost forty cents. A dozen varieties of sandwiches were listed, along with hamburgers, hot dogs and chili con carne. Breakfast items were few but included ham or bacon with eggs and waffles. Many of the dairy products came direct from Sander's own farm in Redmond.

The Sander chain kept going strong well into the 1970s, but as the family business diversified into real estate investments, the Fountain Lunches began to be sold off. None are in business today.

Gil's, Willie's and Fabulous Burgers

These days it is difficult not to notice McDonald's, Burger King and other franchises with their ever-present signage. Only fifty years ago, though, the golden arches and its kin had only just arrived in the Seattle area. There were a few A&W root beer stands and Dairy Queens in the 1950s, but the first McDonald's didn't show up until 1962—south of the city on Pacific Highway. When it opened, the *Seattle Times* thought it necessary to explain to its readers what a franchise restaurant was, as it was such a new concept.

That didn't mean there weren't aspiring hamburger tycoons in Seattle in those days. Gil Centioli was probably the first to build a locally owned fast-food empire when he opened his first burger stand, Gil's, at 4406 Rainier Avenue in 1946. He pioneered the idea—locally, at least—of the nineteen-cent hamburger, an immediate success at a time when the average price for a burger was twenty-five cents. Centioli had previously operated a restaurant at Second and Virginia. He picked up the idea while on a trip to California, where he learned from Jim Collins's Airport Village in Los Angeles how to be successful with low-cost food service. "It's all a matter of volume. Prepared foods and pre-pattied meat eliminate the costly man-hours previously spent getting the food ready for cooking," he said.

By 1954, Gil's had three locations: the original on Rainier Avenue plus one on Broadway and another in West Seattle. Fish and chips, prawns, chicken and fries and pizza had been added to the tried-and-true menu of

Gil's, seen here in 1954, was an early local entry in the nineteen-cent hamburger wars that were soon to sweep the country. *Seattle Municipal Archives, 78970.*

hamburgers, malts and ice cream. A few years later, Gil was able to boast that he had served 915 tons of meat on 14,560,000 hamburger buns over the years. But by 1959, Gil changed direction—out with beef, in with fried chicken—when he obtained the first Seattle-area KFC franchise. Gil's had grown to nine locations by 1963; they still carried his name but were on their way to being converted to KFC outlets. In later years, Gil became part of the KFC organization and opened several dozen of the restaurants around the Pacific Northwest.

Willie's hamburger empire was more modest. It's no longer recalled who Willie was, but the original location at 1823 E Madison was owned by Robert Johnson. In 1951, he tried to liven up his burger stand by adding a merry-go-round, but the permit was denied; neighbors claimed it would be too noisy and cause traffic disruption. Willie's, like Gil's, was an early entrant in the nineteen-cent hamburger business (three for forty-nine cents) and eventually added two more locations: one on Aurora Avenue and another in Everett. The little chain survived into the 1970s.

Fabulous Hamburgers grew by buying existing burger stands and slapping the Fabulous name on them. The first Fabulous seems to have been the former DeLite Lunch at 2201 E Madison. By 1954, there were six Fabulous locations, most of them in the eastern and southern parts of the city. No nineteen-cent burger here; its claim to fame was a double burger—two one-pound hamburgers on a large bun with onions, lettuce, tomatoes and a slice of Tillamook cheese—for fifty cents.

TRIPLE XXX ROOT BEER

It's no surprise that Prohibition was hard on the nation's breweries, distilleries and saloons. Most closed; a few survived by retooling their production lines to make ice cream, malt extract, dyes for commercial use and even pottery. Down in Texas, the Galveston Brewing Company saw it coming—the state had passed its own prohibition statute in 1916, four years before the Eighteenth Amendment took effect at the national level—and, by 1918, had reinvented itself as a soft drink business called the Southern Beverage Company (though it also produced a "non-intoxicating cereal beverage" called Galvo).

Southern Beverage's first soft drink was a sparkling coffee-flavored beverage called Javo. By 1919, it was producing Triple XXX ginger ale; a year later, root beer was added to the line. It wasn't long before the other products were discontinued, as Southern Beverage staked its future on Triple XXX root beer.

At first, the root beer was sold through the usual outlets, such as grocery stores, but in 1921, the company started advertising complete outfits for operating a Triple XXX root beer outlet. Employing a distinctive design for the soft drink stand—a giant barrel—and the slogan "Makes Thirst a Joy," within a few years Triple XXX barrels were popping up all over the southern states. By 1925, the brand was so well known that Southern Beverages changed its name to the Triple XXX Company.

In the late 1920s, the company embarked on an aggressive marketing campaign to introduce Triple XXX root beer out West. Barrels appeared in Utah, Nevada and Montana, and 1929 saw ads in Seattle and Spokane papers for Triple XXX Thirst Stations, as the company called them. At least nine Triple XXX barrels went up in Spokane within a year. The Seattle area had about half that number.

Two of the earliest Seattle barrels were along the Pacific Highway (Highway 99) south of the city—one at 3301 Fourth Avenue S and another four and a half miles farther along on E Marginal Way, a site now occupied by the Museum of Flight. Their designs are nearly identical: a big barrel, nearly twenty feet tall and displaying the Triple XXX logo, surrounded by wraparound doors encircling the windows where customers' orders were taken.

O.E. Kuehnoel opened a Triple XXX barrel at 2822 Rainier Avenue in 1931, and there was another north of the city at 6815 Roosevelt. All of them sold food in addition to root beer. As chain operations, they were expected to dispense nothing but Southern Beverage's drinks, but they had leeway as to what food items they handled. The Fourth Avenue S location sold Ju-Cy Pig barbecue sandwiches; the E Marginal Way barrel also served barbecue sandwiches (though apparently not Ju-Cy Pig) as well as chili, oysters and Sunfreze ice cream. None of these early barrels had much by way of inside seating; customers ordered at the window, picked up their orders and either ate standing or in their autos.

Things changed in 1940 when H.J. Rutherford introduced a new design for Triple XXX restaurants. Rutherford had opened a Triple XXX barrel in Renton—the usual early-barrel type—eight miles south of Seattle in 1930. A decade later, he came up with a revolutionary new look: a giant silver barrel (sometimes two) displaying the Triple XXX emblem atop a streamlined, neon-striped building that provided both curb service and indoor seating.

This 1930s-vintage Triple XXX on E Marginal Way is an example of the early style of barrel that the franchise used. *Seattle Municipal Archives, 10242.*

In the early 1940s, the Rutherfords revolutionized the design with double barrels, a streamlined, round-cornered façade and neon piping. *Seattle Municipal Archives, 18871.*

119

His Renton location was the first to get the new look, followed shortly by a remodel of the old Triple XXX barrel on Fourth Avenue S (which he owned in partnership with O.E. Kuehnoel).

Next came two new Triple XXX barrels north of the city, one at 8401 Aurora Avenue and the other at 7845 Bothell (now Lake City) Way. The Rutherfords also operated two outlets in Spokane and at least one in Portland, Oregon. It was a family business: H.J. (better known as Harry) was the patriarch and continued to manage the Renton location; son A.S. (Archie) ran the Aurora Avenue and Bothell Way locations, while another son, L.W., moved to Spokane to look after things there.

Then and now: The original Triple XXX barrel on Lake City Way still sits above its building, now used as a Chinese restaurant. *Washington State Archives Puget Sound Regional Branch.*

The Rutherford-owned Triple XXX barrels weren't the only ones in town, though. A man named Ruff owned a Triple XXX at 544 Elliott and another in Ballard on Fifteenth Avenue NW. C.J. Rusden had a barrel at 1300 Olive Way; he also owned a Triple XXX in Everett. North of the city was a Triple XXX at 125th and Aurora Avenue; southbound, barrels were located along Pacific Highway S at 148th in Riverton Heights and at 200th near Angle Lake. Almost all of them opened in the 1940–42 timeframe.

Menus differed among the Triple XXX barrels. Since they were independently owned, the only obligation to the Triple XXX Company was to carry that brand, and only that brand, of soft drink—no Coke, no Pepsi, no 7 Up. Beyond that constraint, food and fountain items varied widely. In early days (prior to the golden years of the 1940s), sandwiches and fountain drinks dominated the menu with hardly, if any, dinner meals listed. An early menu for Rutherford & Kuehnoel's Triple XXX on Fourth Avenue S was typical, with seven types of hamburgers, over a dozen sandwiches and a few plate lunches and specials, such as hamburger steak smothered in chili. After the barrel received its facelift in 1940, a revised menu added T-bone and cube steaks, a ground round steak dinner, chicken fried steak and roast beef. Fountain drinks—floats, shakes and sundaes—continued to be popular. Even the early menu offered a limited breakfast.

It's been claimed that there were hundreds of Triple XXX barrels around the country—several dozen in the Pacific Northwest alone. Today, there are only two: one in Issaquah, Washington, and the other in Indiana, both of them of more modern vintage than those described here. What happened? The reasons aren't clear. The popularity of root beer continues—A&W has plenty of outlets around (perhaps being owned by Yum Brands, parent company of Taco Bell, KFC and several other fast-food franchises, had its advantages). Perhaps the rise of fast-food franchises sounded the death knell for Triple XXX. The giant barrels—unmistakable roadside icons—disappeared. Some of the buildings were repurposed as drive-ins.

By the mid-1960s, Triple XXX had no presence in Seattle. The only reminder of the city's original Triple XXX barrels still stands at 7845 Lake City Way. Today, the building houses a Chinese restaurant, but the telltale giant barrel on its roof gives away its original identity.

4

In the Neighborhoods

Former mayor Greg Nickels once described Seattle as a "city of neighborhoods"—127 of them according to the city's website. How did they come to be? Some of them were once independent towns. Others grew around transportation corridors—in early days, at stops along the interurban trolleys north and south out of Seattle; later, as the automobile became part of the scene, along highways or at important road junctions. The Green Lake neighborhood grew near the lake of the same name. The University District, as its name suggests, grew up near the University of Washington. Others? Who knows why? They each have their own story to tell.

Seattle's neighborhoods were tied together by a web of arterial streets. Many neighborhoods had (and still have) their own business districts, and it was natural for restaurants to appear both in the local downtowns and along the main routes between them. Industrial areas also attracted eateries—workers in factories and around the harbor needed someplace to do lunch. Overall, the quantity of restaurants in Seattle's outliers exceeded the number available in the central business district.

BELLTOWN

Seattle's Original Neighborhood

In the 1880s, Seattle was a fairly compact city on the shore of Elliott Bay, clustered around the site of Henry Yesler's mill and hemmed in on the east by remnants of dense forest. About a mile to the north, another community—Belltown—had arisen with its own business district, mill, wharves and residences. What stood between Seattle and Belltown was Denny Hill, several hundred feet in height and, until it was washed away by the Denny Regrade project, a barrier to easy travel between the two places.

It's known that eateries and at least one hotel were established by the time of the great fire of 1889. The Dakota Restaurant was located at 2417 Front Street, the New Orleans was located at the corner of Front and Battery Streets and Mary Yates and Claude Brown also ran restaurants in the neighborhood. Belltown escaped the flames, and the day after the fire, Bell's Hotel (also called the Bellevue House) was said to be the only restaurant left in Seattle. Richard Dodge, proprietor of the Bellevue Dining Room, went to great lengths to take care of the hungry men and women who plodded north from the burn zone in search of a meal.

By the turn of the century, there were at least four restaurants in Belltown, along with a saloon and two confectioneries. The district experienced little growth for the next few decades, even after Denny Hill was removed. In 1940, Herman Doder was running Herman's Cafe at 2309 First Avenue, the Bell Town Cafe was at 2207 First and Christian Steen had another restaurant up the block at 2219.

A new and different Belltown Café appeared in 1979 at 2313 First Avenue, just as the area was beginning to revive. The café's menu offered chicken breasts stuffed with prosciutto and mushrooms, a pork-sausage-and-rice mixture wrapped in cabbage leaves and creamy soups and fish mousses, along with several vegetarian entrées. Co-owners Ben Marks, Phil Messina and Pat Tyler highlighted family recipes; everything—bread, sauces, dressings, desserts—was made on-site. Today a Brazilian-themed restaurant, the Grill From Ipanema, occupies the site. Belltown, having been rediscovered and rebuilt, is considered one of the most desirable (and expensive) places to live in Seattle.

ALONG THE WATER

Even longtime Seattleites are surprised to learn that the city has 200 miles of waterfront—about 54 miles of saltwater shoreline and another 147 miles along Lake Washington, Lake Union and the Ship Canal. With views westward toward the Olympic Mountains and east to the Cascades, it's no wonder that many restaurants have chosen the waterfront to call home.

The early settlers probably didn't take scenery into consideration when the first restaurants appeared downtown. Any restaurant built on Front or Commercial Streets was on the waterfront—at the time, Elliott Bay lapped up almost to the streets. It wasn't until the 1930s that restaurateurs began locating their eateries along the water specifically to take advantage of the views.

Among the first was Crawford's Sea Grill, on Elliott Avenue about a mile northwest of the downtown core. In July 1940, the *Seattle Daily Times* announced the opening of the Sea Grill at 309 Elliott Avenue. Veteran restaurateur C.C. Crawford had been planning it for ten years; designed to take advantage of the sweeping view of Elliott Bay, it was built and completely equipped for $31,000. The glass-enclosed main dining room seated 188 patrons and provided an unobstructed view of Puget Sound and the Olympics. Crawford's motto was "a showplace on the shore of Puget Sound"; his goal was to specialize in "serving the widest variety of sea foods, all prepared on a specially designed broiler, with olive oil used exclusively in the preparation." The menu featured all kinds of seafood: scallops, lobster, snapper, salmon, smelt, sole, tuna, clams, shrimp, oysters, abalone and halibut, plus juicy broiled steaks, chicken and turkey roasted to perfection.

Only five months after opening, the restaurant had become so popular that an addition was constructed to increase the seating space. Unfortunately, C.C. Crawford didn't have much time to savor his restaurant's success, as he passed away in 1942. J.E. Meaker took over for a few years before selling out to Nick Zanides and moving to Tacoma, where he opened a Crawford's. Zenides remodeled the Sea Grill in 1948, creating a congenial, modern, marine ambiance with an interior décor of ship ornaments, seashells, marine life, fishnet curtains and other decorations stressing marine atmosphere. A cocktail lounge, the Coral Room, was added, along with a garden where it was claimed five hundred varieties of roses were grown. Ivar Haglund bought the property in 1965 and moved his Captain's Table there from its original Fifth Avenue location. The Captain's Table closed in 1991, and today a medical facility occupies the property.

Crawford's Sea Grill, its tower spelling SEA FOOD in large neon letters, was at water's edge on Elliott Bay. *Author's collection.*

The Ocean House opened in 1941 just one hundred yards farther along at 375 Elliott Avenue. Initially owned by Evelyn Howie, within a year, it was taken over by Jennie Mangini, with Wener Gloor as seafood chef. Not surprisingly, the Ocean House specialized in seafood but also offered broiled steaks and roast chicken. Lunch was served daily. In 1973, the Ocean House closed; all the equipment was auctioned off. A year later, a new Ocean House appeared at 920 Aurora Avenue, quarters previously occupied by Les Teagle's; it closed in 1979. Today, there's an office complex on the site of the original Ocean House—the later Aurora Avenue site is an office tower.

Skipper's Seafood Restaurant was at 208 Elliott, where the Homewood Suites hotel is today. The vaguely ship-shaped restaurant was built by Ernest Hilsenberg and Curt Kremer in 1942. The nautical theme included a lighthouse, pilot house and porthole-style windows; inside, tables were decorated with charts, and the walls were hung with pictures of ships. A 1960 visitor commented:

> *Skipper's has been one of the best restaurants to get the small oysters, Olympias, Quilcenes and Cove, cooked so gently to make them tender. The other types of seafood are the best ever and served in true nautical fashion. Having two congenial hosts, there has always been one of them standing by to greet the patrons.*

In 1960, the restaurant became George Olsen's Seven Nations, with a decor that "connected East and West in a contemporary mode with an international feeling. Objects of art from India and South America stand out against the white natural woods of the interior…[and] the waiters wear white jackets and French aprons." It didn't last long; by 1962, a Chinese restaurant, the Double Joy, had moved in. Two years later, Stuart Anderson took a long-term lease on the building and made it the first of his Black Angus Steak Houses, a chain that eventually grew to over one hundred locations.

The Norselander, at 300 Third Avenue NW, specialized in "everything edible that swims on Northwest waters." The restaurant opened in 1951 on the top floor of the Norway Center, a modernistic L-shaped building just off Elliott Avenue. Specialties of the house included the Captain's Dinner (salmon, oysters, shrimp, lobster), prawns with fluffy rice, crab Newburg and Alaska shrimp curry, along with deep-fried prawns, crab or oysters; clams; salmon; trout; and other non-seafood dishes such as steaks, chops and poultry. Roy Peterson was the owner, with Ole Madsen as manager and Bill Clark the chef. The Viking Room was the cocktail lounge, with a marine theme of fishnets hanging over the walls and an entrance of sea-roughened

208 ELLIOTT AVE. W., SEATTLE, WASH.

Ship-shaped with porthole windows and a lighthouse tower, everything was nautical at Skipper's. *Author's collection.*

pilings. The Norselander survived into the 1980s; now even the building is gone, demolished in 2008.

Of Danish descent, Holger Nielsen introduced smorgasbord to the Seattle waterfront when he opened the Selandia in 1951. (*Selandia* is the Latin name for the Danish island of Sjælland.) Not long after Nielsen threw the doors open, a *Seattle Times* restaurant critic raved: "In the course of a scant five months the Selandia has earned itself a reputation seldom attained in less than a period of years....The Viking table's 72 square feet of surface is laden for your pleasure with not less than fifty-five varieties of savory taste-thrills."

The lavish smorgasbord included Scandinavian specialties such as *rullepolsa* (Danish spiced meat roll), *leverpostej* (Danish liver pâté), *biff à la Lindstrom* (a Swedish version of ground steak), *sylta* (head cheese), Swedish meatballs and brown beans and planked Dansk *hakkebof* (ground sirloin tip sautéed in brown butter with pan-fried onions). More traditional items included poached salmon, shrimp, crab, roast beef and boiled tongue. A house specialty was *skidden* eggs, "a Nielsen invention made up of hardboiled eggs buried in a creamy mustard sauce." The table always held at least four varieties of cheeses, deviled eggs, stuffed tomatoes and salads. Dessert included apples baked with cinnamon and Swedish pancakes with lingonberries. Nielsen advised diners to make at least three plate-filling circuits around his laden table. The smorgasbord dinner was available daily from 5:30 p.m. with a more limited lunch version from 11:30 a.m. until 2:00 p.m. An à la carte menu, with entrées more familiar to Americans, was offered all day. Popular though it was, the Selandia only lasted for about nine years; it had disappeared by 1960.

On Seaview Avenue, where Salmon Bay meets the sound, is Ray's Boathouse. Ray Lichtenberger built a boat rental and bait house at this site in 1939, adding a coffee shop a few years later. In the 1950s, Marvin and Dorothy Rosand opened Rosand's Seafood Cafe and ran it for about twelve years. The restaurant became the Breakwater, then the Viking, before being absorbed into the boathouse complex and simply called Ray's Boathouse. Ray's has burned and been rebuilt twice and is still in business on its choice piece of real estate with territorial views of the sound and the Olympic Mountains.

Several well-known restaurants were located along Westlake Avenue on the edge of Lake Union. Franco's Hidden Harbor was within the Marina Mart at 1500 Westlake N, a complex of shops oriented toward the maritime trade. John Franco ran the place in partnership with his father, Marco. The Hidden Harbor revealed itself in 1954, billed as "something new in Seattle

Not to be outdone, Selandia also had a tower with its name in neon and an awning-covered entrance. *MOHAI, PEMCO Webster & Stevens Collection, 1983.10.16743.*

dining…nestled in the Pacific Coast's finest yacht marina.…A shellfish specialty house, this is the only Seattle restaurant on waterfront level. Surrounded by yachts. Meals served on open dock if desired." Marco and John had previously operated Franco's Cafe on Western Avenue; after World War II, they sold it and bought the Marina Grill in the Marina Mart, which they recalled as "a seven-stool lunch counter and cigar counter upstairs and only two small rooms downstairs," and completely remodeled the place. The restaurant was actually located over the lake, so whenever a serious plumbing problem developed, a diver had to be called in to solve it.

For many years, the chef was Poppa John (real name, Themistokles Georgeos Karamanos), who in his early days had worked at the Brown Derby in Hollywood, California. The lunch menu featured salads of avocado and fresh Dungeness crab, shrimp louie, Dungeness crab louie, Dungeness crab omelet, crab and cheese dip, Dungeness crab on toast and cheese sauce and sliced turkey breast with bacon and asparagus spears topped with a house-specialty cheese sauce. Dinner entrées varied daily but often included braised sirloin tips, fried Pacific baby clams, prawns kebob Hawaiian and what a restaurant reviewer called "an astonishing array of seafood dishes"—oysters and crab, broiled salmon, grilled halibut, grilled filet of sole, prawns, scallops, lobster tail, shrimp and abalone. Somehow, steaks—from filet mignon to T-bone—also crowded onto the menu along with other non-seafood dishes. Today, the Marina Mart is still there; the Hidden Harbor is long gone.

Oyster Pepper Roast

½ green pepper, finely chopped
2 tablespoons olive oil
1 cup catsup
¼ cup water
2 tablespoons lemon juice
½ teaspoon Worcestershire sauce
1 dash soy sauce
1 dash Tabasco
50 to 65 oysters
Parsley
Toast points
Lemon wedges

In a saucepan, sauté finely chopped green pepper in olive oil until the peppers are tender. Add and blend 1 cup catsup, water, lemon juice, Worcestershire sauce, soy sauce and Tabasco sauce.

Add oysters to sauce and cook until done. Serve in individual casserole dishes garnished with parsley, toast points and lemon wedges.

Fresh Dungeness Crab Fry Legs

3 tablespoons butter
24 to 28 jumbo crab legs
1 ounce sauterne wine
20 large button mushrooms

Melt butter, add crab legs, wine and mushrooms and sauté for 3 minutes.

Marco Franco looks a bit uncomfortable surrounded by adoring waitresses in this 1956 photo. *University of Washington Special Collections, JEW0422.*

Moultray's Four Winds was at 900 Westlake, at the southern end of Lake Union, and opened in 1955, a year after the Hidden Harbor. Chris and Bill Moultray built their restaurant atop a former 1900-era ferryboat called the *City of Everett*. The pirate theme—"Look for the Pirate Atop the Boat"—carried over inside the restaurant, where waitresses dressed in buccaneer costumes served up seafood, steaks and prime rib. Creole-seasoned dishes were a specialty. By 1965, the Four Winds had become the Surfside 9, a dance club. The following year, the bilge pumps that kept the old ship afloat failed, and the *City of Everett* sank to the bottom of Lake Union. It was raised but promptly sank again, this time for good.

The Wharf was part of the million-dollar Fishermen's Terminal project constructed by the Port of Seattle and completed in 1952 at the south end of the Ballard Bridge. The Wharf Restaurant and Coffee Shop overlooked the fishing-fleet moorage, largest on the West Coast, and included a taproom and separate cocktail lounge.

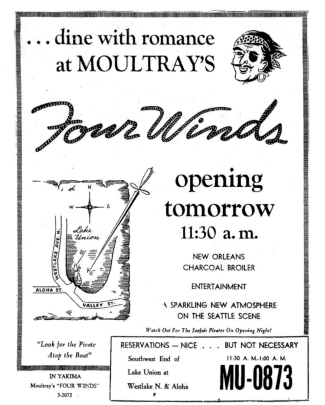

Right: Moultray's was pirate country; a pirate figure atop the old ferryboat beckoned guests to board. There was also a Moultray's in Yakima. *Seattle Times*.

Below: Golden Anchors sat atop the *City of Everett*, the same recycled ferryboat that later was used by Moultray's Four Winds. *MOHAI, Seattle Post-Intelligencer Collection, 1986.5.15.70*.

It's said that the Wharf had a split personality; Jack Curle, the manager, said he had two separate restaurants and cocktail lounges under the same roof:

> *They are served by the same kitchen, but each caters to a completely different clientele. On one side are the hard-working and roughly dressed commercial fishermen whose boats are moored nearby. The coffee shop and Moby Dick cocktail lounge cater to them, while the plush dining room and fancier Mermaid Room entertain more genteel family and club groups.*

The Wharf grew over the years, eventually reaching a seating capacity of four hundred and becoming a popular nightlife destination, booking many musical acts and other entertainment. The Wharf made it into the 1980s before vanishing; today its place as Fishermen's Terminal's premier dining place has been overtaken by Chinook's at Salmon Bay.

On the Lake Washington side of Seattle was the Golden Anchors at 180 Lakeside Avenue, near Leschi Park. It opened in 1945 aboard the *City of Everett*, the same ill-fated ferry that later carried Moultray's Four Winds. Nearby residents were opposed to the idea of a dine-dance place operating in their quiet neighborhood, but the city eventually issued a license over their objections. Perhaps because it was afloat on fresh water, not salt, the Golden Anchor's menu didn't offer much seafood; typical fare included fried chicken, pot roast and sirloin steak. The Golden Anchors doesn't seem to have lasted long; it was offered for sale after only a year and a half of business, and the old ferryboat was towed over to Lake Union to meet its ultimate doom.

Queen Anne

Queen Anne Hill, one of the so-called seven hills of Seattle, defines the skyline two miles north of downtown. There are actually two Queen Anne neighborhoods: one at the south base of the hill around Queen Anne, Mercer and First Avenues and another at the top of the hill a mile farther north (and three hundred feet higher) along Queen Anne Avenue.

Lower Queen Anne developed first, as settlers cleared off the trees at the foot of the hill to build homes. Upper Queen Anne didn't take off until a streetcar line built up it in 1902; before then, the grade was considered too steep and the hill too densely forested to be developed.

Restaurants began appearing in both Upper and Lower Queen Anne around 1930. The Queen Anne Cafe, at 15 Boston Street, atop the hill, had opened by that year. Also on Boston, on the west side past Queen Anne Avenue, was the Hill Top Cafe. Several restaurants owned by Lena Grollmund and Herman Peterson gathered at the top of the counterbalance (so-called as an assist to streetcars climbing the hill) to service hungry trolley riders. In the 1950s, the Red Snapper Cafe could be found at 1833 Queen Anne Avenue.

In Lower Queen Anne, Blanche J. and R.A. Matthews were the proprietors of Matt's Log Cabin, a hamburger shop, in 1934. Matt's was located at 435 Queen Anne Avenue. Another Queen Anne Cafe—no relation to the one on top of the hill—was run by Thomas Jensen at 527 Queen Anne in the 1940s. A restaurant called the King Grill, 605 Queen Anne, was in business in 1951. The entire character of Lower Queen Anne changed when the Century 21 Exposition came to town; located only a few blocks from the fair site and the iconic Space Needle, the neighborhood benefited mightily from the overflow business.

WESTLAKE AVENUE

Westlake Avenue originates in downtown Seattle and for many years was the main route north out of the city toward the Fremont, Phinney Ridge, Greenwood and Green Lake neighborhoods. Aurora Avenue and later Interstate 5 carry the bulk of north–south traffic, but Westlake remains an important arterial. Not surprisingly, a number of cafés and lunch places sprang up along Westlake, particularly in the light industrial district between Denny Way and Mercer Street.

Built of logs and looking like a Wild West stockade, the Bungalow, at 905 Roy Street, disappeared long ago. *Washington State Archives Puget Sound Regional Branch.*

There were the Dart In Cafe, Roy's Cafe and the Westlake Grill within a few blocks of one another. Just north of Denny was the E&B Cafe (later known as the J&K Cafe; it's not known who E, B, J or K were). The Bungalow, a burger joint and tavern, was at 905 Roy Street, a block west of Westlake. It appeared in 1940 but was gone by the end of the decade. The sites of all these eateries have been overwhelmed by the explosive growth of the South Lake Union district.

Fremont

Because Westlake Avenue hugs the east side of Queen Anne Hill in a narrow stretch of land along Lake Union, there wasn't much room for restaurants to build up other than those actually on the waterfront. At the north end of Queen Anne Hill, Westlake merges with several other streets to cross the Fremont Bridge (built in 1917) into Fremont.

Even after being discovered and gentrified, Fremont (which modestly bills itself as "the center of the universe") seems frozen in time; most of the buildings date to about 1910. The community grew with the early timber industry; it sits at the outlet of Lake Union, an ideal spot for sawmills. Once a separate town, it was incorporated into Seattle in 1891. During the heyday of streetcars, Fremont became an important intersection for trolley lines running north, south and east.

Over the years, a number of restaurants functioned in "downtown" Fremont, including the Metropolitan Cafe at the corner of Fremont Avenue and North Thirty-Fourth. The Fremont Drug Company originally occupied the building, but it had become a café by 1914. Now it's a Starbucks. Just up the block was the Club Cafe. Around the corner where North Thirty-Sixth Street heads west to Ballard was the Spa Cafe, run by William and Verna Seder. In 1955, William Seder, despondent over financial problems, took his own life by turning on all the gas burners on the kitchen stove; before he did so, he saved his pet parakeet by taking its cage out onto an open porch. He was only thirty-seven years old. In later years, a typical neighborhood bar with live music occupied the Spa's location; today, it's a vegetarian restaurant.

Across the street from the Metropolitan stands a building that has been home to restaurants since at least 1910. It was first the Bryant Cafe; after a few years as a drugstore, it became Peggy's Fountain Lunch and, in the 1970s, the Dancing Machine Tavern. Between 1981 and 2012, it housed

Costas Opa, a fine Greek restaurant sorely missed by Fremocentrists, as the locals call themselves.

Next door on Thirty-Fourth Street was the Fremont Cafe, operated for many years by Nick Theotokis. A few feet east on Thirty-Fourth was the Aloha Cafe. North of Fremont, heading uphill toward Phinney Ridge, stood the Hob Nob Cafe at 4909 Fremont Avenue. In earlier days, it was called the Woodland Sandwich Shop; by 1968, it had become the Djakarta, an Indonesian restaurant. There's an apartment complex at that location today.

PHINNEY RIDGE

Fremont Avenue intersects North Fiftieth Street; turn west onto Fiftieth, follow the road as it curves north a few blocks later and you're on Phinney Avenue as it heads north to the Greenwood district. On the east side of the street is Woodland Park, one of Seattle's largest parks and home to the Woodland Park Zoo. It was natural that cafés and lunch counters would go up near the park to take care of visitors; over a half dozen could be found along the ten-block length of Phinney Avenue bordering the park.

As early as 1928, there was a fountain lunch–hamburger place at 5409 Phinney; it later became McGrath's Park View Lunch. The Woodland View Cafe was located at 5817 Phinney Avenue; Val's Cafe, at 6020 Phinney, was just north of the park. The 1932 city directory listed Hans Romstead, John Manos, Paul Davison and Mabelle Patten as operating restaurants along this stretch of Phinney. (In those days, it was common for restaurants to be listed by the owner's name.) All of these places have vanished.

Still standing at 6117 Phinney is the distinctive building long known as La Boheme. Looking like it was constructed in the front yard of a house, its English cottage–style design makes a distinctive sight. La Boheme opened soon after the end of Prohibition in 1934 and served a limited menu of hamburgers, steaks and chili—"the finest ever turned out by the hand of man." Known to regulars as "La Bow," it changed ownership in the late 1990s and is now Sully's Snow Goose Saloon.

Another neighborhood favorite, recently closed, was at 6412 Phinney Avenue. In early days, it was known as the Snack Bar, but by the time Jeanne Mae Barwick took over in 1988, it had long been renamed the Phinney Ridge Café. Weekends found customers waiting on the sidewalk to get through the doors. Specialties included smoked salmon benedict, breakfast

La Boheme

offers the finest ✦

HAMBURGER

CHILE

✦ or STEAKS

Ever turned out by
the HAND of MAN

──── 62nd and Phinney Ave. ────
NEAR WOODLAND PARK

La Boheme, looking like an English cottage, could have been mistaken for a private residence. The building still stands along Phinney Avenue. *Author's collection.*

burritos, homemade cinnamon rolls and an unusual breakfast pairing called Shake and Eggs—a milkshake served with eggs done as you like 'em. Mae's Phinney Ridge closed in 2013—another casualty on the dwindling list of Seattle's classic cafés.

Just up the street from Mae's at 6557 Phinney, where the street makes a jog to the west and continues up Greenwood Avenue, a little café called Marian's Lunch operated for a short time in the early 1950s. After a spell as home to various types of stores, the vacant building was purchased by Sharon and John Hughes and opened as a specialty restaurant called Eggs Inc. in 1970. The specialty was omelets—always cooked to order by either John or Sharon (while the other waited on tables), almost always with a line of customers waiting to get in, the place was so popular. The house favorite was called the Five-to-One: ham, black olives, mushrooms, cheddar cheese and onions. Other omelets had names like the El Paso, Barcelona, Bavarian, Canadian and Dungeness. Lunch-sized omelets were made with three eggs; five eggs went into the dinner version. Eggs Inc. eventually added other items to the menu for folks with dietary restrictions to eggs, including sandwiches, homemade pies and two new specialties: beef burgundy and chicken breasts in orange sauce.

What was Costello's Cafe at 6724 Greenwood Avenue in 1951 became the Stumbling Goat Bistro. In the 1930s, Grace and Louis Perkins ran the Emerald Confectionery and Lunch at 6732 Greenwood. By 1968, it had become the 68th Street Tavern; until recently, it was the Kort Haus, a hamburger place. The building housing both the Stumbling Goat and the Kort Haus was purchased by real estate developers and is scheduled for demolition, though both restaurants hope to reopen in the new building.

Another burger place was Matt's Hamburger, a small shop with only nine stools and two tables located at 7118 Greenwood. Matt's was open twenty-four hours a day in 1936, when a fried chicken dinner cost just twenty-five cents. A few years later, it had become the Ridge Cafe; in 1951, it was called Lou La's Grill. Later yet it was the Greenwood Cafe. An art gallery later occupied the premises.

In 1951, Noble's Fountain Lunch was located at 7307 Greenwood; it later became the 4-Rs Cafe and, by about 1970, was the Harbin, Seattle's first northern-style Chinese restaurant. The Harbin moved out, and the Greenwood Mandarin Restaurant moved in, with an extensive menu (over one hundred items) featuring special dishes such as palace beef, garlic chicken and princess chicken. The Greenwood Mandarin closed in 2014, and the building was demolished to make way for a bank branch.

Another location with a long restaurant history is 7419 Greenwood. John McGuirk was operating there as early as 1932. In the 1960s, it was Farrell's Cafe, whose slogan was "Bring the Family for Sunday Dinner—Eat Better for Less." For many years, it's been Yanni's Greek Cuisine.

GREENWOOD

The intersection of Greenwood Avenue and North Eighty-Fifth Street defines the Greenwood neighborhood's business district. Over the years, several dozen restaurants have come and gone along this quarter-mile-long stretch of Greenwood Avenue; no old-timers remain, but many have appeared to take their places.

In 1930, Bill Fenton opened Creamland at 8402 Greenwood Avenue, when he was just eighteen years old. He worked seven days a week in the shop, often getting in at one o'clock in the morning to start making his ice cream. In 1958, robbers broke though Creamland's back door and made off with $550, of which $374 was nickels—that's over eighty pounds' worth. After forty-seven years, taking only a single vacation during that time, Bill Fenton retired after scooping his last ice cream cone in October 1977. New owners

Darryl and Pat Ryan took over for another dozen years and kept intact the old Creamland ambiance. Across the street was the Wee Hamburger Shop. After years of accommodating non-restaurant businesses, today the building is home to Kouzina, a Greek restaurant.

In 1951, the building at Eighty-Fifth and Greenwood, once occupied by the City Drug Store, was taken over by Randle's Cafe. The name soon changed to Jacken's Grill. Jacken's featured full-course dinners in a family atmosphere with cocktails by an open fireplace in the Stardust Room, a separate lounge. In 1964, a complete steak dinner cost $2.50; prime rib was $3.00. Tuesday night was an all-you-can-eat smorgasbord from 6:00 until 9:00 p.m. Jacken's was still Jacken's in 1980 but a few years later became DiMaggio's, where an all-you-can-eat salad and pasta bar—six choices of pasta, four different sauces—was priced at $5.95. Currently, the building serves as an events center called Greenwood Square.

There's an interesting bit of hamburger shop history on the west side of Greenwood north of Eighty-Fifth. In the 1930s, John and Florence Ring

Johnie's Cafe was shoehorned in between two buildings in Greenwood, just north of Eighty-Fifth Street. *MOHAI, Seattle Post-Intelligencer Collection, 1986.5.12382.1.*

The Doodle Sack Drive-In, as it looked in 1956. "Doodle sack" is a slang term for bagpipes. *Seattle Municipal Archives, 75756.*

operated Babe's Hamburger Shop at 8601 Greenwood. They apparently sold the place in 1936 and moved a few doors south to 8635, where they opened Johnnie's Hamburgers. One hundred feet farther along, but twenty years later in time, sat Johnie's Cafe, a burger joint with nine stools and four booths, at 8523 Greenwood. If there was a connection linking Johnnie's and Johnie's, it's been lost over time. Between them were a dine-and-dance place called Verlou's and a Chinese restaurant, the China Inn.

Marie Nordquist was the original owner and namesake of Marie's Cafe at 8549 Greenwood. The story goes that she hired a cook from Oregon, a man named Harold Smith, who brought with him a recipe for blue cheese salad dressing that quickly became a house favorite. They began bottling the dressing in Marie's basement for sale to customers, and its fame spread. In the 1950s, Smith bought the café from Marie, took on Werner Ferber as a partner and set up a bottling works to expand the salad dressing production. They marketed the dressings through several supermarket chains, and within a few years, the dressings business had far surpassed the restaurant, with over $1 million in annual revenues. Over twenty other varieties were offered, including creamy Italian garlic, thousand island and apple glaze, though the blue cheese dressing remained the most popular. Meanwhile, the café struggled along, running afoul of the liquor control board and health

Scotty's mascot fish was decked out in top hat and cane, as the cover of this menu shows. *MOHAI*, Seattle Post-Intelligencer *Collection, 1986.5.15.90.*

department numerous times in the late 1970s. By 1983, Marie's had become the Baranof, still Greenwood's favorite neighborhood bar. Marie Nordquist passed away in 2008. The dressings live on, though today they're made in California, not Greenwood.

In 1951, a place called the One Hundred Per Cent Lunch sat in what is now the Safeway parking lot at 8728 Greenwood Avenue. Across the street and a block north was the Doodle Sack Drive-In at 9009 Greenwood. It lasted for about ten years before being replaced by apartments.

West on N Eighty-Fifth from the Greenwood Avenue intersection was Hazel's Cafe. Scotty's Fish & Chips was up the street at 323 NW Eighty-Fifth. Owner E.W. Robert "Scotty" Wylie operated his seafood place for sixteen years using a fish-and-chips recipe he claimed was handed down from father to son at the Cannon Mills Place Fish and Chip Shop in Edinburgh, Scotland. His menu also listed grilled halibut and salmon; fried filet of sole, shrimp and clams; and oysters in season. Around 1950, Scotty relocated to 8318 NW Eighty-Fifth, and the Fish Net Cafe went into his original location. Also along this section of Eighty-Fifth was a place called the Rattleyboo Cafe at 802 West. It apparently didn't last long.

GREEN LAKE

Two business communities developed at Green Lake—one on the east side, another three-quarters of a mile away at the lake's northern end. On the east side was Warling's Restaurant at 7115 Woodlawn Avenue, a block away from the lake and adjacent to the Green Lake Theatre. Cliff Warling opened his restaurant, described as "the Northwest's most modern and distinctive," in 1949. That year, restaurant reviewer Nat Lund found Warling's "a wise choice for folk in a steak-eating mood" with nine different varieties; top of the line were the New York–cut sirloin and porterhouse, which came with a tossed green salad, potatoes (baked, french fried or au gratin—a house specialty served en casserole with a mild cheese sauce), rolls and beverage for $2.75. Other broiler items included chops, lobster tails and Chinook salmon with melted butter. Filet of sole and butter-fried chicken served with hot baking powder biscuits and honey were also on the menu. Lund described Warling's as a good lunch choice also, with decor "as tasty as the food—restful green walls, with stylized fish, and soft cove lighting" and a fourteen-seat bar with a mirrored ceiling and real bar chairs instead of stools. By 1969, Warling's had become the Little Red Hen, which it still is today.

Just down the street from Warling's, Raymond Buell's Fountain & Grill was a prototypical neighborhood hamburgers-and-milkshakes sort of place. Burgers and a dozen different kinds of sandwiches were on menu along with short-order steaks, chili and fish and chips. An entire page of Buell's menu was devoted to ice cream mixed drinks (shakes, malts, ice cream sodas and floats), sundaes, freezes and soft drinks. Buell's also served limited breakfast fare: ham or bacon with two eggs (seventy-five cents) or a ham and cheese omelet for eighty cents. Buell's was located at 7101 Woodlawn Avenue. A few steps away were two more lunch counter places: Green Lake Lunch & Billiards at 415 E Seventy-Second Street and the Green Lake Bowl Cafe on Ravenna Boulevard.

A block away from Buell's, facing onto the lake at 7116 E Green Lake Way, was the Hula Hut Barbecue & Freeze. Although it had already been around for four years, the Hula Hut celebrated its grand opening in 1954 with nineteen-cent hamburgers, hot dogs, milkshakes and homemade apple pie courtesy of Peggy, formerly with the Green Apple Pie in downtown Seattle. Kids got free balloons and could enjoy a ride on the merry-go-round; leis and something called Hawaiian Freeze Pies enhanced the feeling of being on the islands. A 1971 fire seriously damaged the Hut, and it apparently did not reopen.

Palestine-born Saleh Joudeh arrived in Seattle by way of Italy in 1974, beginning his culinary career as a burger flipper at the nearby Green Lake Bowling Alley. A few years later, he took over a restaurant in the U District and renamed it Avenue 52. After a slow start, Saleh's cooking began to garner rave reviews from local restaurant critics. In 1982, with his lease at Avenue 52 expiring, he moved to Green Lake and created Saleh al Lago (Saleh on the Lake). It is said that, at a time when most Seattleites' concept of Italian food extended about as far as pizza, lasagna or spaghetti and meatballs, he introduced them to risotto, calamari and other classics of Italian cuisine. It was a sad day for Saleh's regular clientele in 1999 when he was forced to close due to health issues.

At the north end of the lake was William Bryan's restaurant, built in 1947 and originally called Bryan's Fine Foods. By 1956, the restaurant had been renamed Bryan's Lake Terrace Dining Room and made its mark on Seattle's fine dining scene, featuring the freshest of seafood and steaks. Holiday dinners (turkey or prime rib) were long a tradition at Bryan's, and reservations were a must-have on weekends. Bryan sold his restaurant in about 1960, but the new owners kept the name for a number of years. Bryan's was located at 7850 N Green Lake Way.

MAGNOLIA

Northwest-bound out of downtown Seattle, Elliott Avenue runs along the bay for two and a half miles before turning north and becoming Fifteenth Avenue W on its way to Ballard. Just at the curve, the Magnolia Bridge carries traffic over railroad lines and port facilities up onto Magnolia Bluff and its small but prosperous business district, Magnolia Village. A couple of lunch counters were located here (the Magnolia Food Shop and the Magnolia Bowl Snack Bar, at 3212 and 3316 W McGraw, respectively), as well as a more upscale restaurant called Tenney's. Verl and Alma Tenney, the owners and cooks, were well known for their homemade pies baked fresh daily: French apple, wild blackberry, pumpkin and pecan, among other flavors. By 1968, Tenney's had become GG's Restaurant, under management of Don and Clara Aust. Today, it's an Austrian-themed steakhouse called Szmania's. Tenney's was located at 3321 McGraw. A few feet away at 3420 McGraw, and open as early as 1947, was the Village Grill, offering "good home cooking at moderate prices." Still in business in 1960, it has since been replaced by a Chinese restaurant.

INTERBAY

Back on Fifteenth Avenue W, literally in the shadow of the Magnolia Bridge, in 1931 appeared what was billed as "a new concept in marketing": the Mid-City Market, Seattle's first drive-up shopping center. Today the idea

The M&J was a little storefront place, one of several along Fifteenth Avenue that catered to workers at nearby industrial operations. *Seattle Municipal Archives, 65936.*

of a supermarket or other large stand-alone store providing its own parking lot is taken for granted, but at the time, it was a revolutionary concept just beginning to become popular in California; until then, store patrons usually had to contend for street parking spaces in congested business areas. Under a single roof, with plenty of free parking, the Mid-City Market was home to a grocery store, meat market, dairy store, fruits and vegetables, even a service station—and Mrs. Helen Lea's Mid-City Lunch restaurant. The Mid-City Lunch changed its name several times across the years and for awhile had a neighboring restaurant, the Cove Inn; both of them were still in business into the 1940s. (The Mid-City Market building still stands, though heavily modified, as the Builders Hardware and Supply Company.)

Just north of the Mid-City Market were the Terminal Cafe and the Stewardess Cafe, facing each other across Fifteenth Avenue at 1601 and 1606 and marking the start of the industrial Interbay district with its massive railroad and shipping facilities. The appropriately named Interbay Cafe stood at 3053 Fifteenth Avenue; a few hundred yards north on the corner with Dravus Street was Hansen's Café, and at 3204 was the M&J Cafe, typical storefront, short-order places catering to workers at the rail yard. The Fisherman's Cafe, farther along on Fifteenth at the junction with Emerson Street, drew its customers from nearby Fisherman's Terminal, home to hundreds of fishing boats and other watercraft.

BALLARD

Incorporated in 1890, Ballard's early economy was based on sawmills and shingle factories and its access to open water (it sits on the north edge of Salmon Bay). By the time its citizens voted to be annexed by Seattle in 1906, Ballard had become a bustling town with a business district stretching along Ballard Avenue and a few side streets. Completion of the Ballard Bridge in 1917 brought Fifteenth Avenue across the Lake Washington Ship Canal about a quarter of a mile east of the original downtown; access from Fifteenth Avenue and the bridge to Ballard Avenue became more difficult after the bridge opened, and Market Street eventually developed into Ballard's new downtown commercial district.

Ballard's 1890 eating establishments included the Queen City Restaurant and Chop House and restaurants run by Burden & Linder, L.P. Levasseur, Carrie Rolff and Elizabeth McDonough. The Queen City Restaurant was still serving a decade later and had been joined by the Ballard Oyster House and the Home Restaurant. They had all disappeared by 1910.

One longtime resident of Ballard Avenue was the Owl Cafe & Tavern. The Owl opened as a saloon in 1904 and over the years was known by several different labels—saloon, café, tavern—and sometimes straddled the fine line of the law. In 1935, owner Emil Einess, aware of an impending police raid to seize his slot machines, called the department and told them not to bother—thieves had broken in the night before and stolen them. The Owl was still going strong in the 1980s as a bar with live music but had disappeared in the next decade after nearly one hundred years in business. The building that housed the Owl still stands, remodeled but basically intact, at 5140 Ballard Avenue.

Hattie's Hat, another longtime survivor at 5231 Ballard Way, is the latest in a string of restaurants to occupy those premises. As early as 1924, Harry Pettyjohn was running a soft drink–lunch counter there. The Old Home Restaurant, under Bror Johnson and (later) Carl Anderson, was a longtime tenant. By 1955, it had become Malmen's Fine Food, owned by Gus Malmberg, open twenty-four hours a day with cocktail service and "the mellow old Scandinavian flavor that made it a rendezvous for gourmet." In 1971, Hattie's moved in along with Aunt Harriet's Room, the cocktail lounge. Forty-plus years later, Hattie's remains Ballard's favorite funky old-time restaurant. "Malmen" is still spelled out in small tiles on Hattie's threshold.

In the early 1940s, Albert VanSanten had a restaurant at 5429 Ballard Avenue called the Vasa Sea Grill. (*Vasa* is Swedish for "ship.") By 1952, a cocktail lounge, the Patio Room, had been added, and Francis King had been taken on as a business partner. King, the leader of a café orchestra in Seattle's early days, played the violin in the restaurant until his death in

home of The GREEN APPLE PIE

The Home of the Green Apple Pie was located at 521 Pike Street. It's unclear why a red apple, rather than green, was featured on the menu cover. *MOHAI, 2009.86.1.*

KIRKPATRICK'S - Seattle's Outstanding Restaurant

The Georgian Room

Above: Earl Kirkpatrick was involved in many Seattle restaurants over the years. His biggest achievement was Kirkpatrick's, at 416 Union Street.

Left: The Georgian Room in the Olympic Hotel issued a series of colorful menus featuring idealized scenes from eighteenth-century royal courts.

Left: Maison Blanc was housed in an elegant 1880s mansion with another restaurant, the Rathskellar, in a basement building fronting Marion Street. In the upper-left corner is a vignette of owner and chef Charles Joseph Blanc. *MOHAI, 2009.71.*

Right: The Paul Bunyan Room was a 1960s addition to Frederick & Nelson's food service, with Paul and his famous blue ox, Babe, portrayed on the menu cover. *MOHAI, 1993.43_box4_folder19.*

Frederick & Nelson's Tea Room served much more than just tea, as the cover of this seafood menu illustrates. *MOHAI, 2009.86.*

Right: Claire Colegrove's Northold Inn exuded the ambience of a Tudor-style English inn with its half-timbered façade, dark woodwork and polished copper ornaments.

Below: The layout of the Purple Pup, another Colegrove restaurant, was typical of its time: long and narrow with a counter and stools and booths lining the opposite wall.

NORTHOLD INN, SEATTLE, WASH.   YE OLDE GOOD PLACE TO EAT.

INTERIOR OF THE PURPLE PUP, SEATTLE'S MOST ATTRACTIVE RESTAURANT, TIMES SQUARE—SEATTLE.   116651

Above: This Triple XXX menu dates to the early 1920s—it lists Triple XXX cola (a short-lived product) along with the company's mainstay root beer.

Right: Day or night, Clark's Round the Clock was always open at 1001 Olive Way. *MOHAI, 1986.15.7.*

Left: A giant smiling fish served as a backdrop on Crawford's colorful menu. Located right at water's edge, Crawford's guests had a great view of ship traffic on Elliott Bay.

Below: The Norselander, on the top floor of the Norway Center, featured an elegant dining room with cloth-covered tables and a high-level view of Elliott Bay.

SEATTLE'S *Only* RESTAURANT

SPECIALIZING *Exclusively* IN

SEA FOODS

208 ELLIOTT AVE. WEST ☆ SEATTLE ☆ Proprietors: CURT KREMER and ERNEST HILSENBERG

Left: Skipper's Galley played up the nautical theme. The restaurant was boat-shaped, and patrons walked a gangplank to get aboard.

Below: The Wharf was two restaurants in one: the upscale dining room seen here and a working-man's café adjacent, both served from the same kitchen.

THE WHARF • Seattle, Washington • ALder-0088

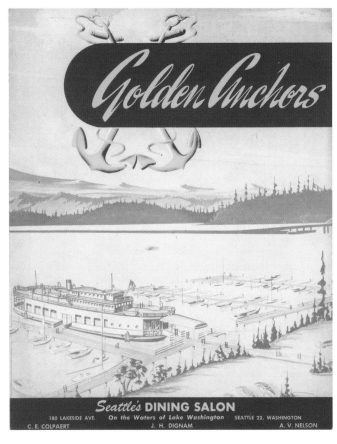

Left: Moored in Lake Washington aboard an old ferry boat, the Golden Anchors was accessible off beautiful Lake Washington Boulevard. *MOHAI, 1996.30.3.3.*

Below: The interior of Manning's, at the corner of Fifteenth and Market Street in Ballard, was the epitome of Googie-style coffee shop architecture in Seattle.

Right: Carl Broome's menu cover fittingly depicted a broom. This menu dates to the 1940s, after Broome had closed his Wallingford location. *MOHAI, 2014.3.1.2.*

Below: The Coon Chicken Inn, on Bothell Way, was one of a chain of three, the others (also pictured here) being in Salt Lake City and Portland.

Carl
BROOME'S
Menu

Nothing is done in a hit-and-miss way in this restaurant. We take particular pains to select the best of fresh meats, choice cuts, and prepare them ourselves. Recipes are tested, and never altered. You will find everything we serve consistently good, wholesome, and tasty.

"HE SERVES MOST WHO SERVES BEST"

314 BROADWAY North, SEATTLE

AT SALT LAKE CITY, UTAH

AT PORTLAND, ORE.

Nationally Famous – COON CHICKEN INN – 8500 Bothell Way – SEATTLE, WASH.

The Igloo floats on an icy island on this menu cover. A penguin takes an order from a drive-up boat while a polar bear roams the parking lot.

A well-dressed couple—she in furs, he in a tux—enters the warm glow of King Oscar's on Aurora Avenue in this period postcard.

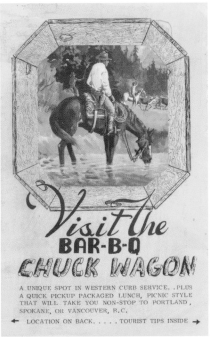

Left: A pirate—looking the worse for wear—graces the menu cover of the Jolly Roger, a roadhouse on Bothell Way. *UW, MEN036*.

Right: The cowboy-themed Bar-B-Q Chuck Wagon was also on Aurora, just north of King Oscar's but a world away cuisine-wise.

Above: In later years, when Power's Pancake Palace took over the Twin T-P's, the gleaming steel teepees were painted orange and blue.

Left: With a lovely señorita on the front and a dashing caballero on the back of its menu, Cook's Tamale Grotto played up its Spanish essence.

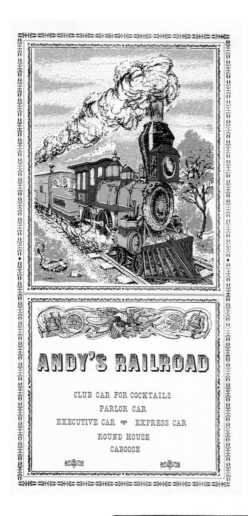

Left: Andy's Diner, housed in a set of repurposed passenger cars on Fourth Avenue South, took the railroad motif to the max with swizzle sticks shaped like train-crossing signs and paper engineers' caps for the kids.

Below: Once the crown jewel of Seattle's roadside architecture, the Twin T-P's opened in 1937 on Aurora Avenue (Highway 99) across from Green Lake.

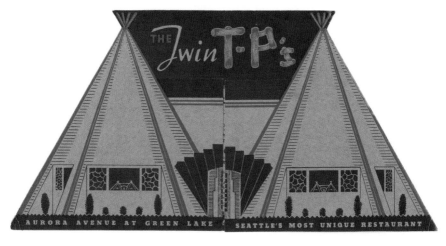

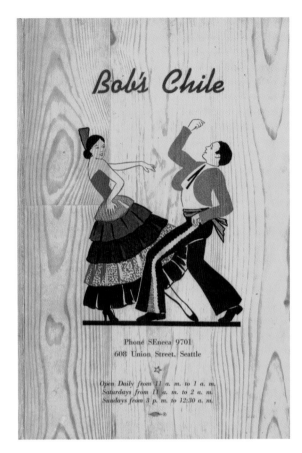

Left: Bob's Chile repeated the Spanish theme a few years later, but this time the couple—slightly stylized—were dancing together on the menu cover. *MOHAI, 1986.15.93.*

Below: The imposing façade of the Gim Ling Restaurant (later the China Gate) loomed over Seventh Avenue South.

Trader Vic's Outrigger in the Benjamin Franklin Hotel offered a colorful menu depicting idealized South Pacific scenes.

Left: The China Pheasant was a dine-and-dance roadhouse on Highway 99; its menu was half American, half Chinese food items.

Below: Bamboo partitions, thatched canopies above the tables and hanging bunches of bananas created an exotic atmosphere at the Kalua Room, in the Windsor Hotel at Sixth Avenue and Pike Street.

1956. The Vasa was another smorgasbord place—they called their version a Vasabord, available every Friday and Saturday evening from 5:00 until 9:00 p.m. and daily for lunch. The Vasa was still in business in 1979; today, the building is occupied by the Peoples Pub, a German restaurant.

Elsewhere along Ballard Avenue were Blossom's Lunch (also called the Corner Cafe and Bob & Nancy's Cafe) at 5133 and the Swedish Kitchen at 5203 Ballard. The Fern Cafe, 4833 Twentieth Avenue, was a block off Ballard Avenue toward the water. The Fern specialized in hot cakes and waffles and put up lunches for workers along Ballard's waterfront; it called itself "the home of the best T-bone steaks in town"—only forty-five cents—but seems to have been in business for just a few years in the 1930s. As early as 1907, there was a restaurant at 5203 Ballard Avenue; by the 1950s, it was called the Swedish Kitchen. In contrast to the already-developing persona of Ballard as a Scandinavian stronghold, Thomas Chinn had his Chung Sun Cafe at 5133 Ballard Avenue, where the Sunset Tavern is today.

John Kenney opened the Driftwood Cafe around 1936 at 5416 Fifteenth Avenue, a short block south of Market Street. By this time, Market (originally called Broadway) had become the commercial district and was the main route connecting Ballard with the Wallingford and University Districts to

The entire staff took a break to have their photo taken in front of the Fern Cafe. Unfortunately, none of them are identified. *Ballard Historical Society.*

the east. The restaurant's name changed a few years later—it became the Driftwood Inn—and by 1959, it had relocated to 1442 Market, still adjacent to the busy Fifteenth Avenue–Market Street intersection. Its advertising urged customers to "follow the crowds to the Driftwood Inn" for chicken, steaks, oysters and fish and chips served with courteous service in a pleasant atmosphere. Under Art Saulness's management, the Driftwood became a bit upscale, with charcoal-broiled steaks and a variety of seafood dishes; they also introduced Ballard to pasties, the meat-and-potato turnovers brought to America by immigrants from Cornwall, England. After thirty-five years in business, Art and Marjorie Saulness closed the Driftwood Inn in 1979. Both of its locations are now parking lots.

Summer 1947 saw Noble's Chicken Dinner Inn open at 1718 Market Street, in the building now occupied by Don Willis Furniture. It became the Spud Nut Shop in 1951, "spudnut" being a potato-based doughnut sold by a chain of stores that originated in Salt Lake City in 1940 and grew to over three hundred stores (of which about thirty-five remain). In the 1950s, Mr. and Mrs. William Markham sold their Spud Nut Shop to Mr. and Mrs. G.B. Gore; it was gone by 1958.

On Twentieth Avenue, half a block north of Market, was the Plantation. Originally named Snyder's Southern Food, its specialty was New Orleans French Creole cooking: marinated shrimp in remoulade sauce, Dungeness crab legs with cognac, poached halibut filet with lime-butter sauce and beef medallions with sauce Marchand de Vin. John Wilson was part owner; Willard Lillquist, the manager; Chef Barbara Sandoval studied haute cuisine for two years in Paris. The Plantation was still there in 1977; today, it's the Golden City Chinese Restaurant. Another Creole-Cajun restaurant, Burk's, was located a few blocks off Twenty-Second Avenue. Terry Burkhardt's cooking was more rustic than fine French Creole, with emphasis on jambalayas, gumbos and étouffées. It closed in 2005.

Barbara Sandoval's Crème de Cognac

Blanc mange base, or vanilla pudding to serve 4, prepared according to recipe except minus ⅓ cup of the milk
⅓ cup fine cognac, or 1 part Grand Marnier to 1 part fine cognac to equal ⅓ cup
¾ cup whipping cream, whipped
Shaved almonds

Cook blanc mange or pudding to thickened stage. Remove from heat. Stir in cognac or combination of cognac and Grand Marnier. Cool. Fold whipped cream into cooled pudding. Serve in 5-ounce brandy snifters with shaved almonds on top. Yield: 4 servings.

Farther along on Market Street was a cluster of short-order lunch counter places: the Hasty Tasty Snak Bar, at 5401 Twentieth Avenue just south of Market; Matt's Hamburger, 2213 Market Street; Power's Fountain Lunch, 2216 Market; and the Royal Cafe, 2307 Market, which in 1936 offered lunch for twenty-five cents and Sunday dinner for only forty-nine cents. The Roxy Cafe, at 2023 Market, went through several name changes over the years. Oliver Cummings was running a café at that address as early as 1934. At some point, it was called the Sunshine Dairy Lunch; by 1951, it had become the Chef Cafe. A trio of Southeast Asian restaurants now occupy the premises.

The Cream Inn Cafe appeared at 2311 Market Street in about 1940. It was owned by Folle and Hanna Pihl and is now a cocktail lounge called Hazlewood. The building next door at 2319 Market has a long restaurant history. As early as 1918, Lena Foster was running a restaurant at that spot. The building did a stint as a Dunlap Radio store until Albert VanSanten (later of the Vasa Sea Grill) opened an eatery there. Albert Selleck bought out VanSanten and ran Selleck's Cafe there during World War II. By 1946, it had become Gunnar's Cafe, owned by Bennet Blumlo; Elbert and Veronica Cope took over in 1957 and operated Gunnar's for another ten years until they retired. Heavily remodeled, the building has been home to one of the Azteca Mexican restaurant chain's locations for nearly thirty years.

At the western edge of downtown Ballard were Matt's Cafe at 2409 Market (now Hamburger Harry's) and Andy's Cafe across the street at 2442 Market; Andy's became Smitty's when Chester Smith ran it in the 1950s. A quarter mile farther west, where Seaview Avenue curves north toward Shilshole Bay, the Totem House served up fish and chips. Somewhat modified (and with an expanded menu), it's part of the local Red Mill Burgers chain. Across the street and of more recent vintage, Hiram's at the Locks was an excellent place for steaks and seafood with a great view of boat traffic through the Ballard Locks. Hiram's arrived in 1976, underwent a name change to the Pescatore Fish Café, reverted back to Hiram's and finally closed in 2003.

On the east edge of Ballard, at the corner of Eighth Avenue where Market Street makes the long climb up Phinney Ridge, Ed Davis had a restaurant

Above: A totem pole looms large over the Totem House, at the west edge of Ballard, in this 1955 photo. *Seattle Public Library, spl_wl_res_00139.*

Left: King Eddie's Dina Buffet soon after it opened in 1954. It's likely the man walking through the door is the king himself, Ed Davis. *Seattle Municipal Archives, 78527.*

he modestly named King Eddie's Dina Buffet. Ed was already known in Ballard for "the biggest hamburger in the world" and excellent steaks at the Davis Cafe, his place on Twenty-Fourth Avenue and Sixty-Seventh Street. In January 1954, the *Seattle Times* announced the opening of King Eddie's "new eating establishment at 8th NW and Market Street….Food that is fit for a king, queen, prince and princess will be ready day and night. Whether it is a steak or a snack, a dinner or a donut, King Eddie promises supremacy in service for 24 hours every day." The new place was decorated "with the Mother Goose type caricatures of royalty," and the house specialty was potpies. The King's empire didn't last long; it was apparently gone within a few years, and today, the Ballard Mandarin Chinese Restaurant occupies the former castle.

Back on Fifteenth Avenue, restaurants lined the street from the Ballard Bridge all the way to Sixty-Fifth Street, nearly a mile north. Just across the bridge, across from still-surviving Mike's Chili Parlor, stood Peters' Chanticleer at 4700 Fifteenth Avenue. Franklin and Ade Peters operated the Chanticleer for over twenty years before selling out in 1961 to Joe and Sharon Neyman. Originally from Butte, Montana, where pasties were (and still are) a popular lunch item, the Neymans possibly took a hint from the nearby Driftwood Inn and began making and selling pasties in their small café.

On the northwest corner of the Fifteenth Avenue–Market Street intersection stood one of the most distinctive pieces of roadside architecture in Seattle: Manning's Cafeteria, part of the Manning's chain of coffee houses, though the only one done in what is called the Googie style. Googie architecture originated in Southern California in the late 1940s (the name comes from a now-gone coffee shop in West Hollywood), and by the 1960s, Googie-style restaurants could be found throughout the country. Stylistic elements included upswept roofs, curved and sharply angled shapes and lots of glass and neon. The Manning's building, designed by Bay-area architect Clarence Mayhew, was constructed in 1964. Sited where it was, at Ballard's busiest intersection, it served as something of a greeting and gateway for residents and visitors. Manning's operated from 1964 to 1983, served good food at affordable prices and became a gathering place for neighborhood regulars. After renovation in 1984, it reopened as a Denny's. The doors closed in 2007, and despite vigorous opposition from preservationists, the building was demolished in 2008.

North on Fifteenth were the Three Sisters Cafe, the Red Robin Cafe and Fifteenth Avenue Fish & Chips. The Three Sisters Cafe, at 5912 Fifteenth, was earlier known as Liden's Sandwich Shop. It later became an antiques store and today is the site of a Taco Bell. The Red Robin Cafe (not to be confused with the later Red Robin Gourmet Burgers chain) was located at 6117 Fifteenth Avenue in 1951. Fifteenth Avenue Fish & Chips, at 6409 Fifteenth where the street makes a slight jog on its way to Crown Hill, apparently didn't last long, even with nearby Ballard High School as a potential customer base.

Leary Way, the connecting link between Ballard and Fremont, hosted a number of restaurants over the years: the Chat 'n Chew, just east of Ballard at 1440 Leary Way; the Cottage Cafe (also known as the Little Place), 3624 Leary Way, now home to Alberona's Pizza & Pasta; the Cornell Cafe, 4302 Leary, where a hamburger stand was operating as early as 1939 and lasted until 1971; Birdie's Cafe (later the Double VV Cafe), an "industrial lunch room" owned by Emma Tuckey in 1940, 4358 Leary; and Bergin's Lunch at 5242 Leary—in 1973, it was the D&W, and today it's the Señor Moose Café.

CROWN HILL

The Crown Hill neighborhood is centered on Fifteenth Avenue and Eighty-Fifth Street, another busy intersection of connecting arterials. In the 1930s, a small business district grew up around the intersection, of which a few buildings remain today.

A bit south of the intersection, at 8037 Fifteenth, was a place called the Twin Chestnuts. In 1946, owner Lawrence Simpier was robbed by a gun-toting man wearing a child's pink bandana for a mask. Kitchen worker Roy Parker tried to hit the robber with a glass of malted milk but missed and was shot at; luckily, he was only slightly injured. In the 1960s, it became McGrath's Twin Chestnuts, open for luncheon and dinner only with "moderately priced home-cooked foods." These days it is the Original Pancake House, an offshoot of the original Original Pancake House in Portland, Oregon.

At 8332 Fifteenth Avenue was Higgse Ice Cream Lunch, a hamburger shop–soda fountain place that vanished in the early 1950s. Next up were the Crown Hill Lunch and Christian's, across the street from each other at 8505 and 8506 Fifteenth, respectively. The Fiesta Cafe, a dine-and-dance place owned by Peter Desimone, went in at 8517 Fifteenth shortly after the repeal of Prohibition; by the 1960s, it was a live music bar called Mr. P's, and today it's Centerfolds, an adult entertainment club.

The Harvester Restaurant began as the Brill & Spalding Tavern. In the 1960s, the Harvester advertised "delicious steaks, chicken, seafood served in pleasant neighborhood atmosphere" with cocktails in the Trophy Room. The restaurant suffered $200,000 worth of fire damage in 1979 due to faulty wiring of a stove hood and didn't rebuild. Its site is now in the Value Village parking lot.

Another early place was Johnnie's Hamburgers, 8521 Fifteenth. It's mentioned in 1939 when it was held up at 2:15 one morning by two armed men—one with a gun, the other a knife—who ordered burgers and, when served, pointed a gun and robbed the cash register of about thirty-five dollars. It later became Johnnie's Char Broiler, open twenty-four hours a day except Sunday, featuring rib-eye steak and eggs cooked the way you like them. Now it's the parking lot of a Pizza Hut.

George Louie's, possibly Seattle's most far-flung Chinese restaurant in its day, opened in 1955 just off Fifteenth Avenue at 1471 Eighty-Fifth Street. In later days, George's wife, Rose, recalled the locals being unfamiliar with Chinese food and that the Louies had to introduce them to this different, new cuisine:

When we first opened, people—the only Chinese food they are used to or knew about or would even bother to eat would be fried rice, chow mein, noodles, things like that. But gradually we expanded and included spicy dishes and more ethnic dishes. And people at first were skeptical, but they tried it and liked it. So we kept adding to it.

North of the Fifteenth–Eighty-Fifth intersection, Fifteenth Avenue becomes Holman Road and curves northeast to meet up with Greenwood Avenue. At the curve were three more eateries: the Coffee-Up Restaurant, at 9016 Holman; Little Acorn Cafe at 9053 Holman; and a different Crown Hill Lunch at 9081 Holman. They are all long gone.

LAKE UNION/FAIRVIEW

Fairview Avenue runs from the north edge of downtown Seattle to Lake Union through an area that, back in the day, was a zone of warehouses and light industry with a few scattered residences. Consequently, the restaurants were oriented to the working class. They included the Fairway Lunch

Counter at 204 Fairview; the Fairview Cafe, owned by Blodwen "Bobbie" Blomquist on the corner of Fairview and Mercer; and Messmerized Chicken 'N Chips, 609 Fairview. The Little White Kitchen was in business under Victoria Bourgault's management as early as 1933 at 713 Fairview. Next door and twenty years later, Modesto and Joseph Colasurdo had their M&J Cafe; it later became the B&A Cafe and went out of business in 1976. To the northeast, where Fairview merges with Eastlake after a short run along Lake Union, was the Lake Union Cafe (the original, not the same-named place a mile to the north these days).

EASTLAKE

A route of the early Pacific Highway, Eastlake Avenue was a major thoroughfare into and out of Seattle. Northbound from downtown, the highway passed through several distinct neighborhoods—Eastlake, the University District and Roosevelt—before turning northeast onto Bothell Way (Lake City Way today) and eventually to Everett and points north.

There were a few small cafés along Eastlake near its junction with Fairview. A lunch room at 1206 Eastlake, opened in the 1920s, became the Baum Cafe under Hazel Baum's ownership. Just up the street was the New Shamrock Cafe, another early lunch place that lasted into the 1950s.

Another complicated thread of Seattle restaurant history: in the late 1940s, Les Teagle opened a restaurant at 304 Eastlake Avenue. Around 1955, he sold it to Harold Frye and found a new spot along Aurora Avenue. Frye renamed the Eastlake Avenue location, calling it Harold Frye's Charcoal Broiler, and happily served lunch and dinner (and cocktails in the Sage'n Sand Room) until 1960, when it was taken by freeway construction.

Undeterred, Frye found a waterfront location on Lake Union at 2501 Fairview and opened Harold's Satellite (the "satellite" moniker was chosen in keeping with the space theme of the upcoming Expo 21 fair). On the menu were seafood kabobs, lobster tails, salmon steaks and other seafood specialties, along with the usual steaks and prime rib. Unfortunately, Frye didn't prosper in the new location; the Satellite closed after about two years, though Frye went on to open yet another restaurant in North Seattle. The vacant Satellite was purchased by Roy Myers, previous owner of the Richelieu Cafe in downtown, and renamed the Riviera. In 1969, it became the Hungry Turtle and was later known as the Landing.

On a slight rise overlooking the University Bridge, just off Eastlake at 3272 Fuhrman Avenue, was the first restaurant in the chain of Red Robin Gourmet Burgers. The story is told that its history began with Sam's Tavern in the 1940s. Sam, the owner, sang in a barbershop quartet, and one of his favorite songs was "When the Red, Red Robin (Comes Bob, Bob, Bobbin' Along)." He liked it so much that he changed the tavern's name to Sam's Red Robin. While it makes for a good yarn, it doesn't appear to be accurate. As early as 1930, the Bridge Cafe—it later became Bee's Corner Cafe—was at this address, and a 1942 classified ad announced that Tommy Dace, well known in local musical circles, "must sell the Red Robin, 3272 Fuhrman Avenue."

Whatever the facts, it's certain that Red Robin was a well-established name by the time Gerry Kingen purchased it in 1969. A newspaper comment of the day captures the Red Robin's early ambience: "very old-tavernish; loud jukebox, a line of hunched shoulders and long hair at the bar; at the tables a mix of old-timers and college kids just discovering the place," with the scent of marijuana detectable, particularly on the open balcony that overlooked the Ship Canal.

It wasn't until the mid-1970s that Kingen started to serve hamburgers—at first only the usual varieties, but eventually offering twenty-eight different types of burgers—and the place exploded in popularity. Kingen began selling Red Robin franchises; a second Red Robin opened in Yakima in 1979

Bee's Corner Cafe occupied 3272 Fuhrman long before the first in the Red Robin chain took over in the late 1960s. *Washington State Archives Puget Sound Regional Branch.*

The first Red Robin, progenitor of the chain, as it looked circa 1970. *Washington State Archives Puget Sound Regional Branch.*

and another in Portland the following year. By 1985, the Red Robin chain included 175 restaurants and corporate headquarters were moved to Irvine, California. Today, the total number of Red Robins worldwide tops out at over 500 locations.

While all this explosive growth was happening, the original Red Robin in Seattle continued dishing out burgers to a steady clientele—until the corporation decided that the building was too out-of-date and not worth rehabilitating. It closed in 2010, and the building was removed.

University District

Eastlake Avenue becomes Roosevelt Way after crossing the University Bridge. Half a mile to the east is the University of Washington (UW) and the aptly named University District. When the UW relocated from downtown Seattle to take advantage of buildings left by the 1909 Alaska-Yukon-Pacific Exposition, this lightly populated area was known as Brooklyn. It didn't take long for the university to bring explosive growth to the neighborhood.

In short order, a mile-long business district of restaurants, clothing stores and movie theaters had sprung up along Fourteenth Avenue (soon to be renamed University Way, commonly called the Ave) to service students and faculty. Dozens of cafés and lunch counters fed hungry students on the run between classes. A few fine dining places intermingled with the cafés, and two hotels anchored the northern end of the district.

At the southern end of the district were such places as the Portage Bay Grill, the Snack Shop, the U&I Cafe and the Club Cafe. At 4136 University Way was an outlet for a small local chain called Fabulous Burgers, which had five other locations around the city. In 1953, fifty cents would buy "two of the most fabulous hamburgers you ever ate"—quarter-pound hamburgers, each on a large bun with onions, lettuce, tomatoes and a thick slice of Tillamook cheese. Howard's Restaurant was a typical storefront eatery at the corner of Forty-Second and the Ave. Just up the street were Opal's Grill and Harvey's Kitchen.

Among the earliest eateries was the Olympia Cafe at 4003 University Way, in business since at least 1932 with frosted refrigerator pipes spelling out the café's name in the front window and an old-fashioned "Booths for Ladies Only" sign on the door. Longtime owners George Apostolou and

Howard's was one of several dozen restaurants along University Avenue catering to students and faculty from the nearby University of Washington. *University of Washington Special Collections, SEA3554.*

John Soldano were legendary for feeding hungry and sometimes penniless students; noted architect Victor Steinbrueck recalled that, when he was a student, "George and John always made certain we had plenty to eat, really loaded us up on mashed potatoes and gravy, plus big portions of meat and crusty bread—stuff that really stuck to your ribs." The price? Thirty-five cents. Steinbrueck remembered the Olympic as "real, not synthetic—something difficult to find these days," but even in 1965, it was one of the last remnants of an earlier generation of restaurants. The Olympic was the last restaurant on the Ave to sell meal ticket books.

The greatest concentration of restaurants on the Ave was along the two-block stretch between Forty-Third and Forty-Fifth Streets. The Columns Cafe was at 4302; opened in the late 1940s, it was gone by 1965. Next door was a hamburger stand called Rod & Dean's. The Lun Ting Cafe, at 4318 University, featured barbecued spareribs, egg rolls, won ton soup and almond chicken and was open only for dinner. Near the busy intersection with Forty-Fifth Street was a group of fountain lunches: Leo's Fountain Cafe at 4342 University, Norm's Fountain at 4344 (now occupied by Bartell Drugs, which had its own fountain service) and Graham's Restaurant & Fountain at 4701 University Way.

Farther along the Ave as it headed toward the Ravenna neighborhood, Hasty Tasty Cafe (5247 University) was a favorite for hamburgers and milkshakes. By 1980, it had become Avenue 52, a restaurant that combined Syrian and Italian cuisine. On the menu were fettuccine, chicken Bolognese and other Italian dishes, along with Syrian specialties such as shish kabob and "upside down" chicken (layers of boneless chicken, deep-fried cauliflower and seasoned rice). Avenue 52 closed when owner Saleh Joudeh moved to Green Lake to open Saleh al Lago.

Among the fine dining spots on the Ave were Lee's Broiler and the Robin Hood Grill. Lee's, at 4553 University, occupied a spot previously home to Sandy's Grill. In 1956, a seven-course steak dinner cost $2.15; the sauerbraten dinner was $1.55. Lee's was open for lunch and dinner, "a continental flavor in an intimate modern atmosphere," with original broiled specialties served Oriental style. When the state legislature changed the zoning for the U District from dry to wet in 1967, Lee's was the first restaurant on the Ave to be granted a liquor license. Still in business in the mid-1980s, today a Starbucks fills the space where Lee's was.

The restaurant at 4334 University had several names over the years. As early as 1923, A.G. Wilds and Roy Hosfield were running the Al Roy Restaurant there. In the 1940s, it was Dick Wiseman's; a few years later, it was Ken's Hamburger Shop. It went upscale in the mid-1950s as Cherberg's Chimes and, later yet, the Robin Hood Grill, with a menu of steaks and entrées (five different types of steaks along with pork chops, veal cutlets, beef liver and bacon and spaghetti); sandwiches, including the house specialty Robin Hood's De Luxe Hamburger (lettuce, tomato, mayo, olives on a toasted bun) and clubhouse, minced ham, chicken salad and grilled chicken sandwiches; breakfast; and full fountain service with sundaes, milkshakes and soft drinks.

In 1923, an elegant apartment hotel, the Wilsonian, opened at the corner of University Way and Forty-Seventh Street. The seven-story brick and terra-cotta structure offered ninety-nine rooms of various levels of luxury aimed at attracting both long-term residents (many of them on the faculty of the university) and overnight guests. Helen Swope of tearoom fame managed the Wilsonian's two dining rooms—the main room, the Peacock, and a smaller Italian-themed dining room called Via Fontana. Within a year, the Peacock Room—"its decorations and furnishings daring in the extreme, yet in compete harmony…a series of moderate-sized rooms afford privacy without the shut-in feeling of the ordinary restaurant dining room"—had become the social center of the University District and was a favorite destination for holiday dinners.

Helen Swope parted ways with the Wilsonian in 1931 to assume management of dining room services at the new Edmond Meany Hotel, located two blocks away at Forty-Fifth and Brooklyn. The Wilsonian's Peacock and Via Fontana dining rooms became casualties of the Depression; the Wilsonian was sold in 1939, but a café continued operating there into the 1950s. The Edmond Meany is now known as the Hotel Deca; the Wilsonian still stands but is not in business as a hotel.

ROOSEVELT

In days prior to Highway 99 and Interstate 5, Roosevelt Way was a main thoroughfare for traffic northbound from Seattle toward Bothell and Everett. Just north of the University Bridge, a number of roadside cafés sprang up near the busy junction of Roosevelt and Forty-Fifth Street, the main arterial connecting the University District with Wallingford and Ballard to the west. Bess N' Nita's Tasty Nook was at 4109 Roosevelt in the 1950s. At 4228 Roosevelt was the Crab Spot, which later became Campos, operated by

Danny and Abel Campos and billed in 1961 as "the only Texas-Mexican style restaurant in Seattle." The Campos brothers learned the restaurant business from their father and had all his recipes, along with the spices and other ingredients "that makes Texas style different from other Mexican foods." Chicken and guacamole tostadas were a specialty; décor included serapes on the walls and an Aztec sundial plate.

D-Lux Hamburger (later called Kirk's Burgers) was located next to Campos. Up the street at 4526 Roosevelt was the Blue Moon Cafe (not to be confused with the nearby and still-extant Blue Moon Tavern). A few doors away was the Red Rooster Cafe; opened in 1939 and operated by Frankie France and Irene Ledwich, it later became Chester's Cafe. Across the street was the Auto Row Cafe at 4551 Roosevelt Way, and two blocks farther north was the Nifty Nook, an eleven-stool restaurant later known as Goldie's Cafe.

Several other eateries were scattered alongside Roosevelt Way as it continued north. For nearly twenty years, Greek immigrant Peter Anastos had Pete's Barbecue at 5300 Roosevelt; it later became the Maple Inn and today functions as Dante's Tavern. Two drive-ins, Ronken's and the Hamburger Round-Up, were a few blocks north. By 1965, the Hamburger Round had become the Taj Mahal Restaurant. It was located at 6106 Roosevelt.

By the 1920s, a business district had risen at the intersection of Roosevelt and Sixty-Fifth Street, and locals and highway travelers had a number of restaurants to choose from. There were the Roosevelt Coffee Shop at 6417 Roosevelt Way and Lloyd's Lunch at 6503 Roosevelt, in business as early as 1934 under H.J. Lane and lasting into the '50s. Clement Arnold had the Rainbow Cafe at 6409 Roosevelt; it later became a Chinese restaurant called the Ming Garden. Another café-turned-Chinese-restaurant was at 6510 Roosevelt; first called the Hollywood Cafe, by the 1950s, it had transformed into the Far West Cafe. H.T. "Ted" Holmes ran De Luxe Hamburgers at 6603 Roosevelt; in addition to burgers, he was well known for his chili. By the mid-1940s, the thirty-nine-seat B-29 Cafe could be found at that address.

The district's premier eatery, as well as one of the earliest, was located at 6521 Roosevelt, where a café was in business by the mid-1920s. By the next decade, it was known as the Wayfair Cafe, owned by Lynette Perry. Egyptian-born Abraham Nakla bought the place in 1947, remodeled it and reopened it as Abie's Grill. "World famous chef Abie," as he liked to describe himself in ads, specialized in $0.85 dinners with a choice of baked spareribs, steamed wieners with sauerkraut, grilled hamburger steak, minced ham omelet, grilled liver and bacon, Columbia River smelts, fried oysters, grilled salmon or halibut steak. Also on the menu were roast beef, pork, turkey, baked chicken, baked ham and a full-course steak dinner for $1.50. Abie's was always open for breakfast—egg dishes, omelets, French wheat cakes and waffles.

In 1948, Abie sold his Roosevelt location and opened a new place just east of the University of Washington in the new Laurelhurst Shopping Center on E Forty-Fifth Street. A colorful character, Abie continued to offer full dinners at moderate prices until his passing in 1959. After Abie departed Roosevelt, the restaurant's name reverted to the Wayfair Cafe, with "lots of good food at modest 'family' prices." Fred and Pat Garski became involved in the restaurant, and by 1951, it had been renamed Garski's Scarlet Tree. Remembered as "a relaxed, friendly atmosphere [that] provides the perfect setting for enjoyment of dinner, luncheon, cocktails or late evening suppers...a Northeast Seattle tradition," the Scarlet Tree served up steaks, full-course dinners, luncheons and cocktails. Two-for dinners were a specialty; the menu offered a choice of regular full-course dinners starting at two for $5.90. Top of the line were steak and lobster dinners priced at two for $10.90 in 1974.

Just north of Sixty-Fifth Street, at 6815 Roosevelt, was the Marnex Drive-In. A Triple XXX Root Beer barrel originally occupied the spot but was torn down in 1940 when the owners chose to open a new Triple XXX on Bothell Way, half a mile north. The Marnex took over the site a few years later; initially a typical drive-in vending $0.19 hamburgers (five for $0.50 with special coupon), milkshakes for $0.19 and a side of french fries for $0.11, by the mid-1950s, the Marnex had evolved into a full-service restaurant with four different steak dinners—filet mignon, club steak, T-bone or rib-eye—ranging in price from $1.00 to $1.65 and a "complete fountain and restaurant menu." Renamed Bojack's Restaurant by 1962, it suffered a major fire that year and apparently never reopened.

WALLINGFORD

Wallingford's compact commercial center grew up astride the trolley line that once ran west along Forty-Fifth Street from the University District before turning south on Stone Way en route to downtown Seattle. Over the years, numerous restaurants intermingled with clothing shops, hardware stores and several movie theaters. At the west end near the Stone Way intersection were the Forty-Fifth Street Cafe (1224 N Forty-Fifth Street), the Wishbone Cafe (1304 N Forty-Fifth) and the Tip Top Sandwich Shop (1400 N Forty-Fifth).

At 1403 N Forty-Fifth Street was Broome's Aristocratic Hamburger Shop, which had the dubious distinction of having been bombed twice in 1935 during a time of labor troubles. Owner Carl Broome rebuilt and within a few years opened two more shops, one on Queen Anne Avenue and another on Broadway. A few blocks farther east were the Chili Bowl Cafe at 1605 N Forty-Fifth and the Green Lantern Cafe and Gus's Steak House at 1618 and 1624 N Forty-Fifth Street, respectively.

Lawrence and Doris Gurney ran Larre's Bar-B-Q in the 1950s, serving up barbecued beef, ham, pork and spareribs for lunches and dinners. Larre's was at 1718 N Forty-Fifth. It later became a Mexican restaurant, the Guadalajara. The Little Wonder Grill was in business at the same time as Larre's at 1927 N Forty-Fifth. Near the historic Guild Forty-Fifth Theatre were the Dixie Cafe and a place called Joe's Snacks in the building now occupied by the Iron Bull Sports Bar at 2121 N Forty-Fifth. Marking the east end of Wallingford, Even's Cafe (later the Chung Mee Cafe) stood at 2301 N Forty-Fifth; across the street was the Little Kit Kat Drive In.

MADISON STREET, THE CENTRAL DISTRICT AND MADISON PARK

Madison Street is the only thoroughfare out of downtown that touches the shore of Lake Washington, running southwest–northeast all the way from Elliott Bay to the lake. Today, it is heavily used by residents of the Capitol and First Hill neighborhoods as well as by commuters wanting to bypass the Interstate 5–State Route 405 bottleneck by getting onto the Evergreen Point Floating Bridge (officially the Governor Albert D. Rosellini Bridge) at Montlake.

What is now a major arterial street had its beginnings as part of a real estate development. Even early in the city's history, Seattleites were making the adventurous three-mile trek from downtown to a pleasant picnic ground and recreational spot on the edge of Lake Washington. In the 1870s, John McGilvra purchased several sections of land in that area for a homestead and had a road constructed to downtown. The rough-cut road became Madison Street, and the old picnic grounds became Madison Park. By the 1880s, a ferry was in place transporting people and freight from Madison Park across the lake to Kirkland. With the rise of the auto age, the ferry route became part of the Yellowstone Trail, one of the country's earliest cross-continental routes. Even after the 1940 construction of Lake Washington's first floating bridge (common name: the I-90 or Lake Washington Floating Bridge; real name: the Lacey V. Murrow Bridge), the ferry remained in service for another ten years.

Restaurants began appearing on Madison, particularly at two neighborhoods along the way: the area between Twenty-First and Twenty-Third Avenues and at its terminus at Madison Park, where quite a commercial district had developed around the ferry landing. There was the Columbus Malted Milk & Sandwich Shop at 1010½ Madison, just east of downtown; it later became the Lock Yuen Cafe. The Tank & Tummy—part café, part tavern—spent about twenty years at 1208 Madison. Across the street was a place that began as Wila's Delicatessen. Robert Harris bought it in the early '60s, renamed it Bob's Cafe and served "delicious breakfasts, luncheon and dinner in congenial surroundings. Luncheons at $1.25…Filet steak sandwich $1.95." Bob's also had a cocktail lounge and banquet facilities.

The Terminal Chop House, another early place, was at 1335 E Madison in 1932. Opposite it across Madison was the Fourteenth Avenue Coffee Shop, 1336 E Madison. Jack MacDougall opened it as a tavern in 1933. In later years, it was owned by Panos Nikolopoulas and Gus Charouhas. The Drum Room Grill was in the same block at 1342 E Madison. It opened prior to 1951 and for a time was owned by Harold Frye, who had several other restaurant interests around the city. Irving Stept was the proprietor in 1966; the same year, the name was changed to Sol's Broiler, but not for long—by the next year, it had become Zed's Broiler Restaurant before reverting back to the Drum Room again. It disappeared circa 1978.

A.R. Smith had a lunch counter called Smitty's Lunch at 1412 Madison as early as 1932. Gordon Sawdy bought it the following year and was still running it a decade later. It was the Taxi Lunch in 1951 and Vi's Cafe three years later. The Cottage Cafe, at 1501 E Madison, was originally owned by Julius Hansen. By 1973, the Cottage was being run by the same Robert Harris who operated Bob's Cafe a few blocks back west on Madison. That same year, Harris was shot to death there; four years later, another murder took place at the Cottage. Still in business in 1978, it is now long gone.

The quarter-mile-long stretch of Madison between Twentieth and Twenty-Fourth Avenues is part of the Central District, for decades a focus of residency for Seattle's black population. Nearly a dozen restaurants and taverns lined Madison in this area. Jimmie's Cafe was at 2004 E Madison. Marion C. Honeysuckle owned the Honeysuckle Recreation and Cafe, 2030

E Madison. Thrasher's Cafe, 2038 E Madison, later became the Casbah Tavern. Floyd Strickler had a card room and tavern at 2047 E Madison in the 1940s; by 1954, it had become the Mardi Gras and was still in business there in 1984.

The Lincoln Cafe and the DeLite Lunch were early eateries in the 2100 block of E Madison, dating to 1932. Charles Barber had a lunchroom at 2229 E Madison in 1940; Carter T. Dawson later purchased it and ran it as Evelyn's Restaurant. In 1972, what had been Trilby's Grill at 2310 E Madison became Willie's Smokehouse. Willie McClenon, a semi-pro football player, renovated a burned-out restaurant with the help of a small-business loan. He installed new booths, counters and a large brick barbecue oven. Willie's specialties were hamburgers, ribs, french fries, chili, ham and eggs, sandwiches and homemade sweet potato pie. For a dozen years, Oscar and Betty Ryan ran Betty's Cafe at 2703 E Madison. Practically all of these places have vanished.

Out toward the end of Madison, in the posh Broadmoor neighborhood, was Nino's Cafe at 4106 E Madison. For a while, there was a soda fountain inside the Broadmoor Pharmacy at 4130 E Madison. The very end of Madison Street at Madison Park supported nearly two dozen businesses during its peak years, including the Bamboo Terrace (4226 E Madison) and the Quality Cafe (4226 E Madison). On Forty-Third Street, which cuts across Madison at its very end, was an early restaurant run by Shields & Hutcheson. Guppy's Fish & Chips, at 1927 Forty-Third N, was just across the street; and to the north, right on the lake, was an elegant place called Elona's Lake Crest Inn. Elona's fixed-price Thanksgiving dinner in 1929 included two seafood cocktails—oyster and crab; creamed chicken consommé; choice of stuffed turkey, roast goose or fried chicken for the entrée; choice of potato (mashed, creamed or candied sweet potato); cauliflower Polonaise; English-style plum pudding with hard sauce; choice of dessert (mince pie, pumpkin pie or Lake Crest apple pie) and ice cream; fresh fruit and nuts; toasted crackers and cheese; and coffee, tea or milk—all for $1.50.

Broadway

In the 1880s, Broadway was a stump road weaving through logged-off land along the top of a ridge that connects three of Seattle's high points: Beacon, First and Broadway Hills. By 1903, a streetcar line had been installed, the muddy road had been paved, Broadway Hill had become Capitol Hill and the location had become a magnet for the well-to-do to construct elegant homes. One hundred years later, Broadway remains the colorful epicenter of Seattle's counterculture and the prime example of the city's diversity.

Just north of Madison, at 1104 Broadway, was the Chieftain Fountain Cafe with a seating capacity of seventy-five. It is now the site of the Silver Cloud Hotel. Several early lunchrooms congregated a block away at the intersection with Union Street: the Broadway Cafe, run by J.H. Smith; Henry Butenschoen's lunchroom, later operated by Don Moore; and a small place owned by Phil Ferran. They all dated to the 1920s and were swallowed up by the district's growth later that decade.

Between Pike and Pine were two places with similar names on opposite sides of the street: the Broadway Center Lunch, 1525 Broadway, and the Broadway Fountain Lunch, 1534 Broadway. The Broadway Center Lunch, initially called the Dairy Lunch, was there in 1918 and owned by Peter Lensinger. After Lensinger committed suicide in 1931 (one of at least a half dozen restaurant owners who did so, including the aforementioned Henry Butenschoen), a name change was made. The Broadway Center Lunch was still in business in the late 1930s.

The Broadway Fountain Lunch, a light lunch and fountain, was open by 1923 and first known as Watson's. In the 1930s, its owners were Mr. and Mrs. Richard Furleigh. It was inside I. Lee's drugstore and in the 1940s was renamed Lee's Lunch; a decade later, it became Dee's Sandwich Haven. The building later became a bank branch and still stands, though heavily remodeled.

Dunham's Confectionery was at the Broadway–Pine Street intersection. Just west at 823 Pine was the Broadway Coffee Corner, and a few blocks away at 611 E Pine Street was Vagabonds House, made to look like a shanty and promising "deliciously different dinners to provide you an adventure in dining."

In the 1920s, the Broadway Dairy Company, manufacturers of Velvet Ice Cream, occupied 1620 Broadway. By 1923, a soda fountain had been added to help sell products. A few years later, the building was sold to the Wise Nut Company, which promptly went bankrupt, and the Palm Cafe moved in. It was later known as the Tiger Lunch. Next door at 1628 Broadway was the Big B Inn. A lunchroom had occupied this spot as early as 1909—one of the earliest in the Broadway district. The Big B Inn lasted for about twenty years, disappearing in the 1950s. Today even the building is gone, replaced by modern construction.

A couple other early lunchrooms were along the 1700 block of Broadway—one run by Margaretta Castor at 1712; another across the street at 1713 with thirty seats was operated by Thelma Madlin. It later became Doris's Coffee Pot and was gone by the mid-1940s.

Broadway makes a name change at Denny Way. Up to this point, the addresses have all been simply Broadway. From this point on, the street was historically known as Broadway N (later changed to Broadway E). Same street, but the addresses seem to start over.

There was a delicatessen lunchroom called the Benton Home Lunch at 106 Broadway N. It was around in the late 1920s and later became the Streamline Cafe. A few doors away was the Pot Pourri at 118 Broadway N; it, too, was a lunchroom/deli combination.

In 1950, Albert Bon leased space in a newly constructed building at 132 Broadway N, moved his Bon's Cafe from 314 Broadway into its new home and left his sister, Sylvia Beck, in charge of daily operations. By 1951, the name had changed to Bon's Congo Room and Grill, with breakfast, lunch and dinner served in modern surroundings. Located as it was in the heart of Broadway's shopping area, the Congo Room was popular for dining and dancing with live entertainment nightly in the cocktail lounge, where the specialty drink was something called the Gravedigger. Sylvia Beck assumed ownership in the 1960s and kept the place going until 1976. The following year, Lion O'Reilly's and B.J. Monkeyshines moved in, keeping the Congo Room's neon monkey sign on the roof.

Leonard Hesse was a partner with Ben Paris in the Snack 'n Tap downtown on Pike Street. After that restaurant closed, he opened his own place—Hesse's Southern Barbecue—in 1935 at 139 Broadway N. Harry Levinson and Carl "Bud" Thompson assumed management of the Southern Barbecue in 1949, and Hesse and his wife took over operation of a restaurant on Mercer Island. By 1954, Hesse's Southern Barbecue had become Selleck's—breakfast, lunch and dinner featuring barbecued beef and homemade pies. Also on the menu were barbecued pork and ham; veal cutlets with country gravy; fried cornmeal or corn fritters with bacon; and over two dozen varieties of sandwiches. Selleck's was gone by the early 1960s.

In the 200 block of Broadway N were several early eateries: Grace Wood's lunchroom, Irving Baker's place and Broadway Bowling & Lunch. In 1932, Fred Stewart had a small café at 214 Broadway N. Ernest Olsson purchased it and renamed it Olsson's Cafe. It later became Andy's Cafe and was still in business in 1979.

Leonard Hesse's Southern Barbecue, at the corner of Broadway and Olive Way, as it looked in 1940. *Seattle Municipal Archives, 18870.*

William Hay leased space at 300 Broadway N in 1937 to open the Checkerboard. By the '70s, it was owned by semi-pro football player Ernie Steele and was a favorite hangout for sports fans, serving "good food at reasonable prices"—steaks, chicken and seafood, with cocktails in the Northwest Room.

Legendary restaurateur Ivar Haglund, well established with his Acres of Clams restaurant on the waterfront, branched out in 1951 with a drive-in restaurant at 305 Broadway N. Predictably, Ivar's had a seafood counter serving fish and chips; but there were also a Chinese bar (with a real Chinese chef—Bob Lan—dishing up won ton soup, fried rice, chow mein, chop suey and egg fu young) and a Mexican bar (chili, tamales and enchiladas—no mention of the chef's ethnicity). Extensively remodeled and expanded in 1963, Ivar's on Broadway was gone by the early 1970s.

Not long after Carl Broome started his Aristocratic Hamburger Shop in Wallingford, he opened a second location at 314 Broadway N. By 1937, both places still featured "Broomburgers" ("the successors to hamburgers"—six varieties including egg, ham and chiliburgers), but more typical café-type fare was also on the menu: several different steaks, including New York cut, chicken fried and ground round steak; something called a Sweep-Steak

Ivar Haglund's second fish and chips bar, Ivar's on Broadway, also served Chinese and Mexican food. *Paul Dorpat.*

(a double patty of chopped beef "reposing in royal splendor on a bed of Mission red beans" topped with an "elaborate spread of mahogany-colored chili" and cheese); fries, onion rings, chili and spaghetti. Breakfast was also served.

Broome kept the Broadway location going for several years after closing the Wallingford store, but by 1945, it had become Bon's Café, and Broome had gone on to manage the Dolly Madison Tea Room. Bon's moved to new quarters in 1950; the old location became Sylvia's Cafe (under Sylvia Beck).

In the 1960s, it was the Luau Barbecue, still operated by Bon; the Luau lasted for about four years before becoming DeCaro's Barbecue in 1964. Later still it was the Broadway Restaurant.

Paul Wolter had the Nite Owl Cafe at 420 Broadway N in the '30s. On the other side of the street, Norm's Cafe, a favorite neighborhood hangout, moved into the Broadway Market in 1928 and moved out fifty years later. There was also a Broadway Lunch in the market for several years, right next door to Norm's.

In the next block north was the Blue Goose at 516 N Broadway; opened in the 1930s with Donald Hargrove as proprietor, by 1942, it had changed into the Chung Hing Cafe, "Chinatown on Broadway," specializing in Chinese and American dishes. After thirty years and several different spellings of its name (Chung King, Chun King, among others), it was still there as the Shan Hai, one of the first restaurants in Seattle to feature northern Chinese cooking, in 1975. Later still it was called the Macfong-Ho.

Teddy Thompson had an early lunchroom at 601 Broadway N. In 1940, it was known as Bilyew's, for proprietor Harlan Bilyew. Bilyew's didn't last long; by the next year, Stavig's Cafe took over. Another early lunchroom was owned by Louis Kulander at 606 Broadway N. This became the site of the Jade Pagoda Cafe, featuring "the fabulous cooking artistry of the Orient and the dining delicacies that are America's favorites," with authentic Chinese decorations and a rockery aquarium.

Owned by Jimmy Woo and founded by his uncles in 1943, the Jade Pagoda was long a Broadway favorite for Chinese cuisine, readily distinguished by its Chinese-style tiered tile roof. Jimmy Woo passed away in 1981; his wife, Pearl, and son Bryant continued the family business until closing in 2006. Nearby was a restaurant called the Bit of Sweden, apparently not related to A Little Bit of Sweden on Sixth Avenue downtown. It opened in 1962 with John Hanson as chef and was well known for Swedish pancakes.

RAINIER AVENUE TO COLUMBIA CITY, RAINIER VALLEY AND RAINIER BEACH

Rainier Avenue originates east of downtown off of Jackson Street and follows the west shore of Lake Washington—sometimes close, sometimes nearly a mile away—to Renton, ten miles south. South of Empire Way, where the early Highway 10 followed its own course to Renton, Rainier passes through several neighborhoods—Columbia City, Rainier Valley and Rainier Beach—each with their own business districts. There were restaurants all along the way.

Eve Pronger purchased an old lunchroom at 3107 Rainier and transformed it into Eve's Hamburger Lunch in 1932. She continued to run it with her husband, Clyde Richardson, for a number of years. In 1959, it was called the Doodle Sack Drive In, possibly a branch of the Doodle Sack on Greenwood. The Richardsons finally cashed out in 1962, selling the place for $70,000 to a developer who wanted to build a mini-mart on the site. A bit farther south, at 3410 Rainier, a hamburger stand called the Square Meal Restaurant was in business as early as 1929.

Kane's Cafe, at 424 Rainier, was another husband-and-wife operation run by James and Hilda Kane. In 1942, Hilda incurred the wrath of the law for playing the jukebox too loud and was fined fifteen dollars. She didn't like it; she appealed; and she won. The Kanes were still running the place into the 1960s, when it became a go-go joint. There was still a restaurant at that address in 1981; today, it's a parking lot.

Until it was annexed to Seattle in 1907, Columbia City was a separate town with a thriving business district, a busy sawmill and electric streetcar connections to the big city. The centerpiece of the town was the Columbia Hotel, a three-story brick structure originally built as a private residence. First called the Hotel Dakota, it was renamed in 1903 and continued in business until 1920. A famous guest was Buffalo Bill Cody. The hotel was well patronized for its Sunday roast beef and chicken dinners—all you could eat for twenty-five cents. Today, the restored building is used for apartments with a restaurant on the ground floor.

The Columbia Cafe, next door to the hotel at 4914 Rainier, started out around 1915 as Mayfield's. In the 1930s, it was operated by M.B. Watts. The café was recognized in 1979 as being one of the first restaurants in Seattle to introduce Braille menus. The Columbia City Ale House makes its home there today. Across the street were the Little Place Cafe and a couple of early lunchrooms run by Robert Metz and Constantine DeMassi.

There was a café called Our Place half a mile south in the Rainier Valley neighborhood. At 5610 Rainier, a lunchroom was in operation as early as 1919. John and Pearl Cummings ran it in the 1930s before selling it to Charles Jarvis. It later became the Friendly Tavern and was still serving in the '80s. Another early lunchroom operator, Joseph Celestine, had a place—Joe's Handy Corner—at 5700 Rainier. By the 1950s, Donald McDorman was running it as the M&M Cafe. Nearby was Ruth's Coffee Shop, which became

The Columbia Cafe was a longtime fixture in downtown Columbia City. Today, the building is home to the Columbia City Ale House. *Washington State Archives Puget Sound Regional Branch.*

a tavern/burger joint after Prohibition was lifted in 1934. The Emerald Isle Cafe was at 5715 Rainier in the '50s, later becoming the Sun Sun Cafe (in the '70s) and the Kuriyama Japanese Restaurant in the '80s.

After its long run south of Seattle, Rainier Avenue finally jogs east to run along the edge of Lake Washington. Here, in the Rainier Beach district, was the Umbrella Grill, open by 1951 with a seating capacity of forty. In the 1980s, a family-run Mexican restaurant, Maya's, moved in. Maya's later relocated a few doors away to 9447 Rainier and is still there. The Broil-Lux was a short-lived café at 9428 Rainier. In 1948, the Rainier Beach Cafe opened in a new building at 9445 Rainier. Originally a hamburger and ice cream shop, proprietor Roscoe Knatcal expanded to beer and wine in the '50s.

AIRPORT WAY AND GEORGETOWN

An argument can be made that Georgetown, not Alki Point, is where Seattle began. Permanent structures were being raised at the Collins homestead there in September 1851 while the Denny party was still shivering in the cold rain at Alki. Georgetown incorporated as a city in 1904—only to be annexed to Seattle six years later. Much of Georgetown's period architecture still stands along Airport Way, formerly called Duwamish Way.

After Boeing Field, Seattle's first commercial airport, was constructed in 1928, city leaders realized the need for an efficient route from downtown to the new facility. Rather than building a new highway, as probably would be done these days, the city simply designated a new route overlaid on portions of seven preexisting streets, and Airport Way was born. It immediately became a major thoroughfare, and restaurants began appearing all along its length from where it departed Fourth Avenue S in downtown Seattle all the way to and including the airport.

On Airport Way's northern end, just south of the important intersection of Highways 99 and 10, was the Gates Coffee Shop, later known as the Airport Cafe. In the 1950s, it was called Al's Coffee Shop, owned by Irving Bamberg; two decades later, it was Walker's Cafe.

The Transit Cafe was located in the Atlantic Street Terminal, built in 1942 at Atlantic Street and Airport Way for the city's transit system. The eatery made no pretensions about its setting: "Atmosphere—don't come! Good food—do come!" was one of its mottos. The Transit was open for breakfast, lunch and dinner; in 1945, $1.35 would buy a full dinner (choice of nine entrées including top sirloin steak, ham and pork tenderloin), salad, coffee and dessert. A few blocks south was the Sixteen Hundred Cafe, 1600 Airport Way, which only lasted for a few years in the 1950s.

The Blue Bird Cafe opened circa 1934 at 1901 Airport Way; by 1951, it had moved across the street to 1906. Paul Kringle was a longtime manager of the Blue Bird. Just south at 2100 Airport Way, Calvin Coolidge Decker and Sam Volpentest had the Transport Grill inside the Transport Truck Terminal. Open by 1952, it was still in business in 1971. A bit farther along was the Truck Trailer Cafe. This stretch of Airport Way was (and still is) lined with light industrial businesses, and many of the restaurants catered to blue-collar workers—nothing fancy, just places to get a quick meal.

At 2701 Airport Way was the Lander Street Cafe, owned and operated by Kenneth and Maude Hutchins for many years. Renamed Eddie's Restaurant in 1967, it went out of business a decade later. Erna's, later Cobb's Cafe, served up short-order fare for over twenty years at 3003 Airport Way.

Peter Rocha was operating a restaurant at 3923 Airport Way as early as 1937. Originally called the Glendale Cafe, it had become Flynn's Cafe by the 1950s. Flynn's was probably the longest-lived of the early Airport Way cafés; it was still going strong in 2007, known for big breakfasts—pancakes and

For fifty years, Flynn's Cafe served up hearty breakfasts and lunches along Airport Way on the way to Georgetown. *Washington State Archives Puget Sound Regional Branch.*

a locally famous specialty, huge sausage, egg and cheese sandwiches—and lunches, where the main attraction was the patty melt. Originally open for dinner (in 1962, a complete Kosher corned beef dinner could be had for $1.25), in its later years, Flynn's reverted to breakfast and lunch only. The building still stands, home to Romio's Pizza and Pasta.

Across the street from Flynn's, and a bit more upscale than its neighbors, Adolfo's Restaurant served Italian food specialties such as veal scaloppini, shrimp *pezzaroli*, stuffed cannelloni, *mastoccioli* with Italian sausage, spaghetti and meatballs and ravioli à la pesto. Its predecessor, the Casanova, was run for many years by Esaia Lozzi until his retirement in 1949. Adolfo's featured Saturday night wine tasting events: sixteen dollars per couple included dinner for two from the dinner menu and "all the wine you can drink in the Gondolier Room." In later days, Adolfo's became Goldie's Airport Way; it is still in business as Bogart's.

Edward Loeser and Bertha Westow had a combination tavern and café at 4740 Airport Way by 1934. Elmer Bailey purchased the place in 1950 and renamed it Dinty Moore's. It had disappeared by the 1970s. Just south of this point, Airport Way crosses over a dozen railroad tracks and drops into downtown Georgetown.

A Japanese sushi house now occupies 5503 Airport Way, an address with a long restaurant history. Charles Ogden had an eatery here in 1932; a few years later, it was known as Fay's, under twenty-year-old proprietor Emma

Woods; by the next decade, it was Don's Cafe, then Frenchie's Cafe and finally Jim's Cafe in the 1950s. The Georgetown Sandwich Shop opened around 1932 at 5545 Airport Way

Over the years, many restaurants lined the five blocks of Airport Way as it passed through downtown Georgetown. At 5629 was the C&L Delicatessen & Fountain, owned by Helen Collins and Eva Mae Lewis. Grace Renninger's Cleveland Cafe (5801), the White Spot Cafe (5821) and the Cafe La France were just down the street, all of them dating back to at least the 1940s. Other early eateries were the Glendale Card & Lunch Room, which by the 1970s was Leo's Ramble Inn, and the Rainier Restaurant (later the Sunrise Cafe). They didn't lack for customers—the original Rainier Brewery was just across the street.

Just south of Georgetown on the way to Boeing Field was Al's DeLuxe Hamburger at 6233 Airport Way. At the airport itself, a lunch counter was in business by 1932. It gave way to the Skyroom in 1940, a plush new dining room opened by Joe Boothby. The Skyroom aimed at attracting more than travelers passing through the airport; its ads invited locals to enjoy dramatic views of airplane activity during a pleasant dinner of choice broiled steaks, seafood or JucyRay Beef. Though the Skyroom survived into the 1970s, passenger traffic declined at Boeing Field after SeaTac airport was constructed, and the restaurant was closed.

Fourteenth Avenue Bridge to South Park

For years, South Park was Seattle's salad bowl. Perched on the bank of the Duwamish River, annual flooding renewed the fertile soils that grew abundant truck crops for delivery to the famous Pike Place Market. The community sits on a main thoroughfare from Seattle to Des Moines and points south, and a small downtown district grew up at the south end of the Fourteenth Street Bridge (now replaced by the new Sixteenth Street Bridge). Several restaurants could be found there before encroaching industrial development drastically changed the character of the neighborhood.

The Nite Cap Cafe, owned by Art Sanders, in business since the early 1940s at 8500 Fourteenth Avenue S, eventually devolved into a typical live music bar. On the same block was Lindgren's Grill; in early days, Dick's Ice Creamery occupied the premises. At 8515 Fourteenth Avenue S, the Cheerie Daze Cafe, a contemporary of the Nite Cap, lasted into the 1970s. Farther south on Fourteenth were King's Burgers at 9133 and Ann's Snack Shack at 9406 Fourth S. Today, downtown South Park is almost devoid of eateries, though a Mexican restaurant is in Cheerie Daze's old home.

SPOKANE STREET TO HARBOR ISLAND

Drive south from downtown Seattle on a major arterial such as First or Fourth Avenue. You'll soon encounter the Spokane Street Viaduct, an elevated roadway that carries huge volumes of traffic between West Seattle and the business district and serves as a main route for long-haul truckers from Harbor Island to the interstates. The imposing structure seems to define the southern edge of the city.

This infrastructure is of recent development, though. Harbor Island, at the mouth of the Duwamish River and at one time the world's largest artificial island, was created in the early 1900s from material sluiced away by the Denny Regrade project and other efforts to flatten Seattle's hills. The viaduct was built in 1940 above grade-level Spokane Street. The West Seattle Bridge is 1980s vintage; there wasn't even a practical vehicle bridge across the Duwamish until 1924.

Portions of Spokane Street survive, though only an echo of pre-viaduct times. In early days, over a dozen restaurants could be found along Spokane Street from its intersection with Fourth Avenue (the route of Highway 99 in pre-freeway days) to its terminus at the base of the West Seattle hill where Avalon Way branches south to climb up to the Junction and Harbor Avenue heads north to wrap around Duwamish Head on its way to Alki Point.

At 228 Spokane Street, the Two Girls' Restaurant—the two girls being Elsie Adams and Rose Sulz—was in business by 1928; that year, it had the misfortune to be robbed three times in two weeks. Edgar Shadbolt later bought the place, described as an attractive thirty-six-seat lunchroom, just as Prohibition ended. He converted it to a tavern, which at the time probably seemed like a money-making opportunity, but it was gone within a few years.

The Dutchman Cafe, at 101 Spokane, took the reverse route. Initially a tavern, it morphed into a restaurant in 1937, when it began serving home-cooked meals from 6:00 a.m. to 1:00 a.m. As much a roadhouse as a restaurant, the Dutchman featured dancing and floor shows on weekends. Proprietor Charles Moran celebrated the Dutchman's fifth anniversary in 1939 in gala style with a fifty-cent chicken dinner, a musical performance by the Singing Hawaiian Orchestra and favors for all. Still a lively place into the 1950s, for years, the abandoned building huddled under the viaduct until destroyed by fire in 2009.

Harbor Island and its two waterways (East and West) have been the focus of Seattle's transoceanic shipping business for over a century. It was natural that eateries appeared to feed the hundreds of industrial workers who flocked in each day. There were the Brass Tavern Lunch at 501 W Spokane Street and the OK Lunch next door at 515, both of them dating from the 1940s, still in business forty years later but now gone.

A bit farther along, Jim Irwin and Louis Laur were operating the Lumber Inn Cafe at 601 W Spokane as early as 1932. The Harbor Island Inn opened at about the same time, with Harry Cotton as proprietor. By 1936, Mrs.

Above: The Dutchman sat at the busy corner of First Avenue S, where traffic headed for West Seattle and the Harbor Island industrial district turned off onto Spokane Street. *MOHAI*, Seattle Post-Intelligencer *Collection, 1986.5.11359.*

Opposite, top: The Lumber Inn was one of a half dozen lunchrooms scattered among the industrial plants along Spokane Street on Harbor Island. *Seattle Municipal Archives, 50109.*

Opposite, bottom: The Blew Eagle was at the western end of Spokane Street, across from the Youngstown steel mill. *Seattle Municipal Archives, 74965.*

Hagny Klones was operating the café; five years later, Jesse Lee Miller took over and continued to run it until his death in 1983.

West Seattleites have fond memories of Nifty Hamburger at 1102 Spokane Street. H.E. "Jim" Chambers started his first Nifty on California Avenue up the hill in West Seattle in 1931. A few years later, the Spokane Street location opened, and in 1936, a third shop at Second Avenue and Denny Way followed. Unfortunately, Chambers's dreams of building a burger empire didn't work out; the California Avenue shop was sold, and the Denny Way operation failed. The Spokane Street Nifty kept going, though; by 1950, it was known as the Nifty Restaurant and Kayoia Room, owned by Ray Smyser. The restaurant's site was swallowed up by construction of the new West Seattle Bridge in the 1980s.

After crossing the Duwamish River's West Waterway, Spokane Street passes through the Youngstown neighborhood. Originally called Humphrey and renamed after the Ohio City when the steel mill was built in 1905, today it is called Delridge. A number of restaurants lined Spokane Street to cater to the steelworkers, including the Tunnel Inn at 2018 Spokane; Andy's, which opened in the Ship Hotel in 1924 and was still there thirty years later; and the Harbor Inn Cafe, practically next door to Andy's at 2311 Spokane Street. For many years, Sam Emanuel Nikas managed the Harbor Inn Cafe.

On the north side of Spokane Street was the U & Us Restaurant at 2338, described in 1941 as a fully equipped lunchroom with curb service. The Blew Eagle Cafe was a few doors away at 2370 Spokane Street. When opened by Gino Tognarelli in 1934, it was just one of the many taverns that mushroomed after the repeal of Prohibition, but by the 1940s, the Blew Eagle had transitioned into a restaurant serving full-course dinners, short orders and merchant lunches. Italian food was a specialty. Frank Feeney and Lewis Dickerson purchased the Blew Eagle in the early '50s, remodeled the place with a large banquet room available for lunches and dinners and offered a complete breakfast, lunch and dinner service plus cocktails. The Blew Eagle is now gone, another victim of West Seattle Bridge construction.

West Seattle

Alki Point in West Seattle is where it all began, with the arrival of the Denny party in 1851. Today, a monument on Alki Beach commemorates the migrants' landing and the site of the short-lived town of New York Alki

(Alki means "bye and bye" in Chinook jargon, reflecting the hope that the little settlement would eventually grow to rival New York City). Within a few years, practically all the settlers had moved across to the east side of Elliott Bay and Alki Point had reverted to something of a wilderness; even well into the twentieth century, the point was best reached by boat from Seattle.

In 1895, Alfred and Lorena Smith took advantage of Alki Point's rugged beauty to build the Hotel Alki, advertised as "Seattle's favorite summer resort," providing accommodations and serving chicken dinners well worth the long trip from Seattle by boat or horse-drawn vehicle.

The Stockade Hotel replaced the Alki Hotel in 1904. A three-story building with gables and a hipped roof, the Stockade featured massive upright logs supporting the roof and two wraparound porches and gave the building the appearance of a Wild West frontier fort (hence its name). Much of the material used to construct the Stockade came from driftwood cast up on Alki Beach; a fireplace in the lobby was constructed from locally collected stones. A newspaper ad from 1905 highlights the hotel's attractions: over one hundred rooms, plus additional brand-new cottages; ideal scenery and pure air; boating, surf bathing and clam digging for the outdoorsy type; and unsurpassed cuisine and service with a table d'hôte dinner on Sundays. The ad urged visitors to take the steamer *Dix* from downtown Seattle to the hotel—only a twenty-minute trip. Unfortunately, the following year, the *Dix* was involved in a horrific wreck off Alki Point with the loss of over forty lives. The Smiths continued to operate the Stockade well into the 1930s. It was located on what is today the 2900 block of Alki Avenue.

Lonely as it was out on Alki Point in early days, the Stockade Hotel soon had a neighbor—Fir Lodge. William and Gladys Bernard had a home built for them about two blocks east of the Stockade just off Alki Beach, one of the first residences in the vicinity. After several years, the isolation drove them back into downtown Seattle, and Fir Lodge became a clubhouse and weekend retreat for the Seattle Auto and Driving Club. Swend Neilson and Fred Fredricksen purchased Fir Lodge in 1950 and converted it to a restaurant called the Alki Homestead. It was resold five years later to Walter and Adele Foote and sold again in 1962 to Doris Nelson.

It was Nelson who created the restaurant's "bit of old Seattle" theme. Basically a big log cabin with a huge stone fireplace against the main wall, an old-fashioned dining room of tables set with white lace cloths, cut glass and old-fashioned lamps and decorated with antiques, the Alki Homestead's main attraction was simple down-home cooking served family style. A 1975 restaurant review well described the place:

Alki Point was still a windswept, lonely place when the Stockade Hotel opened in 1904. *University of Washington Special Collections, CUR341.*

The Homestead's food, like Grandmother's, is simple. It is basically chicken (pan-fried), steak (grilled) and seafood (deep-fried). Ham and prime rib are also available....The house specialty is country-fried chicken; the crust is crisp and flavorful; the meat was tender and moist. It was perfectly greaseless....Chicken dinners come in two prices. For $4.65 you get four pieces of chicken, soup, salad, mashed potatoes and gravy (or, optionally, a baked potato with a light cheese sauce), vegetables and biscuits. For $5.15 you get the same goodies, but you can have second helpings.

Side dishes were simply prepared: broccoli was just that—broccoli; salads were mostly lettuce, nothing fancy. The baking powder biscuits were served just warm enough to melt the butter.

Doris Nelson passed away in 2004, but her restaurant fell into good hands and remained immensely popular—until 2009, when fire seriously damaged the old building. Almost immediately after the flames were put out, a movement was underway to preserve the old building. As of this writing, it is being reconstructed, and hope remains high in West Seattle that the Alki Homestead will soon reopen.

West Seattle sits atop a ridge extending from Duwamish Head on Elliott Bay to the city limits five miles south. A mile wide and at an elevation averaging about 350 feet, it is Seattle's largest neighborhood. California Avenue runs due north–south along the spine of the ridge and contains three distinct business districts—Admiral, Alaska and Fauntleroy—all of them at important arterial road intersections.

The original town of West Seattle, in the present-day Admiral district, was platted in 1885 when the only practical transportation to Seattle was via steamship across Elliott Bay. Railroad connections were established soon after the turn of the century, and by 1906, a bridge—shared by streetcars, pedestrians, horse-drawn vehicles and early autos—made connections easier. The year 1907 saw a new streetcar route established; crossing the Duwamish, it climbed up Avalon Way and Alaska Street to a junction with an earlier streetcar line running along California Avenue. Though there was hardly any development in the area at the time, within a few years, the Junction, as it came to be called, had developed into a full-blown commercial district.

The beloved Alki Homestead, a West Seattle favorite for sixty years, currently awaits restoration after a devastating 2009 fire. *Author's collection.*

Yet another streetcar junction developed at the intersection of California Avenue and Fauntleroy Way, and it, too, soon attracted businesses.

In the Admiral district, the northernmost of the three, was the Bliss Cafe. Located at 2342 California Avenue and in business by 1920, it was one of the earliest cafés in the district. Emerson Bliss advertised his place as "the outstanding cafe in West Seattle," and located as it was across from the Portola Theatre, it did an active trade with moviegoers. In 1930, the café ushered in a new line of soda and sundaes—"Absolutely new…you've never tasted anything like them"—with a naming contest to be held. By the end of the decade, the Jig Saw Tavern occupied the premises; today, it's an Indian restaurant.

Just north was the West Seattle Coffee Shop, owned by Evelyn Schiermeyer. In 1935, it was witness to a tragedy. A jilted suitor saw his ex-girlfriend through the window of the coffee shop; he attempted to enter but was quickly ejected for being intoxicated and the door locked against him. Breaking in through a rear door, he took a shot at the young woman but missed; he then turned the gun on himself and took his own life. A few years later, Martha Sanger took over the restaurant, serving special Saturday chicken dinners that were so popular they often ran out of food. It had become Nell's Coffee Shop by 1951, becoming Brown's and then Bolton's Coffee Shop a few years later. In 1963 and with yet another name—Bailey's Cafe—it was a popular place for Sunday and holiday smorgasbord.

The mother-and-daughter team of Pearl MacLean and Aris Manes ran the Admiral Fountain & Lunch, opened in May 1942 in the new Admiral Theatre building. It was a small place with a counter, five red swivel-top stools and only one table and served breakfast, lunch and dinner. A Friday tradition was a Thanksgiving-style turkey dinner with turkey, dressing, cranberry sauce and pumpkin pie. Customers remember no one ever leaving hungry—if they had no money, they were assigned chores like washing dishes or hauling garbage.

At the end of the block was Skipper's Galley, a place many Seattleites recall as a surreal dining experience. Immediately after being seated, and before menus or water were presented, plates of food—sliced vegetables, baked beans, meatballs, salads, mixed nuts and many others—started appearing on the table. By the time the menu arrived, most diners were already so stuffed from the appetizers (if that's the correct way to describe them) that choosing an entrée was something of a challenge not made easier by the menu being a two-inch-thick three-ring binder. It took time to work through the menu; meanwhile, the plates of food kept arriving, and all the while, the staff (apparently the owner-chef's entire family) stood by watching in silence. A stack of Styrofoam carry-out containers ready at hand was evidence that few customers finished their dinners; what wasn't eaten was packed up by the helpful staff and ready to go—probably enough leftovers for several days' worth of meals at home.

On Admiral Way just east of California were the Happy Hour Cafe and the Admiral Benbow Inn. Bert and Bill McGonagle opened the Happy Hour in 1950; initially just a snack bar inside a tavern, within two years and under new management, it had upgraded itself to a full-service café serving breakfast, lunch and dinner. Mr. and Mrs. Earl Ridgwell had charge of the place.

Kelly's Admiral Way Cafe was next door at 4212 Admiral Way. Owner Sima Kelly dished up "appetizing meals served in pleasant surroundings...a nice choice of entrees, well cooked and properly served." In 1939, the Sunday turkey dinner cost sixty cents; merchant lunches ranged between twenty-five and thirty-five cents on weekdays. For a short time, Kelly's became Gardner's Cafe & Lounge; purchased by Lloyd and Neisa Longmire in 1950, it was remodeled, redecorated and renamed the Admiral Benbow Inn. It was still in business in 2000.

Back on California Avenue heading south, Charles MacBeth was running Red's Cafe as early as 1934. Red's was open for lunch and dinner with drive-in parking and fountain service. Hamburgers were on the menu along with Spanish or chicken tamales, chili and hot and cold sandwiches. By 1961, Red's had become Eng's Cafe; a few years later, it was the Chalet Buffet, an all-you-can-eat place where breakfast, lunch and dinner each cost about $1.50. The building, at 2605 California, still houses a restaurant these days.

On the east side of California was the Avenue Fish & Chips Shop. Owner Floyd Cady also served Mexican chili. A few doors down, at 2648 California, the Dipper Shop featured its own made-on-the-premises ice cream. The shop received a makeover in 1939, and a lunch counter—the Dipper Grill—was added with sandwiches, dinners and complete fountain service; chicken potpies were a specialty. Practically next door was Nowlin's Lunch. In 1929, Mr. and Mrs. Jerry Nowlin purchased the original Vann Bros. location at 2656 California and renamed it Nowlin's Lunch Counter with lunch, ice cream and candies. Yet another ice cream place, the Lucas Dairy Store, sat right next to Nowlin's at 2660 California.

Several restaurants were scattered along the mile-and-a-half stretch of California Avenue between Admiral Way and Alaska Street. The Seattle city directory lists two restaurants with intriguing names in the 2700 block of California—the Tillicum Teepee and the Indian Inn—but little is known about them. In 1932, Ralph Colbert had a hamburger stand at 2761 California, the address of the Tillicum Teepee; whatever was there was gone by 1954. A 1950 newspaper ad for the Indian Inn (open for dinner only) named Kate and Jim Johnson as the owners. The Freezer, another ice creamery turned lunch counter, was next door to the Indian Inn at 2775 California. In addition to its own ice cream, the Freezer served hamburgers, twelve-inch hot dogs, chili and short-order breakfasts.

Wing Chin owned the Hi Hat Cafe at 3221 California. Its grand opening was in December 1949, with Chinese and American food "served to your taste." Thirty years later, the building had become a real estate office. Nearby was the Icicle Fountain & Lunch, with five booths, ten stools and a fully equipped fountain service. Charles and Emma Lewis started the Icicle in 1949, selling it four years later to a Canadian couple, Kenneth and Beatrice Ritchie.

At 3726 California was Kelly's Drive-In; when it opened in 1952, Kelly's billed itself as "Seattle's newest self service drive-in." An order of Kelly's special chicken and fries cost eighty-three cents; also on the menu were hamburgers (regularly nineteen cents but only fifteen cents with coupon), fish and chips, shrimp and malts. Kelly's was open 11:00 a.m. until 2:00 a.m.

The Junction—the busy intersection of California Avenue and Alaska Street—was a magnet for businesses of all types, with plenty of restaurants mixed in. A block north of the intersection, at 4454 California, was Helen's Fine Foods, serving lunch and dinner, with pancakes a specialty. In 1939, Alice's Grill was just a few feet away on the corner of California and Oregon Streets. Alice Ford prepared all sandwiches and meals in a spotlessly clean kitchen; said a contemporary newspaper review, "The noonday lunches and evening meals served at Alice's Grill have won for them an enviable reputation in this community." Alice's was known for steak dinners but apparently was only in business for a few years in the early 1940s.

Gust N. Pothakos was the owner of Gust's Cafe. There is some uncertainty about its location; Gust may have started in the spot left vacant by Alice's Grill, but by the '50s, he was firmly in place at 4533 California. The restaurant disappeared within a decade. Directly across the street from Gust's was Snyder's Cafe, open as early as 1931 under George Snyder. There's a jewelry store there now.

A longtime West Seattle institution at 4542 California Avenue, Vann Bros. Restaurant actually had its origins up in the Admiral district in the early 1920s. By 1934, brothers Ervin and Rueul Vann had relocated to the

The Vann brothers—Ervin and Rueul—wait to greet guests to their restaurant in this 1952 photo. *Seattle Municipal Archives, 23351.*

Junction, where they stayed for nearly fifty years. Vann Bros. was similar to the Ben Paris shops in downtown Seattle—part sporting goods store, part ticket outlet for sporting events, part café. Over time, the restaurant part of the business took over, with a dining room as well as booth and counter service. Vann's built its reputation on complete dinners with a variety of entrées, particularly seafood and charbroiled steaks—at moderate prices. After Rueul Vann passed away in 1966, Ervin continued to run the place before closing in 1984. Relatively unchanged, today the building is home to an Indian restaurant.

Sandy's Cafe, on Alaska Street just off California, started out as Mac's Hamburger and Waffle Stand. In 1926, Harry "Mac" McCleary moved around the corner to 4710 California, and his old location became Tom's Lunch, owned by Tom Aleck. Tom's was later operated by Hazel Small, and by 1951, it had become Sandy's Cafe, run by Robert and Jessie McLaughlin. The new Mac's continued well into the 1940s, open for breakfast, lunch and dinner and specializing in steaks and chops. The late '40s saw several changes of ownership at Mac's; for awhile, it was the Phelps Cafe, owned by Mr. and Mrs. M.M. Phelps. Sold by the Phelpses in 1950 to Katherine Hayes, it received a new name—the West Seattle Cafe—but was gone within a few years.

The New Luck Toy, a Chinese restaurant at 4718 California, may have had an earlier existence on Spokane Street in the industrial district. By 1950, it was well established at the Junction and remained there for over thirty years. Alan Louie was the owner. Across the street, at 4725 California, was a place that went through a number of name and cuisine changes over the years: opened in 1929 as the Chocolate Shop, by the 1930s, it was one of the outlets for the Manning's Coffee chain. Sometime in the 1960s it became known as the Coffeeland Cafeteria.

The 1970s saw it reborn as the Phoenicia, owned by Hussein Khazaal and featuring Lebanese food and specialties from the Balkans, North Africa and the Mediterranean. The menu listed sixteen different dinners—three choices of seafood, three curries, many vegetarian plates—and particular favorites such as shish kabobs and couscous (lamb shanks simmered in a sauce of peppery vegetables served over rice mixed with raisins). The Phoenicia later moved to Alki Avenue, and the Meenar Pakistani Restaurant took its place; lamb dishes were its specialty. It is now a Japanese restaurant.

The Siberrian, a 1940s-era lunch place open for lunch and dinner at 4728 California, offered up fish and chips, steaks, hamburgers and hot dogs. An order of deep-fried shrimp, chips, salad and toast was thirty cents. Down the block was another Chinese restaurant, the Fong Fong, in business during the 1960s. John's Drive In Barbecue & Freeze occupied the odd-shaped corner at 4803 California Avenue; one hundred yards farther on was the Wagon Wheel Cafe.

Nifty Hamburger, later relocated to Spokane Street, opened its first shop at 4829 California in 1931. R.M. Morse purchased it in 1934 and kept a hamburger stand going there. By 1939, it was a place called the Spot, run by a Mrs. Sellars, known for her clam chowder, cube steak dinners and pies.

The D-G Coffee House, opened in 1942 at 4847 California, offered fried chicken for $0.70, baked ham for $0.65 and potted beef with brown gravy for $0.50—each served with mashed potatoes, two fresh vegetables and buttered toast. By 1950, it had become Anita's Steak House, owned by Dave and Anita Neimi. Four years later, Anita's gave way to Kermit's Charcoal Broiler, with prime rib, steaks, butter-fried chicken and seafood on the menu. The Spencer House later took over; in 1969, its special New York steak, "broiled to your taste," with green salad, choice of dressing, baked potato with butter or cheese, a roll and butter was priced at $2.95. The Spencer House became Phase II; Phase II turned into the Yung Ya, a Chinese American restaurant with "the most relaxing atmosphere, best Chinese & American food at reasonable prices in West Seattle." There's a modern apartment building there today.

Several restaurants sat alongside the main arterial that climbed up West Seattle hill from the end of Spokane Street. Gil's Hamburgers, at Thirty-Fifth Southwest and Avalon Way, was the third and final location of the local burger chain that originated along Rainier Avenue. The interestingly named Laff-Alot Cafe, at 4435 Fauntleroy Avenue with Leilia Scrimsher as proprietor in the '50s, featured chicken in a basket. Saturday, when the Laff-Alot stayed open until 1:00 a.m., was french-fried prawns night.

Mr. B's Double Decker Hamburgers, California Mission–styled with tiled roof and stucco exterior, was tucked into the corner of Fauntleroy Way and Thirty-Eighth Street. Inside was the perfect example of a 1950s diner: a curved counter with milkshake machines and a Coca-Cola dispenser; six booths and ten stools; a gleaming backbar with pies, cakes and chilled milkshake glasses; and a jukebox. In addition to the trademark double-decker hamburgers ($0.45 in 1954), Mr. B's served steak dinners (three different varieties, priced from $1.25 to $1.75 and accompanied by fries, a salad and toast) and milkshakes and malts. Ham and eggs were available at any time for $0.85. The building still exists, in use as a dry cleaners.

Back on California Avenue, Chuck and Terry's Fish & Chips was about three-quarters of a mile south from the Junction. Chuck and Terry Mills opened their shop in the early 1950s and served hamburgers and sandwiches in addition to their mainstay items. The building was enlarged, completely remodeled and renamed Terry's Restaurant in 1962 with full lunch and dinner service. A dining room was added to supplement the original counter and stools; an Oriental garden with a bubbling fountain served for outdoor dining. Terry's featured steak dinners and seafood dinners, but fish and chips were still on the menu. By 1977, the Cretan Bull, a Greek restaurant, had taken Terry's place, and a few years later, one of the local chain of Guadalajara restaurants moved in.

Gino's was an early Italian restaurant along California, opened in 1962 and guaranteeing "real Italian atmosphere." A dinner-only place, Gino's menu listed customary Italian favorites such as pizza and spaghetti along with chicken dishes. Nearby was a short-lived place called Nate & Kate's Restaurant. Across the street from Gino's, the Snappy Lunch Room held sway as early as 1932; in later years, it became Chuck & Sally's Tavern.

The counter gleams, the stools are ready, the specials are posted above the back bar and a smiling waitress is ready to take orders at Mr. B's in 1954. *Seattle Municipal Archives, 78963.*

Several restaurants collected at the California-Fauntleroy intersection. The D&E Cafe, on the northwest corner, served breakfast, lunch and dinner. It later dropped food service and was remade as the White Horse Tavern. In 1941, Lyle and Thelma McAlmond, previous owners of the Gatewood Lunch a few blocks away, opened the Morgan Street Lunch. They advertised the best hamburger in town for ten cents. Sold and resold several times, by 1954, the thirty-seat restaurant had become the Circle Cafe. At 6505 California, the C-Q Coffee Shop, owned by Harry Turban, served breakfast, lunch and dinner with emphasis on fish and chips, hamburgers, sandwiches and daily specials called "big plate meals."

Back at water level along Elliott Bay, Alki Beach was well on its way to being developed as Seattle's playground soon after 1900. Roads began to follow the water's edge toward the formerly isolated point; streetcar lines were planned, and beach cabins started to appear. In 1907, Luna Park rose

Two people—presumably owners Chuck and Terry Mills—pose outside Chuck and Terry's Fish & Chips in 1953. *Seattle Municipal Archives, 24462.*

at Duwamish Head, the largest amusement park Seattle ever had; brilliantly illuminated, each building, ride and attraction outlined in lights, its glitter lit up the night sky across the water from downtown Seattle.

It's likely that the café and other concessions at Luna Park were the first food-service places along Alki, apart from the Stockade Hotel at the west end of the beach. As time passed, the café transformed into a liquor emporium—the best-stocked bar in Seattle. Local outcry arose about the ready availability of liquor to minors and the general dissipation of park-goers; in fact, the effort to get rid of the park was partly behind West Seattle's annexation to the larger city. When the park closed in 1913 and the rides and salvageable building were dispersed to other amusement parks, West Seattle probably breathed a sigh of relief.

At 1317 Harbor Avenue, just north of where California Avenue drops off the hill back to sea level, was the West Side Inn. In the late '30s, when Chad

Ballard was manager, the inn's food offerings were limited to a "Chinese food department" with chop suey, chow mein and other Chinese dishes available for takeout. In 1939, a dining room was added, specializing in something called "diplomatic hamburgers," homemade pies and hillbilly music; southern fried chicken, banquet style, was available by request. In the '60s, a well-known jazz club, the Embers, occupied the building.

By and large, eateries seemed slow to develop along Alki Beach. Jane Ferran had a lunch counter at 2762 Alki in 1932; that same year, Emil Schanno started up a café later known as Sherwood's, serving lunches, dinners, sandwiches, short orders and a special seven-course dinner each Sunday (choice of turkey, chicken, rabbit or steak). By 1939, it had become Crook's Dining Room, operated by Charlotte Crook; still later, it was called the Alki Cafe, under management of Isabel Mitchell.

A place called Eat With Casey opened at 2716 Alki in the '50s; ten years later, it had been taken over by Irene Scovil and was known as Irene's Steak House. The Phoenicia, relocated from the Junction in the 1970s, is now the address's longtime tenant. On the next block east on Alki was Nick's Cafe at 2700, now the site of an apartment building. Today the epicenter of restaurants along Alki is the area just east of the Birthplace of Seattle monument at Sixty-Third and Alki Avenue—where it all began.

5
Along the Highways

Modern highways were late to arrive in the Seattle area. Water, dense forests and mountains determined that the original inhabitants and earliest settlers primarily moved about by boat. Early roads were often no more than cow paths; muddy and impassable in the rainy season, they rarely led directly from one settlement to another. Road-building and maintenance were usually left to local jurisdictions.

In 1911, Washington State passed the Permanent Highway Act, which transferred more road building responsibility to the state and authorized the construction of hard-surface roads to enhance commercial transportation. In 1912, the Good Roads Association joined the effort to improve Washington highways and proposed three major truck routes in the state: the Sunset Highway, the Pacific Highway and the Inland Empire Highway. Seattle sat at the intersection of two of these major routes: the north–south Pacific Highway, which, when tied into same-named routes in Oregon and California, ran the entire length of the West Coast from the Canadian border to Mexico, and the east–west Sunset Highway between Seattle and Detroit.

Passage of the Federal Aid Highway Act in 1921 heavily involved the national government in highway planning and funding. Standards for highway construction were put in place. In 1925, the Bureau of Public Roads, predecessor to today's Federal Highway Administration, approved a plan by the American Association of State Highway Officials to create a numbering system for national highways. Within a few years, highway names were replaced by numbers, which, if less romantic, were at least consistent. The Pacific Highway became Highway 99; the Sunset Highway was renamed Highway 10. (Today, Interstate 5 has succeeded Highway 99; the Highway 10's modern replacement is Interstate 90.)

Major improvements to both highways in the 1920s led to more travel. Autos became affordable, people began traveling for recreation and tourism flourished. The Sunday drive in the country became a family tradition. Roadside businesses—restaurants and cafés, auto courts and motels, service stations and tourist attractions—sprang up to meet the wants of the new generation of motorists. And Seattle was primed for it: over the years, well over seven hundred traveler-oriented roadside businesses appeared along the major highways leading north, south and east out of downtown.

The Pacific Highway Heading North

The Pacific Highway originally followed Eastlake Avenue from downtown Seattle to the University Bridge north on Roosevelt Avenue onto Bothell Way (today called Lake City Way). Just outside the town of Bothell, it swung north toward Everett on what was locally called the Everett-Bothell Highway. (For a few years, this route carried the Highway 99 designation but lost the title to the Seattle-Everett Highway soon after the latter's completion in 1927.)

Roadside businesses were quick to develop along the highway at Seattle's northern limits, where residential development tended to be sparse. Among

The Jolly Roger was an infamous roadhouse along old Highway 99 (Bothell Way) in northeast Seattle. *Shoreline Historical Museum, 2028D.*

This view, circa 1930, shows the Coon Chicken Inn shortly after its opening. *Scott Farrar.*

the most noteworthy was the Jolly Roger at 8721 Bothell Way. The pink stucco art deco building was a notorious place called the Chinese Castle from 1933 until 1935, when it was remodeled and reopened as the Jolly Roger. A dance hall and restaurant with a skull and crossbones flag flying from its tower, the Jolly Roger was popular for many years even though it had difficulty shedding its predecessor's reputation. Declared a Seattle Historic Landmark in 1979, it was destroyed by arson in 1989.

Another famous, though controversial, landmark was the Coon Chicken Inn. It was one of a chain of three created by M.L. Graham, the others being in Salt Lake City and Portland. The Seattle restaurant opened in 1929 at 8500 Bothell Way and underwent several design changes over the years.

Not surprisingly, chicken was the featured item on the menu. The famous Coon Chicken dinner (one dollar) included a shrimp or fruit cocktail, chicken consommé, salad (fruit or lettuce and tomato), southern fried chicken, french fries, Parker House rolls, olives, vegetables, pickles, cranberry sherbet, choice of dessert and beverage. À la carte chicken (portions of a quarter, half or a whole chicken), chicken with noodles, fried chicken sandwiches and chicken pies; various types of sandwiches such as clubhouse, tuna, shrimp salad, baked or fried ham, pimiento ham and roast pork; hamburgers; and several varieties of salads rounded out the menu.

Attached to the main Coon Chicken building was Club Cotton, a nightclub that opened in February 1934 with great fanfare. As many as 250 people could be accommodated by the club. Dining, dancing and entertainment by the Club Cotton Merrymakers were offered on a nightly basis with no cover charge. A limited menu of food items from the inn was available at the club.

Club Cotton closed along with the Coon Chicken Inn in the 1950s, and both have long since disappeared. While it is understood that usage of the word "coon" in this context is racially insensitive, the Coon Chicken Inns were a significant part of the American roadside and cannot be overlooked. At the time, there were many restaurants that went by names such as Mammy's Shack and other derogatory terms. In fact, Blake's Mammy Shack, another southern-style chicken dinner place, was just a mile or two farther up the highway.

At one time, there were so many chicken places along this part of the Pacific Highway that local newspapers printed guides. There were the Check 'n' Double Check, Rebel's Inn, Lemm's Corner and the Dixie Inn within a short distance of one another. And if the potentially derogatory implications weren't already clear, there was Henry the Watermelon King—"Real Southern Watermelons Our Specialty."

Not all was southern- (or chicken-) influenced, however. Several famous eateries as well as more conventional cafés and lunch counters lined the highway between Seattle's city limits and Bothell. The Porterhouse Eagle Inn was well known for its porterhouse steaks and Friday seafood buffet. Another famous restaurant was the Plantation, open as early as 1926 and later known as the Green Parrot Inn, the Mountonian and the Manor. Chicken (of course) was on the menu, along with steak and trout dinners. Not far from the Jolly Roger was the wonderfully named Winnie Winkel's Inn, about which little is known. The Wishbone Dinner House was along the highway at Kenmore. At 9824 Bothell Way, and only recently closed, was the Italian Spaghetti House and Pizzeria, a longtime favorite of North Seattleites.

HIGHWAY 99 NORTH VIA AURORA AVENUE

By the mid-1920s, the old Pacific Highway via Kenmore was falling out of favor as being too long and circuitous, and motorists were clamoring for a more convenient direct route between Seattle and Everett. Highway planners proposed a main road that would follow a nearly straight line south from Everett. Once in the city limits, the route would follow Aurora Avenue (then called Woodland Park Avenue) along the west side of Green Lake to a high bridge crossing over the Lake Union Ship Canal and skirt the east side of Queen Anne Hill into the central business district.

Most of the plan came true in 1927 when the Seattle-Everett Highway opened: a marvel of modern highway engineering with two paved lanes and two more (one each direction) reserved for future expansion if the need developed (which didn't take long). But there was a problem—after twenty-five miles of straightaways, smooth curves and gentle grades, the highway suddenly terminated at Green Lake, three and a half miles north of downtown.

What stood in the way of completion was Woodland Park—ninety-one acres of greenery and open space the city had purchased from pioneer businessman Guy Phinney in 1899. Engineers called for cutting the new highway through the park, and in 1930, the Seattle City Council voted its approval. But vociferous objection, most notably by the *Seattle Times*, delayed construction for several years, and in the interim, vehicle traffic had to traverse several routes around Green Lake to avoid the park—for instance, following Green Lake Way to Stone Way, crossing the Fremont Bridge and taking Westlake Avenue into downtown. This wasn't exactly the direct route drivers had been promised.

Construction finally happened 1932; the Aurora Avenue Speedway, as it was called, was built through the park, overlaying portions of West Green Lake Way and Linden Avenue at the north end. The Aurora Bridge (formal name: the George Washington Memorial Bridge) opened the same year, the last link of the highway to be completed, and Aurora Avenue (soon to be designated part of U.S. Highway 99) became the newest and fastest way to get into or out of the city from the north.

Suddenly the terminus of Aurora Avenue at Denny Way became a very busy place. What had been an area of mixed-use residences and open space now found itself home to businesses catering to the motor trade. No fewer than six service stations can be counted in a 1930s photo of the intersection.

Restaurants weren't lacking either. Among the first to take advantage of the new highway was Bob Murray's Dog House, originally located at 714 Denny between Aurora and Dexter Avenues. The Dog House opened in 1934 under co-owners Bob Murray and F.S. Knuppe. Born in Aberdeen, Scotland, Bob Murray managed several theaters—the Blue Mouse and Music Box—after arriving in Seattle. Described as a "prominent sports enthusiast," he became involved in wrestling in 1936 as a promoter and match-arranger for the Western Athletic Club while continuing to operate the restaurant. Though Knuppe remained involved for several more years, the place rapidly became known as Bob Murray's Dog House, a name it retained for nearly sixty years and under several different owners.

Murray relocated in 1954 when the Battery Street Tunnel was built through, or more correctly below, the Aurora/Denny intersection. The junction had been at street level, but the tunnel was some twenty feet below grade and involved construction access ramps between Aurora and Denny. Murray felt that the new alignments made it difficult for his customers, so he relocated the Dog House to 2230 Seventh Avenue, about a tenth of a mile away. The old location became Dick Odman's Broiler, at least until 1971.

The Dog House was an immediate success from the day it opened. A 24/7 operation, it attracted a motley lot of customers and became famous for and took pride in its blue-collar, greasy spoon reputation—some of it deserved, some not. A mural behind the counter depicted its mascot pooch and doghouse and "All Roads Lead to the Dog House" slogan. The same themes were repeated on the menus, and for a time, the restaurant sponsored a baseball team called the Bowwows. In the cocktail lounge (stocked with "the usual booze"), organists played requests of show tunes and television theme songs and sometimes whistled their way through an entire set.

Former Seattle City Council member Jean Godden recalled:

> "What'll it be, honey?" was the phrase used by lippy apron-clad waitresses. The clientele was heavily blue collar: cops, musicians, night-shift workers, journalists, janitors, cabbies and serious writers looking for a slice of urban life.... The fare was basic, comforting and cheap, even by the standards of the times. One of the menus (probably dating from the 70s) shows Rib Steak (tenderness not guaranteed) with fries and a salad for $1.25. Also on the menu, Bob's special burger—double super with onions and fries—55 cents. Then there was The Pooch—a hamburger that speaks for itself.

Seattle Times columnist Erik Lacitis wrote of a visit in 1984, when lunch specials were $3.50 and dinner specials $5.95:

> I was finished with the salad. The waitress took the fork out of the bowl and placed it by my dinner plate. "You'll be wanting to keep this," she said. You bet that The Dog House is one of the original recyclers. Why give you two forks when one will do?

A winsome pup graced the menu cover of Bob Murray's Dog House on Denny Way. *University of Washington Special Collections, MEN005.*

My baked potato came with butter. I asked the waitress if there was sour cream. "No," she said. You bet that The Dog House is a direct kind of place.

Nobody challenges the authority of a Dog House waitress, average age about 50. It'd be like swearing at your mother.

But the food was good, he said:

On one recent visit, I tried the grilled fresh salmon steak ($6.50 for the special dinner). It was nice and moist and flaky. A few days before that I had paid twice that much for salmon cooked about the same, only served by a guy with an operatic Italian accent.

I've also tried the deep-fried Louisiana prawns, "served with our delicious barbecue sauce." At $6.50, I got a plateful of prawns. So they weren't sautéed in a delicate wine sauce. They were big and fresh and juicy. Some days you just feel like eating deep-fried stuff.

No matter what you order, a meal for two, including a couple of drinks from the bar, shouldn't run more than $20. It's not going be a dinner that'll get raves in Gourmet *magazine. But like the waitresses, it will be an honest meal.*

The place even gained literary fame: mystery writer J.A. Jance used the Dog House as a locale for her protagonist, retired Seattle Police Department detective J.P. Beaumont.

After Bob Murray passed away in 1970 his wife, Petie—remarried to Bill Boudwin—operated the Dog House up to her own death in 1980. In later years, it was owned by Laurie Gulbransen, who started as a waitress in 1934, became manager in the 1940s and assumed ownership by the 1970s. The story was that the restaurant had been willed to her by Murray after his death.

When the Dog House closed in January 1994, it received eulogies befitting a famous personality, which by that time it had become. It was replaced by the Hurricane Café, itself now a victim of Seattle's South Lake Union area urban growth.

At the Denny-Aurora intersection was the Carnival Drive-In. Next door, Ernie Hughes and Ralph Grossman opened the Igloo at 604 Denny Way in 1941. Self-described as the "most novel restaurant in the West," it consisted of two igloo-shaped domes joined by an ice tunnel–like entryway between them, in keeping with the igloo theme. Above the twin domes was a neon sign flashing the restaurant's name and the image of the smiling face of a fur-clad Eskimo with a rainbow on either side. At the time the Igloo opened, there were practically no other buildings around, and it must have been a spectacular sight that easily drew in travelers from Highway 99.

Inside, the Igloo offered booth and counter seating for ninety-six; outside was parking space for one hundred cars. Indoor waitresses wore white uniforms with blue-dotted aprons. Curb service was provided by waitresses who originally wore what was described as "mounted police uniforms," though by the '50s the uniforms had become the ubiquitous car-hop attire: short skirts, puffy blouses and tasseled cowgirl boots. A staff of as many as twenty-seven inside and outside workers might be on the job at any given time.

The Igloo threw a party for its second anniversary in June 1943. "All Seattle is invited to join in," said its ad in the *Seattle Times*:

> *Two years ago we opened our doors for business...a novel drive-in dining spot that specialized in delicious food. Now, in spite of food rationing and restrictions, you still get fine food, well served in booth, counter or in your car. You'll find, too, that we've grown during these past two years....We don't serve beer or wine...but we do have a splendid selection of fountain specials, as well as complete meals and short orders. You will enjoy the service of the courteous, beautiful and well-trained girls....If you have not been one of those who have visited The Igloo...Mr. Ralph Grossman and Mr. Ernest Hughes and their staff would like to meet you and serve you.*

A 1941 menu listed the usual short-order items and sandwiches plus the Igloo hamburger (toasted bun, cheese, relish, pickle, mayonnaise and lettuce for fifteen cents), the Husky hamburger (giant sized, with french fries for twenty-five cents) and the St. Bernard hot dog (with chili for twenty-five cents). A pounded farm steak (what we'd today call a chicken fried steak) with country gravy and fries cost fifty-five cents, while the Sea Shore Dinner (crab cocktail, scallops, salmon, filet of sole, oysters, fries and tartar sauce) would set you back sixty-five cents.

The Igloo served up a hearty breakfast and was especially proud of its fountain service. In addition to typical ice cream, sodas and sundaes, the Igloo featured several specialties, such as the Sun Valley Banana Split (three scoops of Danish chocolate, vanilla and strawberry ice cream), the Mt. Rainier Revel (Danish vanilla and chocolate, caramel-topped, with nuts and whipped cream) and the Mt. Baker Special (pineapple and orange sherbet topped with strawberries, crushed pineapple and whipped cream).

Irene Wilson, a waitress, recalled how busy the Igloo was in the 1940s: "I liked working outside better. More freedom. Outside, you only had to worry about your tray. Inside, they had to bus the tables." She enjoyed her time at the Igloo and particularly the effort her boss Ralph Grossman put into creating a homelike atmosphere for the workers.

By 1954, the Igloo had been acquired by the local Sanders chain, and two running penguins had been added to the sign above the domes along with awnings above the windows. The Igloo was outside the construction zone of the new Battery Street Tunnel—a 1954 photo clearly shows it to be well away from the new off-ramp between Aurora and Denny—but for some reason both it and the Carnival disappeared at about that time.

North of Denny, Aurora remained largely residential for a number of years, though businesses gradually began moving in. My Pal Cafe at 410 Aurora was open by 1938; in 1960, it was owned by Mr. and Mrs. Lawrence Crane. At 421 Aurora, Emma Gordon operated a ten-stool, four-booth lunch room called the Green Hat Cafe as early as 1933. The restaurant at 702 Aurora went through probably more name changes than any other in Seattle—at least eight. From humble beginnings as the Aurora Tavern in 1934, it had become the Aurora Cafe by 1941. Between 1947 and 1951, it was Kirkpatrick's Coach Inn, owned by Earl Kirkpatrick and managed by Glenn Vickers. Kirkpatrick sold the place in 1951, and the name changed to Sutherland's Coach Inn, specializing in prime rib dinners with cocktails in the Tally Ho Room. Sold yet again and apparently completely remodeled, the restaurant reopened in 1954 as Taller's Charcoal Broiler.

Taller's took out a quarter-page ad in the *Seattle Times* to announce its grand opening with a menu featuring complete lunches and dinners, steaks, seafood, chicken, spaghetti and homemade pies. Thoughtfully, the owners provided a display window opening onto Aurora so that passing motorists could watch the charcoal broiler in action. By 1963, Taller's had became the Hippopotamus Restaurant, run by Dick Komen and L.E. Kirkham, who also owned Bud's Burger Haus at 2424 Aurora. In 1975, it was Murphy's; two years later, it became La Mancha, operated by Richard C. Mancha and advertised as a Mexican smorgasbord featuring everybody's favorite dish, menudo. The end came in 1980 when La Mancha quit business and all the restaurant equipment was auctioned off.

In the early 1950s, brothers Ralph and Edmund Messert realized that following in their father's footsteps in the cemetery monument business wasn't what they had in mind. They owned a long, narrow piece of land along Aurora Avenue and decided that it would be an ideal location

Right: Taller's windows faced onto Aurora Avenue, letting motorists observe the charcoal broilers in action. *Seattle Municipal Archives, 78405.*

Below: Two penguins danced atop the twin domes of the Igloo, at the corer of Aurora Avenue and Denny Way. *Seattle Public Library, spl_wl_res_00228.*

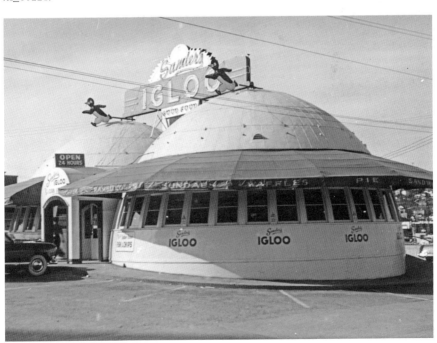

for a hamburger stand. After doing their research, including several trips to California to get a firsthand look at the newest drive-ins there and learning about the local drive-in business from Gil Centioli of Gil's Hamburgers on Rainier Avenue, they opened Dag's Beefy Boy at 800 Aurora in 1955.

Dag's (a nickname of their father's) specialized in nineteen-cent hamburgers (six for ninety-seven cents). According to *Seattle Times* columnist John Reddin, Dag's claimed to sell four hundred steers' worth of beef a year plus four tons of french fries a week. Introducing their signature Dagilac and Dagilac II burgers in the 1970s, Dag's pulled in traffic off the highway with a readerboard displaying witty and occasionally perplexing mottos such as "Feel Wanted—Dag Wants You to Eat at Dag's" and "Dagilac II—Poetry in Hamburger." They even earned a place in fast-food history with a new concept: left-handed burger buns.

By 1961, Dag's had added several more locations: Rainier Avenue at Empire Way and Fourth Avenue S at Lander Street. Both locations sported interesting features like ceramic tiles across the front of each building and glassed-in stainless steel kitchens in full view of customers. Sadly for its many fans, Dag's closed in 1993.

Les Teagle's was just one hundred yards up the highway from Dag's; gastronomically speaking, it was a world away—a high-end dinner house with fine linen tablecloths and silverware, with exposed wood beam ceilings

Dag's was as well known for its humorous signs as for the nineteen-cent burgers it sold by the truckload. *Paul Dorpat.*

and a view overlooking Lake Union. Teagle's first restaurant, located at Eastlake Avenue and Thomas Street, east of Lake Union, was operated by his wife, Rita. By 1960, he had established his namesake restaurant at 920 Aurora. Larry and Margaret Anderson of the *Seattle Times* remembered Teagle's as a "ritzy spot we went to on our way to formal dances."

Teagle retired in 1965, and the restaurant was purchased by Dave Cohn, a well-known Seattle restaurateur. The new owners kept Teagle's name—it was now known as Teagle's After Five—and continued the tradition of fine dining. After a 1966 visit, *Seattle Times* food critic Everett Boss portrayed Teagle's as "a gustatory gratification that will not soon be forgotten, having been enchanted by the astonishing continental cuisine and service…a jewel in the crown of our Queen City—an absolute must for the adventurous palate."

Danish-born manager Palle Wilms and chef Bob Frandsen created a menu offering seafood selections, including Oysters Villeroy, Lobster Newberg, Prawns Orly, King Crab Legs Orly and Sole After Five (their signature dish, sautéed sole covered with crab meat, béarnaise, asparagus and sliced crab legs); Veal Oscar; Russian Stoganoff ("a tantalizing creation of choice tenderloin beef with fresh mushrooms, sour cream, spices and a touch of wine"); and standards such as prime rib, tenderloin, filet mignon and lobster. The dessert highlight was crepes—strawberry, pineapple or chocolate.

In 1968, Jack McGovern's Encore replaced Teagle's, with "prime rib and a gracious dining atmosphere…specialties of the house." Two years later, the Encore became Dickinson's Table, "a new experience in fine dining" featuring prime rib ("sold by the inch!") and a steak and lobster combo for $5.75. Dickinson's didn't last long; the following year, Jack McGovern re-acquired the property and reopened as Acapulco, a Mexican restaurant where chef Arturo Cota guaranteed authenticity in his cuisine. In 1972, it was the Lulubelle Restaurant; a year later, it became the Ocean House, the name it kept until ceasing business in 1979.

Few businesses developed along the section of Aurora Avenue that clung to the edge of Queen Anne Hill. One exception was the Tiger Inn, which opened for business almost immediately after dedication of the Aurora Bridge in 1932. Owned by Mrs. N.H. Dahl, the inn's specialties were "superb hot roast beef," chili and hamburgers. By 1936, the location had been taken over by the Aurora Furniture Company. Today, its location, 2556 Aurora, is the parking lot for Canlis, Seattle's most esteemed restaurant.

Teagle's was practically next door to Dag's but a world away, culinarily speaking, with linen tablecloths and an impressive view of Lake Union. *Seattle Municipal Archives, 26749.*

Just north of the Aurora Bridge was Dee's Cafe at 3818 Aurora, a small place that lasted for a dozen years before silently disappearing. Long after Dee's had disappeared, a takeout chicken place called the Broaster opened in 1962 in the next lot north.

Ida & Gene's was another restaurant that developed multiple personalities over the years. Located at 3926 Aurora, it was opened in 1954 by Ida Floresca and Genevieve Laigo and advertised the finest steak and chicken in Seattle. By 1962, it had become the Lapu Lapu, with "unusual and distinctive Philippine cuisine, reminiscent of the romantic South Pacific Isles…Delicious Chicken Adobo for a taste thrill. Real Mango ice cream will be an enjoyable finish to your 'adventure' in dining Philippine style." Chef Luiggi's Restaurant had moved in by 1976; three years later, it was the Bamboo Tree Restaurant, and the following year it became the Siam Restaurant. A hotel, Staybridge Suites, now occupies the site.

At 4012 Aurora was Wright's Cafe. Owner Carl Belasco had an interesting history: orphaned with two brothers when tragedy struck the family farm in Nebraska, he was sent to Boys Town, the home for at-risk youth made famous by the 1938 movie in which Spencer Tracy played the role of Father Edward Flanagan, its founder. Belasco came to Seattle in 1928 and learned the restaurant business from Mrs. Chauncey Wright, widow of the well-known restaurateur. After she died, he bought one of the Wright restaurants from her estate. He kept the name when he moved to his own place on Aurora in 1940. Wright's became a popular meeting place for north-end civic organizations such as the Kiwanis. In 1946, Belasco moved Wright's to a new location a few blocks away at 4220 Aurora, and 4012 became the home of the La Patina Inn and, by 1956, Casa DiNapoli, owned by Dan Catone. Wright's was gone by 1960.

Mr. and Mrs. Ernest J. Leak operated several restaurants, including one in Puyallup, another along the Mount Rainier Highway and a third called Leak's Little Canyada Inn on Pacific Highway S in Des Moines. In 1948, they opened Leak's Chicken Dinner Place at 4132 Aurora. An all-you-can-eat chicken dinner for $2.50 was the featured menu item, along with choice steaks and homemade pies. Leak's had apparently disappeared by 1958.

A block farther north was Helen's Roundup at 4252 Aurora. Opened in 1954, it had become the Quality Pancake House by 1963, operating under franchise from the famous Original Pancake House in Portland. A wide variety of pancakes—Alaska Sourdough, Old Yankee Yeasty Buckwheat, French Pancakes with sec suzette topping and German—were on the menu, along with standard breakfast fare such as eggs, ham, bacon and waffles. A few years later, the American Oyster House was at that address. Pancakes were still on the menu; it's recorded that in 1968, co-owner Mildred Milbrad was fined fifty dollars for slapping a customer after he complained about the restaurant's specialty pancakes.

With twenty years of experience in the Seattle restaurant business, Thomas Jensen opened King Oscar's Smörgåsbord in 1940. Unfortunately, Jensen, who had operated the Waldorf Hotel dining room, Jensen's Queen Anne Café, the Wild Cat Cafe on Westlake and the Hi-Ho Cafe on lower Queen Anne, passed away a few years later, leaving his wife, Amy, to run the restaurant until son Bill Jensen took over operations after his discharge from the army.

Describing a visit to King Oscar's in 1949, *Seattle Times* columnist Nat Lund recalled: "The smorgasbord itself is the main feature, and the huge silver candlesticks hidden, so awash are they with Scandinavian delights." Among the variety of dishes were korvkoko (chicken livers and barley topped with tart lingonberries), liver paste, herring in sour cream, pickled beets, Swedish brown beans, steaks cooked "old country style" (sautéed, not broiled), cold roast beef, smoked salmon, homemade crock cheese, various salads (macaroni; fruit; tomato and cucumber; and cottage cheese) and rice custard pudding. Bavarian Chicken Breast en Casserole and Swedish pancakes filled with chicken and mushrooms were house specialties.

Bill Jensen claimed a smorgasbord wasn't the real thing unless it had at least sixty different items on the buffet table. He gladly provided novices with advice on how to approach a smorgasbord: "It should be eaten in four courses. First, the fish and appetizers. Then the salads, cold meat and pickles. Third, the hot dishes—Swedish meatballs, beans, ham. And lastly, the cheeses." Dessert, if the diner felt it to be needed after sampling all the dishes, was Swedish pancakes served with lingonberries and homemade syrup. Customers unfamiliar with smorgasbord, or unwilling to try something new, could order off a complete menu of American dinners, specializing in salmon, oysters, broiled lobster and prawns.

King Oscar's was located at 4312 Aurora, housed in what once had been an elegant private mansion with two massive chimneys and typical Victorian trim. A twin-gabled Bavarian-style façade was added to give the place an authentic feel, and the Scandinavian mountain chalet theme was continued inside with dark wood, tapestries and vibrant colors throughout the restaurant. Originally open only for dinner, it added lunch service in 1968. The Fjord Room, a cocktail lounge, was upstairs from the restaurant with a view out over Lake Union. A novelty drink for two called "the Voyager" was served in a bowl with miniature Viking ships afloat in it.

In 1977, King Oscar's became the Cedars of Lebanon, owned by Wajih Alawar and hailed by food critic John Hinterberger as "an oasis of Middle Eastern cuisine in the shifting sands of fast-food emporiums that line Highway 99." It later became Simonetti's, an Italian restaurant. Even after the name changes, the King Oscar Alumni Association, made up of those who had enjoyed dining at the old King Oscar's, held reunions there. The building was extensively damaged by fire in 1984 and eventually demolished.

Bavarian Chicken en Casserole

6 chicken breasts
Flour
Salt
Ground pepper
¼ teaspoon thyme
½ cup butter
1 tablespoon dehydrated chopped onion
¼ cup chicken broth
½ cup white wine
12 slices ham, cooked
½ cup light cream
1 teaspoon parsley flakes

Shake chicken in flour with salt, pepper and thyme. Sauté breasts in butter until brown. Add onion, broth and wine. Simmer, covered, 30 minutes. Stuff ham slices into slits cut at each side of breasts. Stir cream and parsley into broth and pour over chicken in individual casseroles. Bake 10 minutes at 350°. Serves 6.

At 4900 Aurora was the Chuck Wagon Bar-B-Q, its neon sign highlighted by the head of a bull and flashing out what was on the menu: barbecued spareribs, ham, beef and hamburgers. Carhops dressed western style, complete with silver dollar–studded leather belts, provided curb service. Located as it was near the south end of Woodland Park, the Chuck Wagon made a specialty of providing a "quick pickup packaged lunch" (spareribs, French bread, salad, coffee, knife, fork, spoon, paper cups and plates and napkins) to take into the park and enjoy picnic style. The Chuck Wagon survived into the 1990s but has been replaced by an office complex.

Just north of the Chuck Wagon, Aurora begins its tree-lined, three-quarter-mile run through Woodland Park—the long-disputed section once known as the Aurora Speedway—to emerge at Green Lake. Straight ahead at 7701 Aurora stood the crown jewel of Seattle's roadside architecture, the Twin T-P's.

Herman Olson conceived a novel design for a roadside attraction: a restaurant constructed in the shape of two huge adjoining Indian teepees. He registered his design (he called it a "resort building") with the U.S. patent office, obtained a construction permit in 1936 and got busy. In March 1937, his vision, the Twin T-P's, opened to great fanfare.

Per its name, the Twin T-P's consisted of two Indian teepees constructed of crimped metal fashioned over concrete forms with an interconnecting entryway. The teepees stood nearly twenty-five feet tall and were outlined with neon lights. Located where it was, on busy Aurora Avenue just across from beautiful Green Lake, the Twin T-P's was an amazing sight and immediately became popular both with local and passing motorists.

Each teepee housed a spacious dining room. The main dining room, in the southern teepee, held fourteen booths that seated 56 persons with additional tables accommodating 18 more. A huge open fireplace occupied the center of the room. The second teepee contained seating accommodations for another 40 persons with a counter, booths and fountain service, for a total seating capacity of about 115 customers. The kitchen was located behind the lobby-like entry and took up portions of both teepees. Restrooms were upstairs on the second floor of the lobby.

The café was inspired by Indian designs. Massive murals on the walls, created by artist Alan Nothhof, depicted native lives and legends. Each mural (eight in all) had a name and portrayed a specific subject, such as *Chief Seattle, Famous Chief of the Duwamish and Suquamish Tribes, Friend of the White Man*; *Striped Wolf, Indian Warrior*; and *Morning Star, Tribal Beauty*. The ceilings were painted with designs based on Northwest Indian motifs.

In 1939, the menu offered two price options for dinners: $0.85 and $1.10. For the latter price you would get a choice of cocktail (fruit, shrimp or crab) or soup, a salad with French dressing, choice of New York–cut sirloin steak or half a pan-fried chicken, hot biscuits with jelly and a dessert: pie, cake or ice cream sundae. À la carte items included chicken potpie and chicken fricassee. Sandwiches, such as baked ham, sliced chicken and tuna fish, cost between $0.20 and $0.35. Several distinctive sandwiches were also on the menu, including fried Willapoint Oysters and a Monte Cristo, as well as the ever-popular T-P Burger.

The Twin T-P's pride was its fountain service. Original fountain specialties—most of them named after the murals—included the Chief Seattle Sundae (two scoops of ice cream on split banana, chocolate, marshmallow topping, whipped cream and nuts; thirty cents). The Morning Star Sundae (vanilla ice cream, orange sherbet, pineapple, fresh banana ring, whipped cream and cherry) was also thirty cents. The Striped Wolf Sundae (just twenty-five cents) had vanilla ice cream (double-dipped), Dutch chocolate topping and shaved chocolate, whipped cream and chocolate decorettes.

In August 1939, veteran Northwest restaurant man Frank Holzheimer took over operations, with Homer Richards replacing Arthur Apgar as chef. Walter Clark purchased the Twin T-P's in 1941, adding it to his growing restaurant empire, and the name changed to Clark's Twin T-P's. With a new manager and chef (Meigs Close and James Cheek, respectively), Clark modernized the restaurant by "blending an historic background with today's latest ideas in food service…smart surroundings, delicious dishes to whet every appetite, modest prices to meet the most careful budget!" Among other changes, the booths were redesigned to provide a better view of Green Lake, and the T-P's began staying open "from morning 'til way past midnight, at counter, booth, or table."

The story goes that around 1942, Clark offered a job to an old friend who was looking for work—a fellow named Harland Sanders. It seemed that Sanders was less interested in flipping hamburgers than working on his chicken recipes, however, and he soon parted company with the Twin T-P's, returning to his native Kentucky to find fast-food fame as Colonel Sanders with his Kentucky Fried Chicken franchises.

The Twin T-P's were remodeled again in 1949, and prices increased: luncheons were now $0.85, dinners $1.50. By 1958, Walter M. Power had bought the place and renamed it Powers' Pancake Palace. The teepees were painted orange; a huge waffle was installed over the entryway, and a giant stack of pancakes adorned the side of the south teepee. In 1968, the old name was restored, but by the late '70s, the spelling had changed: it was now the Twin Teepees, and it remained for the next thirty years.

The restaurant suffered a fire in July 1997 and a more serious blaze in June 2000. Claiming the expense of repairs and necessary upgrades such as removing asbestos and lead-based paint were too expensive, the current owner applied for a demolition permit. In July 2001, the restaurant was bulldozed—an event that still haunts the memories of Seattle's historic preservationists.

Seventy-Second Street marked the beginning of the busy Aurora shopping district. As real estate became valuable, residences lining Aurora sprouted storefronts in their front yards within a decade; practically the entire six-block stretch to Eightieth Street was filled with shops, restaurants and service stations.

The Aurora Grill was a storefront café at 7301 Aurora run by Mr. and Mrs. Rau from about 1948 to 1957. Next door at 7305 was Mac's Barbecue. Eunice Marshall ran it for several years before illness forced her to sell it in 1932. New owner George McLaughlin occasionally took out an ad in the

The Twin T-P's as it looked in 1942, when it was part of Walter Clark's restaurant empire. *Museum of History and Industry, 1983.10.17115.1.*

Seattle Times, urging readers to "take the family to Mac's Barbecue for a real treat." By 1948, it was the Meet Me Here Tavern, apparently no longer in the restaurant business. Pep's Hamburgers was another early eatery at 7317 Aurora and was still in business in 1964, though the place was practically demolished by a runaway truck that year.

Hildegard's Chicken Dinner Inn was an elegant dinner house that shared the building at 7401 Aurora with a bicycle shop. With fine linen tablecloths and napkins, flowers and candlesticks on its tables, windows masked by wood-slat blinds and heavy drapery and mural-painted walls, Hildegard's projected an aura of genteel dining. Owned by Hildegard Allen with Stan Asmundson as chef, Hildegard's opened to diners in 1946 and soon became well known for charcoal-broiled steaks and butter-fried chicken. Duncan Hines recommended Hildegard's. By 1957, Diamond Jim's occupied the premises, and Hildegard had moved on to manage the Tropics Motel restaurant and lounge. Still standing, the building is a motorcycle shop today.

The next two blocks saw a number of restaurants come and go in a twenty-year period, among them Matt Fogarty's Restaurant at 7404 Aurora;

a place called A Real Cafe at 7501, which went through five owners in eight years before becoming the A.C. Tavern in 1937; the Woodland Restaurant at 7606, open as early as 1928; the Kodiak Cafe at 7608; the Royal Cafe two doors away at 7616; and Florence & Marie's Coffee Shop, located at 7617 Aurora Avenue and also known as the Huddle Cafe.

At 7701 Aurora Avenue stood the Dixie Flyer Diner. Soon after arriving in Seattle in 1945, Virginia natives Clifton and Edna Prichett realized that their new home city lacked a modern dining car—the type of classic stainless-steel-and-porcelain beauty common on the East Coast but rare out West. They purchased a 1946 "Challenger" model from the Kullman Dining Car Company of New Jersey and had it shipped across country by railroad for $1,000. While they waited nine months for the building to arrive, the Prichetts built a kitchen, pantry and restroom behind where the diner would be located.

The Dixie Flyer opened in January 1947. The gleaming new dining car immediately became popular with Seattleites and, as something of a novelty in the Pacific Northwest, attracted scores of curious tourists and long-haul truckers, as well as locals frequenting the busy Aurora shopping district. The diner was open from 8:00 a.m. until 2:00 a.m. daily except Tuesday, when the staff—the Prichetts; Mrs. Prichett's sister, Grace Woods; Edith Snipes; Martha Freckleton; and ex-navy chief commissary steward Johnny Clautier—took a well-deserved morning off. The four large booths and fifteen stools seated thirty-one people, and there was often a line waiting to get in. Off-street parking for twelve autos was offered, with a rear entrance for those wanting to avoid Seattle's legendary rainfall.

The Dixie Flyer's staff took pride in their southern hospitality and home cooking, always served with a smile. The menu offered daily fifty-cent lunch specials as well as T-bone steak dinners, hamburgers and hamburger steak. The diner became famous for its Denver sandwiches and for serving breakfast—buttermilk hotcakes and ham and eggs—at all hours. The Prichetts put in plenty of elbow grease to keep their diner sanitary and shining; baked goods and pastries were displayed in built-in glass cases, and food was kept in tightly covered stainless steel pots.

Despite several years of success, by 1952, the Prichetts were apparently encountering personal difficulties. In June that year, Clifton and Edna Prichett were divorced. A month later, an advertisement appeared in the *Seattle Times* offering a stainless steel diner for sale. It's not certain that it was the Dixie Flyer, but no other diner in Seattle matched the description. Apparently no sale took place, because Edna Prichett continued to be listed as the diner's owner in Seattle business directories for the next few years.

In June 1955, the diner was purchased by Andrew Nagy, owner of Andy's Diner at 2711 Fourth in South Seattle. By 1956, the Dixie Flyer had been renamed Andy's Too Diner. For the first several years after Nagy purchased it, the diner was operated by his nephew, Andrew Yurkanin, who functioned as cook, manager, greeter and occasional waiter.

In 1958, the diner was moved from its North Seattle site to 6151 Fourth Avenue S, about a mile south of Andy's Diner. Aurora Avenue was becoming more residential, there was too much traffic on Aurora for motorists to stop easily and there was more business in the rapidly developing south end. The diner's story at its new location, and that of the original Andy's Diner, will be told later in this chapter.

Next door to the Dixie Flyer but preceding it by twenty years was the White Kitchen, at 7909 Aurora, Maybelle Blecker, owner. At 7714 was a delicatessen owned by Lauchlin McLean in 1939. By 1941, new owner Thomas Barber had renamed it Barber's Delicatessen. In 1948, it was Goodall's Fountain Lunch, a fountain lunch, ice creamery and delicatessen; between 1951 and 1956, it became the Peacock Inn. Today it is Pho Thân Brothers, a Vietnamese restaurant.

In 1941, an early health-food place, the Nutburger, stood at 8018 Aurora ("nutburger" being a burger-shaped patty of ground nuts and flavorings). By 1948, Hawley's Drive-In stood there; in 1956, Cafe Avel replaced Hawley's, and Chapala Mexican Dinners took over in 1974. Bill & Paul's Hamburgers opened at 8412 Aurora in 1930, when this segment of the highway was still called Woodland Park Avenue. Almost immediately, it went through the usual changes in ownership, being known as the City Line Cafe for a time—until 1954, Eighty-Fifth Street marked Seattle's north city limit. The café was gone by 1941.

Zip's 19¢ Hamburgers, at 8502 Aurora Avenue, opened in 1955. In 1963, it added Zippydogs to the menu for nineteen cents—same as the burgers; cheeseburgers were twenty-four cents—plus two new locations: First Avenue and Denny Way and Forty-Fifth Street at Roosevelt. They all seem to have disappeared by about 1967. A Jack in the Box now occupies the Aurora location. Although they aimed for the same market, these Zip's don't seem to have been connected to the chain of Zip's Drive-ins started by Robert "Zip" Zuber in Kennewick in 1953; the signage is different.

The quarter-mile stretch of Aurora between Eighty-Fifth and Ninetieth Streets saw a number of lunch places come and go in the '30s, including Walt's Hamburgers at 8511 Aurora and the National Cafe across the street at 8520. In the 1950s, Little Audree's Cafe, later known as the Bob-o-

This Zip's 19¢ Hamburers, part of a local chain of three, was on Aurora Avenue at Eighty-Fifth Street. *Seattle Public Library, spl_wl_res_00229.*

Link, was next door to the National. Mr. and Mrs. A.J. Sauers operated a lunchroom and ice cream parlor at 8816 Aurora. First called Bill's Cafe, it was the Rafters Cafe in 1949 and Tiny Tim's a few years later. The Sauerses turned their attention to building a motel behind the café, and by 1956, the lunchroom had disappeared, with the motel taking over the whole building.

The stone-front building still standing at 8904 Aurora was the White Stone Tavern & Cafe for many years, offering food and drink served in its fireplace lounge. In 1979, its name changed to the Brooklyn Bridge, and it was called Mel's in 1981. Today, the Jade Restaurant and Lounge occupies the site. At 8954 Aurora was Sally's Sandwich Shop, run by Mrs. Sigrid "Sally" Foss in the early 1930s. Offered for sale in 1933, it became the Shamrock Tavern, a typical burgers-and-beer place operated in partnership by Ercole Tiberi and Ralph Pelegrini.

In 1935, Pelegrini suddenly accepted a job offer in Wenatchee and left his wife to look after his interests. She and Tiberi apparently didn't see eye to eye about how the place should be run, so they divided everything 50/50—each took exactly half of the beer, four of the eight bar stools, ten of the twenty toothpicks, one of the two cans of popcorn and so on, though a problem arose when they counted sixty-three napkins—not an even number; so they each took thirty-one and evenly divided the leftover. They even cut the bar counter in half, though they couldn't divide the booths—they were nailed to the floor, and the landlord quashed the idea of ripping them out. Tiberi continued running the tavern for a few more years before selling out to John Ghetti in 1936. It's gone now.

Jack Case ran a café at 9012 Aurora as early as 1937. That same year, a hamburger cost ten cents at the Flying Boots Cafe, across the street and slightly north at 9053 Aurora. They charged thirty-five cents for their special home-cooked dinner. A place called Had's was farther up Aurora at 9418 in the '50s. Sealy's Fish and Chips was at the intersection of Aurora and Ninety-Fifth Street. In 1948, you could grab a quick bite in Doran's Cafe at 9724 Aurora. By 1962, it had become Henning's Charcoal Broiler, open for breakfast, lunch and dinner with steaks, chicken and seafood on the menu. By 1967, Venetti's La Strada Restaurant occupied the address and survived into the 1980s.

The Snow White Cafe, at 10123 Aurora Avenue, opened sometime around 1942 and went through several changes of ownership in the next few years. The interior layout was typical for the times—lunch counter on one side of a long, narrow room, booths against the other wall. In 1954, the café was owned by Thomas Argeris and managed by Gladys Brown. That year, a school bus, swerving to avoid a small child playing in the street, struck the front of the café and caused major damage.

Several cafés clustered near the busy intersection of Aurora Avenue and 105th Street in the 1950s, including the North Park Cafe at 10309 Aurora and Eve's Cafe at 10332. The Bon Ton Cafe was open twenty-four hours a day, serving up fried chicken, steaks and homemade chili. An early arrival, the North Star Cafe, was at 10413 Aurora in the 1930s.

A Triple XXX Drive-in variously known as Lindquist's, Pederson's and Pappy's stood at 12255 Aurora for several years. In 1954, the LeMar Drive-In occupied the spot, and in 1960, it became Smitty's Pancake House. Today it's the location of a newer restaurant, the 125th Street Grill.

The Village Inn was part of the National Auto Village auto court complex at 125th Street and Aurora Avenue. The inn was a squared-log façade to the court's stucco tile–roofed main building and served the basics—hamburgers and beverages (probably a euphemism for beer)—to the auto court's guests as well as highway travelers.

Curly's Drive-In was a bit unusual in that it offered inside dining, complete with a cozy fireplace hearth, as well as drive-up service. Chicken, hamburgers, french fries and fish and chips were on the menu. Located at 12752 Aurora, Curly's had become Art Lee's Chinese Restaurant by 1966.

Today, the site is part of an auto dealer's parking lot. Hugh Sloan operated Dee Dee's Cafe at 12804 Aurora, changing the name to Sloan's Fine Foods in 1956. After Sloan passed away the following year, it became Snyder's Restaurant and was gone by 1964.

At 13104 Aurora was the Port Hole Drive In, a restaurant built in the shape of a ship. Its first incarnation was fairly simple—a modest boat-shaped building containing the kitchen and order windows, with a covered awning on either side to protect drive-up customers from the elements. (They made the ship look like it had wings.) It opened in 1952 and was purchased later that year by Frank Wnukowski, who remodeled and expanded it the following year. A total rebuild took place in 1959—a massive two-story structure with "jet-age, swept-wing canopies extending 150 feet to the highway." Wnukowski named it Frank's Port Hole to distinguish it from its predecessors. Both inside and drive-up service were provided (11:00 a.m.–3:00 a.m. every day) by waitresses in nautical garb. Located as it was near the popular Aurora Speedway racetrack, it was a busy place.

Wnukowski opened yet another restaurant at this same spot in 1965. The Neptune was a complete departure from the earlier ship-shaped design, with a three-peaked roofline sporting the colorful figurehead of King Neptune and three mermaids. The 3,300-square-foot restaurant of

The Village Inn was attached to the National Auto Village, an early auto court on Aurora Avenue. *Washington State Archives Puget Sound Regional Branch.*

masonry and wood-framed glass with stone wainscoting along the front seated 150 customers. Interior decoration was done in tones of beige, white and gold. Predictably, the Neptune featured seafood on its menu. The old Port Hole building remained standing nearby for a couple years, but eventually both it and the Neptune gave way to redevelopment. Today, it's a parking lot.

An early auto court dating back to 1932, the Red & White Cabins, stood at 13575 Aurora. By 1948, it had been renamed the Paradise Motel, and a small café was built along Aurora at the motel's entrance. The Paradise Cafe served up standard fare: steaks, fried chicken, sandwiches, chops, chili, ravioli, malts, shakes and ice cream. A large plate-glass window gave diners a view of traffic out on the highway; the door, set into a corner of the building, was surrounded by glass blocks, something of a fad of the times. There's an auto dealership at that address today. At 14025 Aurora, Swanney's offered fish and chips in the 1930s. A few decades later, the Tik-Tok Drive In opened at 14040 Aurora. Later known as El Chico, part of the building still stands.

Seattle proper ends at 145th Street, the city limit since 1954. This was a very lightly developed region when the Seattle-Everett Highway opened in 1927. The highway ran through miles of cut-off timberland and small farms (often derisively referred to in the city papers as "chicken ranches"). In short order, this stretch of highway became the domain of the roadhouses. By the 1940s, most of those had disappeared, and legitimate roadside businesses started popping up all the way to Everett.

North of 145th Street are the communities of Shoreline, Richmond Heights, Edmonds and Lynnwood. We're getting beyond our main focus now, but a couple of noteworthy places should be named.

Alexander "Jerry" Girard opened the Golden Tub in 1930 and operated it until retiring in 1944. It was located at 14507 Aurora. Farther up the highway was the Hilltop Cafe at 14845 Aurora. In 1935, it advertised that it specialized in fried chicken, a $0.25 lunch and delicious sandwiches. At 15744 Aurora was the Garden Spot café and tavern. In 1951, it became Snuffy's Cousins and was owned by Mr. and Mrs. Tom Horn. Briefly renamed Bob's Grill in the mid-1950s, the original name was restored a few years later. Food reviewer Steve Johnson visited Snuffy's in 1976 and had good things to say about the extensive menu: breakfast served anytime with more than a dozen omelets available; ham, egg and hash browns made with real potatoes for $2.45; and fast and friendly service. Shay's Restaurant took over in the 1980s and is still in business.

Bessie Haines ran the log cabin–style Bessie B Lunch for forty-five years before retiring in 1956. *Shoreline Historical Museum, 65.*

In 1921, Bessie Haines opened a lunch counter in husband Roy's garage to serve passengers at the nearby interurban station. By 1928, she had moved to her own building—Bessie B Waffle Shop and Lunch Room—on Aurora Avenue at N 185th Street. Inside were a dark wood lunch counter and white-painted tables and chairs, with a fireplace and mantel along the north wall. A sign above the door advertised trout dinners. The log cabin–style building replaced the earlier lunch room in the early 1930s, a few feet farther south on Aurora. Bessie's was a familiar landmark for highway travelers as well as locals who met for "coffee hour." Bessie sold the café in 1956 to Mr. and Mrs. William Plouff, who had operated Anabel's Cafe in the Greenwood neighborhood. The café lasted for a few more years but is now gone.

Highway 99 S via Fourth Avenue S and E Marginal Way

Highway 99 heads out of Seattle on Fourth Street S on its run south before turning onto E Marginal Way and eventually climbing the hill above the Duwamish River on its way toward Tacoma. For some reason, this section of the highway didn't develop as many roadside restaurants—in 1951, fewer than a third—as grew up along an equivalent distance to the city's north. But among them were some now-lost gems.

The 4th Ave. Drive-In debuted in 1940 at 1245 Fourth Avenue S. Something must not have gone according to original plans; within a year, it had been completely remodeled and was under new management: R.J. Rusden, who also owned a Triple XXX root beer barrel on Olive Way and another in Everett. Though called a drive-in, it was actually more of a full-service restaurant serving breakfast "the way you like it…fresh-from-the-farm eggs and sugar-cured ham and bacon," a variety of tempting dishes for lunch and melt-in-your-mouth steaks and fresh salads for dinner. Ready anytime were hamburgers, barbecued beef and pork sandwiches and apple pie. Inside were booths and a counter, with outside curb service at all times. Chef Emily Lacey took pride in serving complete Sunday dinners—$1.25 for roast turkey, cocktail, soup, vegetables, dessert and beverage.

By 1962, the drive-in had become Budnick's Chez Paree Restaurant, owned by Richard Budnick and offering "'Steak Bordelaise' that's 'Terrifique'" in contemporary and French décor. It was still Budnick's in 1970 but sliding more into a go-go bar sort of place. The change wasn't successful; it closed a year later.

The 4th Ave. Drive-In was bright, shiny and new when this photo was taken in 1940. *Seattle Municipal Archives, 18872.*

Don Cruikshank, aka Mr. C, moved in in 1973. Mr. C's menu listed fifty different kinds of hamburgers ranging in price from sixty cents to fifty dollars. Each burger creation was named after a state:

Maine—burger steak and grilled prawns

Minnesota—a combination of a third of a pound of beef and a slice of Canadian bacon

New York—hamburger, raw onions and a Kosher pickle

Montana—a burger with three different melted cheeses: cheddar, Monterey jack and American

Massachusetts—it came with a pot of baked beans

Florida—topped with an egg, sunny-side up

Least expensive was the Rhode Island (a child's-size burger—no offense, Rhode Islanders). At the top end was the fifty-dollar Alaska, a ten-foot-long hamburger served on a hardwood plank with fries.

Mr. C said he got the idea from all-burger places in California.

Let's face it, everybody loves a good hamburger. I just decided to add a few dimensions. Like where else in town can you get a hamburger served with stemware and linen napkins?

But the strangest thing was the time a guy called up and ordered one Alaska burger to go. First I made sure he was on the level. And he was. Then I told him that taking out an Alaska burger to go was not an easy thing. He said he could handle it. Sure enough, he showed up with a Volkswagen van and stuck it in the back. I watched him drive off. He had three feet of hamburger sticking out the back.

Mc. C's lasted for a few years before turning into the Meat Market, a cabaret/comedy nightclub. It was gone by 1981.

The spirit of Andy's Diner still resonates with Seattleites. A longtime fixture along Fourth Avenue S, Andy's was famous for charbroiled steaks served in actual railroad cars and its collection of authentic railroad items and pictures. The diner was the brainchild of Andrew Nagy Jr. After four years in Reno working at a hotel restaurant, Nagy relocated to Seattle and in July 1949 opened "a novel dining spot...a regulation steel dining car with the wheels removed and fitted it up as an attractive café" at 2711 Fourth Avenue S, about a mile and a half south of the central business district. In 1956, Andy's Diner moved another mile farther south to 2963 Fourth Avenue S, and it's this incarnation that Seattleites fondly remember.

Nagy's nephew Andrew Yurkanin had joined him in the restaurant business in 1955 as manager and jack-of-all-trades at the soon-to-be-renamed Dixie Flyer Diner on Aurora Avenue. When the former Dixie Flyer was moved to Fourth Avenue S in 1958, Andy Yurkanin followed suit and continued to manage the rechristened Andy's Too Diner. By 1959, he had become a full partner with Nagy and moved uptown, as it were, to Andy's Diner. (The Andys were familiarly referred to as "Big Andy" [Nagy] and "Little Andy" [Yurkanin].)

By 1959, the diner's business was booming. More railcars—a bar car, a club car and an executive car—had been added, and an entrance building had been constructed. Andy Yurkanin recalls the diner's golden years: "We served about 1,200 people at lunch on a good day—we had capacity for 380 people, and we filled the place three times over. We also served between 200 and 400 dinners." The fare was originally typical diner food, with a growing focus on steak and prime rib dinners. Saturday, the busiest night, kept longtime employees Alberta Lemonde and Betty Ayers active. Thornton "TA" Wilson, Boeing Company chairman, was a regular customer, stopping in three times a week.

The Andys began expanding their business as early as 1961, when they decided to create a chain of restaurants based on Li'l Abner, the cartoon character created by Al Capp. Only a single Li'l Abner's saw the light of day, however—apparently hillbillies couldn't compare with railroads when it came to restaurant themes—and by 1964, the concept was defunct. Undeterred, Nagy and Yurkanin opened a string of successful restaurants in the 1970s: Andy's Tukwila Station in 1976, the Eugene Station (now called the Oregon Electric Station) in Eugene in 1977 and Andy's Auburn Station on C Street in Auburn in 1980, among others.

After Andy Nagy passed away in October 1980, Andy Yurkanin carried on until his retirement in 1996 after nearly forty years in the restaurant business. His son ran the restaurant for a few years until it was purchased by two local businessmen. The end came in 2008 when Andy's closed its doors. In a sense, Andy's Diner lives on; its collection of railroad cars is still in place and functioning as a restaurant called the Orient Express. But much to the regret of longtime Seattleites, the old-time diner experience is gone.

A bit south of Andy's was another railroad-car-turned-diner operation, Knight's Diner, at 5717 Fourth Avenue S. There's an interesting backstory about Knight's. Brothers Jack and Frank Knight got into the diner business

Andy Nagy stands on the observation deck of one of the railroad cars that formed Andy's Diner in 1954. *Seattle Municipal Archives, 78429.*

in Spokane in 1932 when they purchased an old railroad coach car, refurbished it and opened their eponymous Knight's Diner near the railroad yards northeast of the city. Within a few years, they had become so successful that Frank Knight moved to Seattle to repeat the story. Originally located at 6159 Fourth S, by 1949, the diner had relocated to 5717, across from Kettell's Drive-In.

In the meantime, the Spokane Knight's went through a few changes. Jack Knight entered the service in 1943, and the diner's new owner renamed it the Valley Diner, soon to be renamed Wright's Diner. In 1950, Jack repurchased Wright's, gave it back its old name and moved it to Division Street, closer to downtown Spokane. The diner moved again in 1992 to Market Street in northeast Spokane, and there it remains today, still popular and often voted "best breakfast in Spokane." The next year—1993—the Knight's Diner in Seattle closed; the railroad car was trucked to Spokane and reopened downtown in 1995 as Frank's Diner, in honor of Frank Knight. Final score: Spokane: 2 old-time diners; Seattle, 0.

Kettell's Corner was a longtime Seattle favorite on Fourth Avenue S at Fifty-Eighth Street, a site occupied in the 1920s by Wray's Service Station

The menu for Knight's Diner was cut to the same shape as the old railroad car that contained it. *Author's collection.*

No. 2. Kettell's Drive-In opened there in the '30s, and by 1954, a full-sized restaurant had appeared. The food bordered on the greasy-spoon type of cooking—no low-calorie, weight-watchers fare on the menu—but Kettell's, with its huge sign (including a blinking neon owl), was always popular with the locals and nearly always full. The restaurant made a specialty of preparing takeaway orders—both lunch and dinner—for workers from nearby industrial areas. Nonsmokers remember needing to hold their breath while wading through a cloud of fumes to get to the nominal smoke-free area. It was a shock to the regulars when Kettell's suddenly closed in 2003. Today, the building contains a gentlemen's club called Kittens.

The year 1958 saw Andy's Too Diner, formerly the Dixie Flyer, being moved from Aurora Avenue to 6151 Fourth Avenue S. Just as the Dixie Flyer Diner had been on the main highway north out of Seattle, this new location was along the principal route out of the city southbound. The relocated diner received a few additions: a rear dining room behind and approximately the same dimension as the original diner; a thirteen- by nineteen-foot, two-story addition built in 1960; and eventually a twenty- by fifty-foot dining room added to the rear of the original dining room. Behind the diner was a small building used for storage.

The name of the diner after its relocation is a bit of a puzzle. Longtime manager Andy Yurkanin remembers it as Andy's Too. Property assessment photos from 1958 and 1960 clearly show a large sign reading "Andy's Too Diner" in front of the diner. But the Seattle business directories for the same period list the Fleet Diner at this address, and a contemporary photo backs this up. It was apparently also referred to as Andy's Two and Andy's Diner No. 2.

This building was a gas station before it became Kettell's Drive-In in 1948. Kettell's Corner later occupied the same site. *Washington State Archives Puget Sound Regional Branch.*

After the Dixie Flyer Diner was transported from Aurora Avenue to Fourth Avenue South, it was renamed the Fleet Diner. *Andy Yurkanin.*

Whatever its name, the diner seems to have remained in this location until 1964. By July of that year, it had moved again to 4125 Maynard Avenue S, about a mile away. It isn't certain that the diner ever reopened for business at the Maynard Avenue site. Property records list M.P. Yousoofian as the new owner, but there is no record of any business at that address for the period 1964–69. Sometime prior to 1968, the diner had met its fate: Seattle city property assessment data for 1969 notes that it had been torn down and was off the tax rolls. A McDonald's now occupies the site on Fourth Avenue S; the Maynard Avenue location is a vacant lot.

Margo's Restaurant at 6519 Fourth Avenue S started life as the Hungry Junction, so named because it sat at the corner where Highway 99 turned onto E Marginal Way on its way south. Originally a log cabin–style café with a portico facing the street, by 1962, Margo's had expanded into an austere cinderblock building. Street-side was a totem pole, a stylized thunderbird bearing Margo's sign. Margo's was open for breakfast, lunch and dinner; specialties included thin hotcakes, thick steaks and kosher corned beef. Cocktails were available in the Pow-wow Room. Like Kettell's Corner a few blocks north, much of Margo's clientele were south end workers, and takeout orders were a big part of the business. Margo's closed in the early 1960s, but part of the building is still in use as a Vietnamese restaurant.

Originally a gas station, by 1937, the Hungry Junction was selling homemade chicken pies—"Tak'em away in crocks"—and Danish ice cream, 7 Up and Coca-Cola. *PSRA*.

The Camel Inn went through a number of name changes over the years. This is how it looked in 1964. *Washington State Archives Puget Sound Regional Branch.*

The famous Budweiser horses parade in front of Verna's Inn on this old postcard. *Author's collection.*

The Camel Inn was another south end restaurant that went through a series of name changes. Opened around 1930 as the Chat & Chew Cafe, it became Leo's Cafe a few years later, then Pat's Place before finally settling on its final name. For a number of years, the Camel Inn was a reputable eatery operated by Dick Phillips, but by the late '60s, it was falling on hard times. The inn—by then, the tavern business overshadowed the café—began incurring liquor permit violations on a yearly basis. An arson fire in 1974 severely damaged the inn, but it rebuilt and struggled on for a few more years. The building, deserted, still stands at 7047 E Marginal Way.

A few cafés lined the highway as it edged the west side of Boeing Field, such as Burnace McNabb's Kitchenette Lunch, a block south of the Camel Inn; Brodine's Lunch and Wally's Lunch, both in the 9100 block of E Marginal; the Little Red School House Cafe, located where the Museum of Flight now sits; and Feek's Cafe, at 10222 E Marginal nearby to the still-operating Annex Tavern. Verna's Inn Tavern occupied a brick building of interesting design at 10440 E Marginal Way. Opened sometime around 1950, Verna's specialized in Italian and American dinners and was open daily from 11:00 a.m. to 11:00 p.m. By the '70s, a topless joint, the Bear Cave, had taken over the building; it is gone today.

HIGHWAY 10 E

Seattleites who remember the Sunset Highway (aka Highway 10) generally recall it passing through the Mount Baker tunnels and crossing the Lake Washington Floating Bridge on its way east. Few realize that the highway's early alignment took it south from Seattle around the south end of the lake via Renton before angling northeast toward Issaquah. This route split off from Fourth Avenue S onto Dearborn, then south via Rainier Avenue to Empire Way (today's Martin Luther King Jr. Way) and on to Renton. There were a few restaurants along the mile and a half of Rainier between Dearborn and Empire when Rainier carried Highway 10 traffic before the route was realigned across the floating bridge in 1940.

The Hitching Post was just south of Dearborn at 1135 Rainier Avenue. Ostensibly a tavern, it also served chicken and steak dinners. It was in business by 1934. The name changed to the Chalet in 1967, became the Brothers Tavern in 1971 and switched back to the Chalet again by 1975. In its later years, the Chalet was what today is called a dive bar: loud music, lots of beer, probably not much by way of food.

Ruby Bailey had a lunch stand at 1348 Rainier in 1932; it later was run by Alice Bridges. At 1503 Rainier was Alice's Grocery and Coffee Shop, which also sold lunches. The Rainier Cafe, a working man's place, was at 1508 Rainier in the '30s. Just down the street, Domonick Yellum opened a tavern in 1933. Five years later, it evolved into the New Italian Cafe and Tavern, run by James Conguista. The New Italian offered typical fare—spaghetti, ravioli, pizza—and was in business until about 1967. All of these places are now buried under the Interstate 90 approach to the Mount Baker tunnels.

Half a mile south were the Bantu Cafe, at 2007 Rainier, and the Siberrian Cafe practically next door. The significance of the names isn't known, though there was also a Siberrian in West Seattle at about the same time. O.E. Kuehnoel's Triple XXX root beer barrel stood at 2822 Rainier, right where Highway 10 turned off onto Empire Way. Kuehnoel's stand was part of the first wave of Triple XXX barrels in Seattle and survived into the 1950s, when it was replaced by a grandiose $100,000 building with covered drive-in stalls for forty-three cars plus regular restaurant facilities inside.

The new Kuehnoel's Restaurant and Drive-In kept burgers and Triple XXX root beer on the menu but aimed to attract a more upscale crowd with

The parking lot at the Bambi Drive-In was torn up for sewer replacement the day this photo was taken in 1949. *Seattle Municipal Archives, 10242.*

steaks and the house specialty, roast sirloin of beef; in fact, the restaurant's name was briefly changed to Kuehnoel's House of Rare Beef. An interesting touch was the Gallery of Contemporary Art, a portion of the restaurant dedicated to displaying work from Northwest artists. In 1967, Kuehnoel sold out to the Standard Oil Company of California (for reasons unknown), and the restaurant's name became the Spindrift. A few years later, Gil A. Centioli of Gil's Hamburgers bought the place and added his name to the marquee. The restaurant's last owners were Bruce and Phyllis Beisold; it disappeared around 1979, and today the site is a parking lot.

Just south of Kuehnel's, Highway 10 split off from Rainier onto Empire Way. In earlier times, this was a fairly lightly developed section of Seattle, and only a few roadside restaurants developed before the official highway alignment switched over to the floating bridge route in 1941.

At the corner of Empire Way and Hudson Street was the Bambi Drive-In, open for breakfast, lunch and dinner with a soda fountain and curb service. Nearby, the M&R Fountain Lunch was at 3927 Empire Way.

Coyne's, one of Seattle's earliest A&W Root Beer outlets, was at 5700 Empire Way, though it didn't appear until the 1950s—long after the highway was rerouted. In the days when a mug of root beer only cost a nickel, A&W sold pizza and chili dogs in addition to its trademark Papa, Mama and Baby Burgers. Coyne's also had an A&W on Twenty-Fifth Avenue NE. Across the street at 5705 was the Empire Way Cafe, owned by Bob and Nel Paulsen.

6

A Touch of the Exotic

Pick up a copy of the current Seattle yellow pages and flip to the restaurants section. You'll find page after page of listings to suit every taste and budget, from fast-food franchises and corner cafés to upscale eateries famous nationwide and drawing from practically every ethnic cuisine on the planet. Today, they're all considered part of Seattle's culinary melting pot. We think nothing of having ravioli one night, jambalaya the next, maybe some chicken Kiev a few days later—and how about some shrimp enchiladas Suiza later in the week?

Time was, though, that eating at a Seattle restaurant meant choosing from a limited number of menu items heavy on steaks and chops, with sometimes a token nod to seafood. Anything outside those familiar boundaries was considered by the mainstream Seattleites to be somewhat exotic. Even Italian dishes long since blended into the great American cookbook—standbys like lasagna or spaghetti and meatballs—seemed out of the ordinary. As late as the 1950s, one restaurant reviewer commented that her meal at a certain Italian restaurant was excellent "if you liked that sort of food" (paraphrasing just slightly).

In truth, eateries offering food other than standard American fare have been in Seattle since the early days. Originally, they may have drawn their support from members of the same cultural group as the cuisine, but over time, the more conventional citizens of Seattle discovered and popularized these new, different, foreign foods. It's interesting to note that when display ads started to appear in the Seattle telephone directory in the 1950s, ethnic restaurants—Chinese, Mexican and Italian—were among the first to make extensive use of them.

Chinese

中国餐厅

It's probable that the native Duwamish considered Anglo-Europeans as a wave of new ethnic arrivals. That notwithstanding, the Chinese are considered the first ethnic culture to establish itself in Seattle once Anglo predominance was a given fact. Nineteenth-century historians recorded instances of Chinese employed in area fish-packing plants in the 1850s, and the esteemed Wing Luke Museum cites Chin Chun Hock as the first Chinese person to settle in Seattle, circa 1860. By the 1880s, the Chinese were well established, so much so that it led to competition with Anglos for jobs and eventually to an ugliness known as the Seattle Riot of 1886, when armed mobs attempted to remove the Chinese from the city. It wasn't until well into the twentieth century that anti-Chinese sentiment abated; by that time, sufficient numbers of other ethnic groups had arrived that the so-called American distaste for foreigners had been somewhat diluted.

Several Chinese restaurants are known to have existed as early as 1879. Possibly named for their proprietors, they included Ah Chu, at the corner of Third Avenue and Washington Street; Ah Jim, on Third between Washington and Main Streets; and Hei Lee Fong, on Washington Street. All three were in the area where the Chinatown district was already rising.

By the turn of the century, Me Wah & Company was conducting a "first-class Chinese restaurant and merchandise" at 318 Washington Street. Yoot Hong had a restaurant in the brick three-story Canton Building at 210 Washington, with Chung Dep two blocks away at 414 Washington. The Prince Chinese Restaurant was near the north end of the business district on First Avenue near Pike Street, and the Shanghai Restaurant was midtown at 214 University. Chas. Louie operated a restaurant under his own name at about that time; by 1909, he was a principal in the Pekin Cafe at Second and Yesler.

In later years, *Seattle Times* columnist John J. Reddin reminisced about Seattle's early Chinese restaurants:

> *For many of us who were reared in this old sawmill town, our first taste of Chinese cuisine came with a prohibition-era visit to Chinatown for a late-hour snack, usually after other restaurants were closed. Like many others, we suppose, we soon developed a taste for chow mein, sweet-and-sour spareribs, fried rice, egg roll and other American-type Cantonese cookery.*

In those days, however, Chinese restaurants (like the many near-by speakeasies in Chinatown) were sparsely furnished. Customers were served at a counter or bare table and the menus were often sticky with soy sauce. It was pretty primitive, to say the least.

In various residential areas, however, it soon became common practice for someone to suggest after a late-hour poker or house party: "Let's all go down to Chinatown and get some chow mein or almond-fried chicken."

While the early Chinese restaurants may have catered predominantly to their countrymen and a few adventurous Seattleites, the Pekin Cafe charted a different course, ushering in a new trend with a mixture of Chinese and American dishes on the menu. Christmas dinner at the Pekin in 1915 was about as Americanized as it could be, with traditional roast turkey the main attraction. The Pekin also introduced live music to the Chinese dining experience; a brief series of performances by the Hawaiian Orchestra proved so popular that Mr. Louie invited them to remain as a permanent attraction at the Pekin.

By the late 1920s, there were plenty of Chinese restaurants in Chinatown (naturally) but also spread around other sections of the city and even out into the developing suburbs. Chinatown (today, officially called the Seattle

The Pekin Cafe, an early Chinese American restaurant at Second Avenue and Yesler, looked much like any other café of the times. *MOHAI, 2002.48.1267.*

Chinatown–International District) hosted restaurant upon restaurant within its twenty-plus acres. Notable examples include the Golden Pheasant Cafe at 307 Sixth Avenue S, opened in 1929 as an "exclusive Chinese restaurant" and surviving into the 1960s. The building that contained it was erected in 1873; now called the Old Main Street School, it is one of Seattle's oldest buildings.

The King Fur Cafe, at 709 King Street, dated from 1930 and under longtime manager Fred Eng was still going strong thirty years later. Its menu was typical of the times, a mixture of Chinese and American foods. Various types of chow mein, foo young and fried rice made up one side of the menu, along with roast pork and duck, shrimp and a few out-of-the-ordinary items like mar hi chicken and lichee duck. Steaks and chops could be had by the less adventurous. A block away at 667 Jackson, the Hankow Cafe advertised Chinese foods delivered to all parts of the city—day or night—as early as 1934. Owned by Suey Kay Lock, the Hankow closed in the '60s.

New restaurants opened in Chinatown as older ones closed in the 1960s. As each one opened, its ads announced it to be Seattle's newest and best Chinese restaurant. The newcomers, such as Art Louie's (421 Seventh S) and the Bamboo Terrace on Maynard, emphasized genuine Chinese décor and a trend toward more authentic cuisine than the Americanized fare of the past. The Bamboo Terrace promised "only authentic Chinese cuisine…exotic foods from the Orient are prepared in original Chinese fashion and served with the distinction of its origin." The usual chow mein and fried rice dishes, while still on the menu, were overshadowed by new and unusual dishes.

Charles Wah's 8 Immortals, opened in 1964 in what had been the Don Ting Cafe, epitomized the new class of Chinese restaurant. The menu included barbecued spareribs and fried meat dumplings; exotic soups such as egg flower, abalone, seaweed and shark fin; chicken wings with oyster sauce, pineapple duck, mushroom chicken balls and ginger beef. All dishes were cooked to order, "different than so-called commercial Chinese restaurants where most dishes are semi-prepared in advance and simply finished when ordered." The food was said to be Cantonese in eight "immortal flavors: Hom, salty; Tom, bland; Teem, sweet; Seen, sour; Foo, bitter; Lot, hot; Heong, fragrant; Gum, golden." For the uninitiated, the 8 Immortals of Chinese mythology were described in a booklet free to guests.

Chinatown wasn't the only place to find Chinese food. As early as 1911, the Nanking Restaurant, upstairs at 1511½ Fourth Avenue in midtown, called itself "the prettiest Chinese and American grill on the coast," with the best lunch and dinner in the city for twenty-five cents. The Nanking

The Hang Chow was a storefront café on Eighth Avenue, the east edge of the downtown commercial district. *MOHAI*, Seattle Post-Intelligencer *Collection, 1986.5.11364.*

moved to new quarters a block away in 1924; its grand opening announced the largest and most exquisitely finished and modernly appointed Chinese restaurant on the Pacific coast. It was gone by 1934.

The Shanghai Restaurant fared better. It opened prior to 1916 at 106 Second S and soon added another location on Pike Street. Half the menu was devoted to Chinese dishes—the usual chop sueys, chow meins and rice dishes—with the other half listing American favorites such as chicken, steaks, seafood and sandwiches. The Second Avenue branch closed in the early 1930s; the location at 711 Pike received a new name—the New Shanghai Cafe—and was still going strong in the late '60s.

Another early midtown restaurant was the King Joy on Fourth Avenue, not far from the Nanking, "where discriminating epicureans may find fellowship in dining with congenial spirits amid ideal environments." The building that housed it was specially constructed for the restaurant with tables, booths and private dining rooms. At 1411 Eighth Avenue, the Hang Chow Cafe celebrated its grand opening in 1934 with free tea and rice cake to all visitors and a special six-course roast turkey dinner, Hang Chow style, for a dollar.

In 1948, Ruby Chow and her husband, Ping, opened a restaurant in an old mansion on Capitol Hill. Over the years, it became one of Seattle's best-known restaurants, recalled as the first upscale Chinese restaurant and the first to introduce Mandarin-type cuisine to Seattle. Authentic cuisine dominated the menu; the only Americanized items were steak and fried chicken. Patrons could select from among several complete dinners (for two or more) or order à la carte. Dinners included the Imperial (barbecued pork, spring rolls, prawns, shark fin soup, Imperial chicken, Mandarin duck, abalone in oyster sauce, ginger beef, cashew shrimp), the Canton, the Mandarin and the Emperor's Feast (which required forty-eight hours' advance notice). Among the individually ordered dishes were Mandarin duck, sesame chicken, *gai ding* (diced chicken with vegetables and almonds), prawns Cantonese (prawns with chopped pork and eggs in black bean garlic sauce), tomato beef curry and pineapple spareribs. After twenty-one years of loving attention to their restaurant, the Chows leased it in 1979; it was bankrupt a year later.

Farther out into the suburbs, the Chung Hing Cafe opened at 516 Broadway in 1942; thirty years later, it became the Macfong-Ho, specializing in both southern and northern cuisine, including sizzling dishes, vegetarian plates and Peking duck. On Forty-Fifth in Wallingford, Tien Tsin introduced Seattle to Szechuan foods in the '70s. In the Rainier Valley, the Topspot—a modern Chinese restaurant with Oriental atmosphere, "where the finest Chinese and American food is served at modest prices"—opened in 1962. After it closed in the early '70s, its neon sign was salvaged and put into storage for several years until 2002, when a new business recycled the sign—minus the S, which had fallen off—to advertise Top Pot Doughnuts, now a successful café chain with over two dozen locations in the Seattle area.

After Prohibition was repealed in 1933, a new breed of Chinese restaurant started to appear in Chinatown and around the city. Though often cloaked in Oriental-sounding names and offering a nominal menu of Chinese foods, in reality, they were nightclubs in disguise. An example was the Chinese Garden on Seventh Avenue S. Originally a typical Chinese café, by 1936, it had evolved into "Seattle's most celebrated restaurant for supper and after-theatre parties—music and dancing every evening after 9." In 1960, the Gim Ling took over the premises, and in 1976, it became the China Gate. Owned by Alan Louie, who had previously run the New Luck Toy in West Seattle, it was well known for dim sum. The China Gate closed in 2010.

Club Maynard, formerly the Pixilated Club at 612 Maynard S, advertised itself as something new in nightclub entertainment with Oriental decorations, floor shows and dancing on the finest finished dance floor in the city. Food—chop suey, noodles and American dishes—was almost an afterthought. It was in business from 1937 to about 1950.

Farther south on Highway 99, at 10315 E Marginal Way, the China Pheasant threw a grand opening party in 1940, promising "the sweetest of music—the choicest of foods at Seattle's newest, quaintest dining and dancing rendezvous." Built by Slim Randles, a Seattle carpenter, and owned by Mar Dong, also the owner of Mar Hotel in the International District, the China Pheasant was known to be a "real swinging roadhouse." In addition to dinner, the restaurant offered music by Bob Harvey, dancing and gambling. It was operated by Harry Lew. In 1945, the police raided the establishment for gambling equipment. Despite the sheriff's best efforts to close the place down, it remained open long enough to run into trouble with the law again. In 1962, the manager was arrested and fined for serving alcohol without a liquor license.

Its opening announcement invited Seattleites to step into the Chinese Temple—"shadowy, rich with Eastern splendor…the hospitality and quaintness of Old China brought to Seattle"—to enjoy Chinese foods served in the traditional manner, drink the beverages they enjoyed and "dance to American dances on a table-smooth floor—to the daring syncopations of a smart American orchestra." Located at 1916½ Fourth Avenue, the Chinese Temple didn't last long; it was gone by 1940.

The Rainbow, at 710 Union, billed itself as "America's outstanding Chinese & American restaurant" with a house orchestra, floor shows three times a day, dancing noon and night, beer and wine and a menu of Chinese and American food. The Chinese theme didn't last long; within a year, it was known as the Supper Club for about a month, and later that year, it was McKenzie's Restaurant. In the '40s, it became John Q. Public's, with a capacity of seven hundred and continuous dancing and entertainment.

JAPANESE

日本料理店

Japanese were later arriving in Seattle than the Chinese; a sizeable Japanese population was not recorded until the 1890s. Japanese restaurants were also slower to develop, and on that subject, there are several confusing factors.

For one thing, at that early time, many restaurants were only listed by the surnames of their owners. It is a tempting but risky assumption that a restaurant with a Japanese-sounding name (e.g. T. Miyasaki) was, in fact, a Japanese restaurant.

Also, it seems that—even more than with Chinese owners—many restaurants owned by Japanese catered to American tastes in the early days. While there were certainly Japanese restaurants serving Japanese cuisine, few of them advertised; in many cases, all memory of them has been lost.

At this late date, the issue of who was first, and how authentically Japanese their restaurant was, probably can't be solved. In later days, it was claimed that the first Japanese restaurant in Seattle was opened by either Toyojiro Tsukono (the Klondike, in 1896) or Osamu Sakamoto in 1897. However, the 1890 city directory lists these restaurants: R. Taniguchi, 106 Weller; Nakagawa & Aki, 2417 Front; Onta, Opa & Mori, 502 S Seventh; and Matagito Tsukuno, 504 Main. A 1909 study of immigrants living in West Coast states found eighty-seven Japanese restaurants in Seattle, of which thirty-six served American meals and fifty-one served traditional Japanese foods. It's known that in 1911, T. Yamashita owned the Sunrise Restaurant at 116 Second S, and K. Nishimura was owner of the Cascade Restaurant, 209 Main Street. Both of them were located in the Chinatown district, but which category the two fell into can't be determined.

Italian

Ristorante Italiano, Mangia e Italiano

As ubiquitous as it is these days, it is surprising that Italian cuisine was late to develop in Seattle. Out of a total population of 230,000, the 1910 census counted only 3,454 Italians, many of whom had originally come to work in the coal mines south and east of the city at Renton, Newcastle and Black Diamond. Nonetheless, a well-known Italian restaurant—Maison Tortoni, first in the city—was doing a fine business at Second and James in those early years.

The City Grill opened in 1909 on Third between Yesler Way and Prefontaine Place. Within a year, and after a change in management, the City Grill announced it was specializing in Italian food. After Joseph McGuire took over in 1931, the restaurant reverted to a typical dine-dance-drink place and closed in 1948. Another early establishment, the American Cafe, described itself in 1911 as the "only Italian restaurant serving a table d'hôte dinner," though what was on the menu—chicken gumbo, consommé, poached filet of sole Marguerite, spring chicken sauté Marengo, Noisette of lamb Rachel, leg of veal and Melba peaches, among other items—sounds more French than Italian.

A place called the Italian Tavern opened in 1930 at 810 Union Street in the old Ambassador Hotel. Managed by Frank Galati, the menu featured Italian dinners with emphasis on spaghetti and ravioli. The following year, the restaurant moved into the St. Regis Hotel and promptly went out of business. A year or two later, the Italian Tavern's quarters on Union were occupied by the La Tosca Cafe. Chef Jack Gustino promised "true Italian cookery at its best" with dinners priced at $0.60, $0.85 and $1.00. Thanksgiving dinner at La Costa—seven courses served Italian style and including a bottle of wine—was $1.25 in 1936. Later owned by Frank and Ruth Petrino, it closed during World War II.

The Italian Village was a popular Fifth Avenue eatery with Joe Santilli as owner and manager. A native of Abruzzi, Italy, Santilli had previously run a small place called Buon Gusto in the Queen Anne neighborhood. In 1933, he bought the old Fifth Avenue Cafe at 1413 Fifth, remodeled and modernized it and gave it a new name. The restaurant was well known for chicken cacciatore, veal scaloppini and bocconcini à la Romana, among other Italian specialties. A full-course dinner cost $1.25, with a choice of seven entrées: filet mignon with mushrooms, roast turkey, lamb chops, pork tenderloin Italian style, roast leg of veal, grilled salmon steak or roast chicken. À la carte menu items included steaks, pork chops, oysters and halibut. When it closed in 1971 after nearly forty years in the same location, a news columnist mourned the loss:

Joe Santilli's Italian Village restaurant was as comfortable as an old shoe. Thousands of Seattleites ate Italian food for the first time there, including young couples on dates who later ate their engagement and wedding dinners at the Italian Village and returned on every anniversary for the next 25 years or more.

The early 1930s saw the opening of the Roma Cafe in the New Richmond Hotel at 310 Main Street. Louis Pettofrezzo ran the café until retiring in 1953, when it was purchased by Bill and John Gasperetti, part of a family who owned and operated a number of places in Seattle and along the

For forty years, Santilli's Italian Village Cafe occupied part of a glass tile–faced building on Fifth Avenue. *MOHAI*, Seattle Post-Intelligencer *Collection, 1986.5.11368.1.*

highways. The Gasperettis not only owned the café, they were also the chief cooks. The Roma Cafe was so good that even competing restaurant owners stopped by for a meal. John Franco of the Hidden Harbor on Lake Union was a regular customer and particularly fond of braised sirloin tips with spaghetti *alburro*.

At a time when Italian restaurants (in Seattle, at least) offered a mix of Italian and traditional American dishes on their menus, the Roma Cafe differentiated itself with a much larger variety of Italian items than its contemporaries. The usual fare like roast chicken and pork, liver and onions and boiled ham were listed, but Italian specialties made up more than half of the menu. Even conventional dishes like Swiss steak and pork tenderloin were given an Italian flavor. In addition to à la carte items, the Roma offered three different special dinners ranging in price from $1.75 to $3.00. Each dinner came with soup, salad, an entrée (pot roast for the lowest-priced dinner, steak or chicken cacciatore for the highest), ravioli or spaghetti, a vegetable, dessert and beverage.

In 1961, the Roma Cafe moved to 220 Fourth Avenue S. Seventeen years later, after nearly a half century of creating quality Italian dinners and pleasing thousands of customers, the Gasperetti brothers decided it was time to retire. The Roma Cafe closed in 1980, and a nightclub, the Komedy Store, moved in. Today, the site is a vacant lot.

The Italian Club of Seattle dates its origins to 1920. In 1937, the club moved into quarters at 620 Union Street, soon to be known as the city's most elegant downtown club, complete with its own members-only restaurant. Costanzo Lazzaretto, better known as Chef Costa, was the longtime chef for the Italian Club; he later opened his own place—Chef Costa—at 167th and Aurora. With its fancy dining room, big cocktail lounge and attentive staff, a dinner at the Italian Club was always a special event.

The American-Italian Cafe, under proprietor Jules Daverso, took over 620 Union a few years after the club lost its lease. Open to the public, the café served dinners from 5:00 p.m. until 11:00 p.m. with sixteen-ounce steak a specialty. By 1949, a buffet lunch service had been added. After a short stint as the Elks Club headquarters, the space became a nightclub—Irving's 620—in 1961. Irving's didn't last long; a year later, it had become Mario's 620, "Seattle's newest and finest theatre restaurant." By 1967, a place called the Fifth Amendment had taken over, followed in 1970 by Apricot Orange, a discotheque. These days, a nondescript parking garage marks the site of the old, elegant Italian Club.

As early as 1932, George Leos was running the Palace Grill at 159 Yesler Way. He sold it to the Daverso brothers, Frank and Jules, in 1946. The brothers were principals in a moving and storage company, Owl Transfer; Jules had been associated with the American-Italian Cafe. The brothers kept the Palace Grill name for a couple of years before renaming it for themselves.

Daverso's claimed it introduced pizza to Seattle around 1948. Pizza was popular on the East Coast but almost unknown out West. When Daverso's started offering it, they had to explain to potential customers what it was ("sort of an Italian pie with tomato sauce and cheese"). Daverso's was more than just pizza, though; in 1949, newspaper writer Nat Lund described what Daverso's "ancient and honorable establishment" (it was only three years old at the time) had to offer: "lasagna alfurno, a special sort of short spaghetti glamorized with ham, sausage, cheese and other assets; chicken fanciers go for the pollo alla cacciatore, a daily feature, as is the justly-famed Daverso pizza."

In 1960, Daverso's opened a second location on Lake Union, at 1844 Westlake Avenue N. Harry Drinkwater, along with the Daversos, took over management of the new restaurant. The expansion must not have gone well, though; within two years, it had closed, to be replaced by a place called Kim's. The Daversos kept the Yesler Way restaurant for another few years, but by 1964, it had become Rudy's Italian Restaurant. Rudy's was still there a decade later; it moved to 423 Second in 1976.

Ciro's, at 109 Pine Street in the Gatewood Hotel, was owned by Jessie Christensen, sister of infamous nightclub owner Frank Colacurcio. In 1931, the Seattle Grill was at this address; four years later, Spiro Boris opened his New Oyster & Steak Shop there. It was the Kwang Chow Cafe in 1940 and the Gatewood Grill ten years later before becoming Ciro's by 1958. Ciro's specialized in pizza and other Italian foods at modest prices, according to its ads, and was open for breakfast, lunch and dinner. The Gatewood Hotel building still stands, in use as apartments, but Ciro's is long gone.

A downtown favorite for many years was the Abruzzi Pizza House at the corner of Pike and Sixth. It opened around 1956 under Carmen Finamore and had wraparound windows so people strolling down the sidewalks could watch pizza dough being tossed. In addition to pizza, Abruzzi's menu listed half a dozen types of spaghetti; lasagna with meat or Italian sausage; and several kinds of ravioli. By 1996, this old-style pizzeria found itself surrounded by the high-rise glass and steel towers of a redeveloping Seattle; inevitably, progress in the form of Niketown gobbled up the building that contained it.

Eastlake Avenue was still lightly populated when the Casa Villa opened its doors in 1936. Located at 1823 Eastlake, the restaurant—an Italian-design villa of white stucco and tile roof—was the creation of Alice and Robert Smith and Herman Stoll. A sign above the entryway bore the Casa Villa's slogan: "A touch of old Italy." It became well known for its seven-course dinners for only $1.00 (by 1951, the price had risen to $1.95), and of course, Italian cooking was emphasized.

In 1959, the Casa Villa was completely remodeled under new owners George DiJulio and Robert Hyde and two years later was chosen to be part of an International Cooking School hosted by Frederick & Nelson, the downtown department store. William Boileau, the Casa Villa's chef, prepared chicken cacciatore for the event and must have done well—the restaurant's reputation for quality dining rose significantly. A 1966 restaurant review commented favorably on the lunch offerings, in particular the Gulfport salad bowl (fresh greens, crab, shrimp, tuna, sardines, hard-cooked eggs and tomato wedges), broiled teriyaki steak, ravioli and scallops. The dinner menu listed broiled lobster tail, tournedos of beef Casa Villa, veal scallopini

Casa Villa was a familiar sight along Eastlake Avenue for over forty years. It later became a Mexican restaurant and has been slated for redevelopment. *Author's collection.*

Marsala, veal parmigiana, chicken cacciatore and a large variety of pasta dishes. Somewhat incongruously, evening music entertainment was provided by 250-pound, electric ukulele–playing "Little Bob" Hrvatin. After Casa Villa closed in 1973, a Mexican restaurant, Casa Lupita, moved in. More recently home to Don Eduardo's Mexican Restaurant, today it is a vacant lot.

Out north on the highway to Bothell, the Italian Spaghetti House and Pizzeria, at 9824 Lake City Way, was doing business by 1954 with family-style pizza and spaghetti and pizzas tossed in view of customers. Long a favorite of north-enders, it closed in 2011. At the other corner of the city was Galletti's Italian Restaurant, at 2311 California SW in West Seattle. In the '70s, it claimed to be "West Seattle's only restaurant serving original Italian dishes" with family dining and moderate prices.

MEXICAN

Restaurante Mexicano

Though it wasn't until the '60s that authentic Mexican restaurants took root in Seattle, the late 1920s saw the city, like the rest of America, develop an appetite for south-of-the-border-style foods—chili, enchiladas and particularly tamales. Street vendors sold them, and tamale shops opened. Blues great Robert Johnson sang about them in "Hot Tamales (And They're Red Hot)"; not one but two musical groups (the Alika Hawaiian Trio and the Goofus Five) recorded a song titled "Hot Tamale Molly." In Seattle, street peddlers like Marcus Joffary, Frank Ray and Charlie Lunan sold tamales from carts. John Kahn had a tamale restaurant at 604 Union in 1924; the Eagle Tamale Parlor was at 726 Pike. Two places called the Golden Tub Tamale Shop opened on the northern edges of the city. Being Italian didn't deter Joe Milani from building a prosperous tamale factory at 2934 Western Avenue.

The earliest shop seems to have been the B&M Tamale Grotto, originally on James Street in 1905 and relocated to Fifth Avenue by 1914. It was only open at dinnertime (special Mexican chicken dinners cost fifty cents). Another early place was Austin's Chili and Tamale Shop, in business by 1915 and owned by Jesse Henderson. For reasons not clear today, Henderson was known as "Dad Austin"—thus the name of his shop.

Austin's had a habit of moving frequently: opened at 313 Pine, it moved to 1907 Fifth Avenue in 1919; then to 1631 Westlake (1920); 517 Pike (1923); and 611 Union in 1931, where it remained until Henderson retired in 1935. Austin's stayed open until 2:00 a.m.—perfect for night owls—with chicken and beef tamales, chili, enchiladas and sandwiches. After Austin's closed, the Chinese Village Cafe took its place at 611 Union.

In 1921, Cook's Tamale Grotto debuted at 721 Pine Street. (Despite shared usage of "grotto," there doesn't seem to have been a connection between Cook's and the earlier B&M.) Clarence and Genevieve Cook ran the place. A menu from 1943 lists what was available: tamales, of course—special chicken or Texas beef tamales (fifty cents and thirty-five cents, respectively; smothered in chili and cheese for an additional twenty cents), enchiladas and chili; also salads, relishes and sandwiches; turkey, chicken (either hot or cold), ham, chili, egg, salami, grilled cheese and a lettuce sandwich with thousand island dressing. In an early example of fusion cuisine, Cook's menu also offered Chinese noodles and spaghetti (Milanese with choice of sliced chicken or fried chicken livers).

When Cook's Spanish Inn opened on Highway 99 south of Seattle in 1948, it turned management of the Tamale Grotto over to Mrs. Emory Holman. Shortly afterward, Cook's relocated to 611 Union Street, which thirty years earlier had been home to Austin's.

Newspaperman John J. Reddin recalled Cook's as being the place where he was introduced to enchiladas. It was still in business in 1956 but had closed by the time Clarence and Genevieve passed away in 1960.

Bob's Chile was in a similar vein as Cook's: chile (Bob always spelled it with an "e"); chicken and Spanish tamales; cheese, chicken and beef enchiladas; and various sandwiches (ham, liverwurst, cheese, salami and chicken, among others). Bob's menu also listed salads, relish trays and spaghetti. Located at 608 Union Street—right across the street from Cook's—Bob's opened in 1932 and survived well into the 1970s. One of the owners, unfortunately, did not: co-owner Robert Kevo was fatally shot while arguing with a customer over a bill in 1968.

One of the first authentic Mexican restaurants was Juan's Mexican Cafe in the Fremont district. By 1945, Juan's was serving up tamales, chili, enchiladas and Mexican dinners. Downtown, Los Amigos and La Fiesta opened their doors in the late '50s. La Fiesta was at 715 Pike, a spot that had held a restaurant on and off since the 1910s. Owned by Chester Espinoza, it was a typical interior arrangement of a counter and stools on the right side, booths on the left. What made La Fiesta different was its sauces—many of them using authentic ingredients such as ground California and pasilla chilis rather than the tomato-based sauces so common. Los Amigos, a couple of blocks away at 906 Pine, took pride in hot Mexican dishes individually prepared. It was gone by 1965. A small local chain of the same name appeared in the suburbs in the 1970s with no relationship to the downtown restaurant.

Another local chain, Guadalajara, had its start when Pablo and Lucy Lopez opened downtown in 1967. By 1974, they were up to four locations: at 1429 Fourth under Pay'n Save; another in Wallingford on Forty-Fifth; and two others elsewhere in the city. A main attraction of Guadalajara was the *chalupa*, a bowl-shaped tortilla shell topped with lettuce, guacamole, sour cream and meat (ground beef or chicken) that Lucy Lopez claimed she invented while working at Bob's Chile Parlor. It later became a staple at local Mexican restaurants.

Pablo's Especial, on Roy Street near the base of Queen Anne Hill, was considered Seattle's best Mexican restaurant in the 1980s. Owner Pablo Knecht specialized in Jaliscan fare rather than the usual Sonoran—no tacos, but 144 different offerings, all original, on the menu, including *sopa de camarones*, *gambas costa brava* (baked acorn squash stuffed with garlicky prawns and a white wine–garlic sauce) and *zarzuela de mariscos* (chorizo, shrimp, scallops, fish fillets, clams). In later days, extensively and hideously altered, the building became known as the Blob.

Greek

Ελληνικό εστιατόριο

Greek restaurant owners have been part of the Seattle scene since the 1910s. The Parthenon was located near the Arctic Club; other early Greek restaurants were a block apart on Third Avenue. Three longtime survivors were the Acropolis, at 315 Yesler Way; the Apollo (403 Second Avenue); and the Sapho, 114 Prefontaine Place, owned by Louis Fakas and Ed Martin (real name: Malevitsis).

The Sapho, located on the ground-floor premises of a triangle-shaped building that fronted on both Fourth Avenue and Prefontaine Way under the Yesler Way viaduct, was a favorite of policemen, bail bondsmen and politicians. When it closed in 1963, the *Seattle Times* wrote its obituary:

The Sapho was one of the last of the old-time Greek restaurants with refrigerated front windows for displaying steaks and melons and other meats and fruit. It also was one of the few "full menu" eating houses where customers had a choice of seven or eight entrees—even late at night

Unlike most of today's short-order restaurants where steaks, chops, hamburgers—even hot beef sandwiches—are cooked to order, the Sapho menu also included a wide variety of ready-to-serve entrees such as boiled finnan haddie or steamed barbecued cod with new potatoes, boiled salmon, braised lamb, boiled ox tongue, baked halibut, roast leg of lamb and dressing, etc.

The old-fashioned, full-menu restaurants are fast disappearing from the Seattle scene. Rising food and labor costs and sparse patronage, especially late at night, have taken a toll. So has the fact that no one wants to put in 14- or 16-hour days, as did the ambitious and hard-working Greek immigrants.

Greek-owned though they were, none of these places served authentic Greek food. That was left up to the Greek Village and TOPS 24, both of which appeared in the mid-1960s. The Greek Village apparently came first, though the date isn't certain. John Nicos of the Greek-American Historical Museum of Washington State described its history:

In 1966 Petro opened the Greek Village in downtown Seattle with Bill Apostolou. Greek culture was coming into vogue with the movie Never on

Sunday *and it was an opportune time to provide Greek cuisine and culture for restaurant patrons.*

Initially they served only lunches when the Village became a major attraction for both Greek and non-Greek customers. Colleen became the financial controller, carefully keeping the books for the Village. Her mother was the chef, giving the food an authenticity not found elsewhere in Seattle. Petro had done some travelling and was able to engage several musicians, including John Tziotis, Nick Halkias, Tony Proios and Eleftheri Retsinas. The music and belly dancing added flavor. Petro and Colleen partnered with Jim Anas for a while but it was primarily the couple that made the Greek Village what they wanted, not only a representation of Greek food, but of the entire culture of Greece.

Petro and Colleen worked at making the Village "first class all the way," even introducing separate menus for men (blue, with pricing) and women (gold, without pricing). After 13 years of operating a fast-moving and successful business, the couple decided it was time to sell the Village in 1979.

Restaurant critic Everett Boss was favorably impressed by the Greek Village on a 1966 visit. On the lunch menu were *avgolemono* (egg-lemon soup); a house salad of romaine lettuce, tomatoes, green onions, feta cheese, Greek olives and Greek sardines; and a list of entrées that included *Stifado en casserole* (a Greek stew of seasoned beef and onions), *pastitsio* (layers of macaroni, ground meat and Greek cheese sauce) and *dolmas* (stuffed grape leaves) in an egg-lemon sauce.

Dinner entrées included *gouvarlakia* (Greek meatballs), *moussaka* (baked eggplant and ground meat), lamb or beef en brochette, shish kebab and a seasoned roast lamb dish called *arnipsito*. Seafood such as broiled trout, salmon, smelts (*marithes*) and *kalamarakia* (squid with white wine) was offered. The non-adventurous could choose from charcoal-broiled steaks and pork or lamb chops. Baklava, a classic Greek delicacy, was for dessert along with several different types of pastries.

TOPS 24 opened in 1963, when business partners George Serpanos, Demo Apostolou and Aleko Gotsis purchased the Madison Cafe on Ninth and Madison. According to John Nicos:

They gave it the name of TOPS 24, because it was to be the "top of the line" and it would be open 24 hours a day. The problem was that none of the three knew how to cook. They flipped coins and George was the winner.

The Greek Village, at 700 Fourth Avenue, had a parking lot on its roof. The Columbia Tower now stands where it once was. *Seattle Public Library, spl_wl_res_00032.*

Demo and Aleko went on to open their own businesses and George hired cooks and wait staff. In addition to the food and drink, live Greek music made TOPS a popular destination for several musicians and appreciative audiences. TOPS was under George's ownership from 1964 to 1978 when George turned the business over to his brother-in-law, George Valaoras. It then became the First Hill Bar and Grill and closed in 2013.

A more recent departure is Costa's Opa in Fremont, owned by Costa Antonopoulos and closed in 2012 after thirty-two years. Loyal customers recall cramming into the small waiting area for their tables to be ready and gazing through conveniently placed windows at the trays of moussaka, spanakopita and Greek potatoes waiting to be served. When it went dark, the SeattleMet website ranked it as the saddest restaurant closing of the year. Not all is lost. Another Costa's, owned by Antonopoulos's brother in the University District, is still going strong.

Russian

Русский Ресторан

More than three decades after it disappeared, the Russian Samovar is still remembered as Seattle's quintessential Russian restaurant. It wasn't the first—the Moscow Restaurant on Lakeview Boulevard preceded it by a few years. By 1928, the Moscow was well known for its Old Russia atmosphere and was a favorite for lunch, dinner and after-theater parties. On the menu were traditional Russian dishes such as *blinchiki* pancakes and *cutleti Kievska*; Russian dark bread always fresh from the oven was served with every meal. Owned by Mr. and Mrs. Nicholas Gorn, the restaurant, described as "a small establishment that resembled a candy house from a Russian fairy tale" with an interior wall mural depicting Russia in winter, was a favorite of University of Washington students. Unfortunately, the Moscow Restaurant stood in the way of freeway construction and was demolished in 1958.

In 1926, Kolia Levienne, on the faculty of nearby Cornish School of Music, created Petrushka as a gathering place for artists, poets and kindred spirits. (The name was taken from the puppet hero of Russian "Punch and Judy" shows.) Located at 729 Harvard Avenue N, at first it seems to have only been a tearoom with light lunches, but it soon evolved into a full-service restaurant with Russian meals, luncheons and suppers prepared by Mrs. Larissa Voitiakhoff.

A few years later, Peter and Larissa Voitiakhoff opened the Russian Samovar in a newly constructed building known as the Loveless Studios at 806 E Roy. It was an overnight success, partly due to the gossip/shopping columnist known as Jean who urged her readers to try the Russian Samovar for "delicious and different foods, served in an Old World atmosphere." On weekends, a crowd of as many as twenty-five often waited patiently for a table.

Among the Russian Samovar's attractions were the hand-painted wall murals depicting the Russian folktale of three children who were lost in the woods but were guided to safety by animals. Other scenes showed the aristocracy of the Russian court in the seventeenth century. Leaded glass windows, dark woodwork and an entry door (some called it a portal) added to the feeling of being transported back to an earlier time. Of course a samovar—a large tea urn—was part of the décor.

Looking like a gingerbread house from a fairy tale, the Moscow Restaurant was on Lakeview Boulevard in the Eastlake district. *Seattle Public Library, spl_wl_res_00128.*

The restaurant closed during World War II, though its tearoom remained open as the Supper Bowl. In the early 1950s, June Simpson bought the place and adopted the name Simpson's Russian Samovar. Ownership changed again in 1978 with Martin and Margaret Farrar, and Simpson's name was dropped.

A 1976 restaurant review by columnist Larry Brown described dinner at the Russian Samovar. On the menu (with explanatory notes for the uninitiated) were:

> chicken Kiev (boneless breast of chicken wrapped around seasoned butter, then dipped in a light batter and fried)
> veal Cordon Bleu (thin strips of veal wrapped around Canadian bacon and Gruyere cheese)
> beef stroganoff (thin strips of beef in a mushroom sour cream sauce)
> Golubsti (chopped beef, onions and seasonings wrapped in cabbage leaves)
> Tefteli (Russian meatballs in tomato–sour cream)

Bastrooma (marinated and skewered beef with onion-tomato sauce)
Okoon v smetna (halibut in sour cream sauce)
Pelmini ("Russian raviolis"—packets of pastry stuffed with dilled beef
 in sour cream sauce)
grilled lamb chops
sirloin steak with sauteed mushrooms
broiled rainbow trout

All entrées came with a relish tray of fresh vegetables (carrots, celery, olives, pickles, tomatoes), borscht, a *piroshki* (meat-filled pastry), green salad, a vegetable dish such as broccoli soufflé, rice, biscuits and rye bread and dessert (pecan pie, blueberry tarts topped with vanilla ice cream). Prices ranged from $4.50 to $6.75. A mini-buffet lunch—salad, cold meats, cheeses, two hot dishes (stuffed green peppers, fried chicken)—was available Tuesday through Friday for $2.00.

When the Farrars lost their lease in 1982 and closed the Russian Samovar, over five hundred people signed a petition of protest about the closure, urging the landlord to reinstate the restaurant. It didn't happen. The Russian Samovar found a new location in Pioneer Square, but the move wasn't successful. A Greek restaurant called Baklava moved in at 806 Roy, and since then, it has seen a string of other restaurants, including Coco La Ti Da, a short-lived dessert lounge; a Spanish restaurant, Olivar; and most recently, Restaurant Marron.

The Troyka was located at 2109 N Forty-Fifth Street in the Wallingford neighborhood. Owner Faina Tulintseff was well known for her piroshkis; it's said she made sensational *golubsti*. Other specialties included *pelmeni* and *plombir* (Russian ice cream). In business in 1961, it was gone by the late '70s.

By 1982, the only remaining Russian restaurant in Seattle was Kaleenka, a small storefront café that opened in 1978 at 1933 First Avenue. The menu contained the usual items: chicken Kiev, beef stroganoff, pelmeni and golubsti. The food was always good, and patrons could sit in the two bay windows by the door and watch traffic going by on the busy street. What made Kaleenka special were the piroshkis. Owner Lydia Venichenko Barrett found they were so popular that she created a traveling booth to sell them at local fairs and festivals. The restaurant closed in 2000, but Kaleenka's piroshkis live on—the booth is still a prominent fixture at the Washington State Fair. Seattle, however, is currently bereft of Russian restaurants.

The Persian Dining Room belongs in a category of its own. Despite its exotic name, the Persian Dining Room served conventional American food.

What made it different was that it was created as a training ground for food service workers. Started in 1933 by Effie Raitt and Margaret Terrell, both of them involved with the home economics department of the University of Washington, future cooks, waitresses, hostesses and managers received practical experience working in a full-scale, three-meals-a-day restaurant environment. Breakfast at the Persian Room was popular among downtown workers; sixty-five cents bought a club breakfast (chilled fruit juice, one egg, two strips of bacon, toast and coffee); Persian pancakes with syrup, juice and coffee was another twenty cents. Pecan and butterscotch pies were dessert favorites. The only nod to Persia was the décor and the names of a few of the items on the menu. The Persian Dining Room was in the Northern Life Tower at 1218 Third Avenue and was in business until 1957.

CAJUN/CREOLE

Laissez Les Bons Temps Rouler

It's a long way from the warm waters of Louisiana's bayous to chilly Puget Sound, but over the years, a few restaurants have managed to bridge the gap. First to open was FranGlor's, at Fifth and Jackson in the International District. Owned by Frances Emery and Gloria Lacey, it was described as "a hole-in-the-wall place with killer red beans, gumbos, jambalaya, cornbread, and the most incredible selection of blues and soul on the jukebox." FranGlor's later moved to 547 First Avenue S; it disappeared in 1990.

Crawfish Alley was in the basement of the Colman Building at 808 Post Avenue, a spot long occupied by the Colman Lunch. Its cuisine is best described as upscale Creole with entrées such as steak Robespierre (sirloin with mushrooms in a brown sauce), chicken jambalaya, oysters Lafitte, stuffed trout Nouvelle Orleans, *poisson en papillote* (cod, vegetables and sauce cooked in parchment), scallops St.-Jacques, filet of sole amandine and poisson Florentine. Appetizers included crab-stuffed mushrooms, chilled Louisiana prawns and Dungeness crab cocktails with soup choices such as bayou oyster soup and gumbo. A special New Orleans dinner for two—soup, salad, steak Robespierre or duck a l'orange, cheesecake or pecan pie for dessert and a bottle of champagne—cost twenty-five dollars in 1976. The restaurant had three dining areas: the main dining room, the bar and the Gazebo Room, all decorated New Orleans style. It was gone by the late 1980s after about fifteen years in business.

Out in Ballard was Burk's Café, Creole/Cajun but leaning more toward the more rustic, earthier flavors of Cajun cooking. "Burk" was owner Terry Burkhardt, who presided over the kitchen of his nine-table eatery. In addition to a printed menu listing the customary jambalayas and gumbos was a blackboard with daily specials such as crawfish in Remoulade sauce, crawfish bisque, blackened red snapper, shrimp Creole and shrimp étouffée. Of course, pecan pie—almost obligatory for a Cajun restaurant—was also on the menu. Jars of pickled okra at each table were a nice touch. Unlike okra as it is normally found in cooked dishes (which most people consider slimy and have an uncontrollable urge to spit out), the pickled variety was crisp, spicy and salty—which probably helped increase Burk's drinks revenue. Burk's was located at 5411 Ballard Avenue and open from 1983 until 2005.

POLYNESIAN

Faleaiga Tahiti

Warm waters, balmy winds, palm trees swaying in the breeze—the romance of the South Pacific has had a hold on the mainland states practically since Hawai'i was discovered in the 1770s. A 1930s post-Depression, post-Prohibition country was ready for happy times; a South Seas vacation would do the trick, but overseas travel was beyond the reach of most people. So why not bring the South Seas home? How about stateside bars and restaurants with a Polynesian motif? By the time Hawaii became a state in 1959—and helped along by Hawaiian-based movies like *Blue Hawaii* starring Elvis—Polynesian, or tiki, culture was deeply ingrained in the American psyche.

Don the Beachcomber is credited with starting the tiki bar craze. Don (real name, Ernest Raymond Beaumont Gantt) opened a bar called Don's Beachcomber in Hollywood in 1933. A few years later, Don moved his bar a short distance, added a restaurant and changed its name to Don the Beachcomber. His tiki-themed restaurant was immediately popular, and by the 1950s, there were several Don the Beachcomber restaurants across the country.

Don's success didn't go unnoticed. Up in the Bay Area, in 1934, Victor Bergeron opened a bar called the Hinky Dink in Oakland. In 1937—the same year Don made his name change—Bergeron unabashedly copied Don's style; he assumed the moniker Trader Vic, and the Hinky Dink became Trader Vic's. Don and Vic were amicable rivals for many years, freely borrowing each other's ideas. Both claimed invention of the mai tai, the rum and fruit juice cocktail still popular today (*maitai* is said to be the Tahitian word for "good"), though the evidence seems to suggest that Vic came up with it first.

Trader Vic landed in Seattle first. In 1949, Western Hotels announced plans to open an Outrigger Room—designed by Trader Vic to resemble a South Seas beach—in the Benjamin Franklin Hotel. Five years later, the Outrigger doubled in size. Filled with Polynesian artifacts and wall décor, the new Outrigger offered escapism from the city—a tropical vacation self-contained within its walls. Behind its beach shanty façade could be found "delicacies prepared right before your eyes in the authentic Polynesian manner." There was the Captain's Room, fashioned to look like the main saloon of an old sailing vessel; the Barbecue Room, where, from a softly lighted vantage point, diners could observe "actual Chinese ovens behind a baffle of bamboo, grass and glass"; and the Garden Room with its lush foliage.

Trader Vic's menu was designed to appeal to both conventional American and exotic South Seas tastes. One page of the menu listed typical fare such as lamb chops, chicken Cordon Bleu and filet of beef along with a few slightly adventurous dishes like beef teriyaki and sesame chicken. The facing page was given over to what the menu called *paké* dinners—complete meals with more exotic items. The Kowloon, for instance, included beef tomato, almond duck, chicken Cantonese, *bah mee* noodles and coconut ice cream. The Macao dinner consisted of pineapple pork, oyster beef, Chinese snow peas, pork chow mein and rum custard ice cream. These days, all of those dishes are familiar to anyone who has ever ordered Chinese takeout, but in the 1960s, they probably seemed unusual and almost alien to taste buds accustomed to steak, potatoes and frozen vegetables.

The Outrigger officially became Trader Vic's in 1960. Twenty years later, when the Benjamin Franklin Hotel was razed to make way for the second tower of the Washington Plaza Hotel (now the Westin), Trader Vic's moved into the Plaza's original first tower. It was the only Trader Vic's in the entire chain that served breakfast. When it closed in 1991, having lost its space in the Westin, longtime manager Harry Wong hosted a closing party.

Phil Wong and Christina Gee have fond memories of their father, Harry Wong, and his time at Trader Vic's. They recall that he first got a job there

The interior of Trader Vic's created a South Seas atmosphere with rattan and bamboo furnishings. *MOHAI*, Seattle Post-Intelligencer *Collection, 2000.107.185.26.01.*

in 1953 as a cocktail waiter in the original Outrigger, working his way up to waiter, dining room captain, assistant manager and manager around 1968. To most of the clientele, Harry Wong *was* Trader Vic's, highly thought of as host and manager and in the same league as legendary Seattle restaurant owners Peter Canlis, Victor Rosellini and Walter Clark. That's pretty good company. Wong may not have owned Trader Vic's, but he acted like he did, in the best possible sense.

Says Christina,

> *I worked at Trader Vic's beginning in June 1969. I was a "coat room girl" hanging up coats, answering the telephone, recording dinner bill charges and sometimes acting as hostess, taking people to their tables. It was the year of the big service industry workers' strike, and I crossed the picket line to help my dad working with a skeleton staff and limited menu.*
>
> *My favorite time to work was June and senior prom season. I loved watching the kids dress up and come to dinner. We younger staff gave them an extra special reception because whether or not they became future customers depended on that one evening out.*

Dad said the busiest day of the year at Trader Vic's was Valentine's Day. Second, Mother's Day. Yes, New Year's Eve was also a huge event! Phil and I once had the luxury of eating dinner there on New Year's Eve, but we had to eat very, very early, probably when the place opened at 5:30 p.m., and had to leave before the prime dinner hour. Definitely we did not get the best table in the house!

Don the Beachcomber didn't arrive in Seattle until 1979 and only stayed for about a year. The fifteenth location in the chain, it was located at 2040 Westlake Avenue N with a fine view of Lake Union and an interior design described as "Grass Shack Moderne." Don's menu listed quasi–South Seas foods such as mahi mahi and Polynesian chicken along with roasts, grills and stir fries. Beachcomber *pupus* (loin ribs, sliced barbecued pork and *rumaki*) were popular, as was a house specialty called *Bahala Na* (duck Mandarin, Lobster Chungking and Chicken Manuu around a bed of fried rice). Like Trader Vic, Don the Beachcomber was famous for potent cocktails with names like the Vicious Virgin, Pi Yi and Missionary's Downfall.

By 1981, Don's had been replaced by a restaurant called Green Jeans. Both chains still exist, though not in Seattle. There are three remaining Don the Beachcombers and over a dozen Trader Vic's worldwide, only a few of which are in the United States.

Seattle could boast of a couple home-grown Polynesian-themed restaurants. The most elegant, logically enough named the Polynesia, was located at the end of Pier 51, a dramatic setting adjacent to the ferry dock with sweeping views of the waterfront, the sound and the mountains. It opened in 1961.

Described as "an authentic segment of Tahiti transported to Seattle's waterfront...authentic not only in décor but in food preparation and service," the restaurant's triple A-frame design—three high-peaked gabled sections rising from a common roof—was inspired by the Polynesian *halau*, or long house. Architect Raymond Peck chose both the form and materials to create a South Seas atmosphere. He designed not only the building but also the menus and costumes for servers, keeping to a basic color scheme of tangerine, gold, black and seal brown throughout.

Interior walls were polished teakwood and grass cloth, deeply carved beams and upholstered benches, rattan chairs and carved figures; lava rock from Hawaii, art carvings and seashells were liberally sprinkled about. Markings on the posts and beams replicated the patterns of authentic ceremonial shields. A spiral fireplace in the main dining room rose from a reflecting pool on the floor to a black metal hood in the ceiling. Three Tahitian luau torches marked the entrance with exposed gas flames.

The Polynesia accommodated 320 diners and was open for lunch and dinner, with distinctly different menus for each. Lunch selections included crab Rangoon, barbecued spareribs, "exotic Polynesian appetizers" and several types of salad: a fruit salad served in a pineapple basket, an avocado supreme salad and chef's and chicken salads. Several omelets were offered: crab, mushroom, shrimp and oyster. Entrées were a choice of Rex sole, poached salmon with egg sauce, oysters mariniere poached in Chablis and herbs, mahi mahi with lemon butter and macadamia nut sauce and chicken à la Polynesia.

The dinner listed a long choice of entrées such as *Sai Foon* (Oriental vermicelli in chicken broth with julienned ham) and Trade Winds Salad (crab lags, prawns, mixed greens and tomatoes with a tart mustard dressing). Specialties included Mandarin duck, beef mushrooms, shrimp Tahitian, Imperial beef, various curries and a special all-seafood dish called the Blue Lagoon (filet of sole, crab legs, mussels, shrimp and scallops poached in a wine and hollandaise sauce). The risk-averse could always choose a steak. Desserts included coconut snowball, fresh pineapple with Cointreau and crepes Hawaiian.

Stephanie Graham recalls a visit in 1967:

> *The occasion was my boyfriend's senior prom. Once inside, I was intimidated by the lush and colorful surroundings. Once seated, I noticed I was by far the youngest person in the restaurant. Most were middle age and older-generation adults dressed quite lavishly. It made me think I was in the company of rich people. Many gawked at the "youngsters" being seated in their formal prom attire.*
>
> *The things I remember most about the inside: a colorful Polynesian atmosphere where the rustic beams were adorned with colorful carvings, tiki torches, palm trees, orchids, cockatoos and grass plants. The water side of the restaurant had cozy tables for four and a view of the sun setting over Elliott Bay. All the tables gleamed of white starched tablecloths, silver flatware and elegant stemware. In the center of each table was a candle in the shape of a coconut, which gave the entire restaurant a shimmer like nothing I had ever seen before.*
>
> *The menus had similar coconuts and tiki-torch drawings. Dinner for both of us was about twelve dollars, including tip, which at that time seemed like a huge amount of money to spend on a single dinner. As we*

left, I remember one gentleman spoke as we walked by him, asking where we were off to. My date responded with our plans, and the gentleman said he remembered when he was young and he hoped we had a nice dinner and would have a fun evening.

In 1975, restaurant reviewer John Hinterberger paid a visit and was impressed by the several entrées he sampled. He also recorded an interesting quote from the manager, Bob Teichman, who, while acknowledging that the food was not authentically Polynesian, said, "In the first place there's nobody around here who would know how to cook it, and not that many Americans would be interested in eating it."

When the state condemned Pier 51 in order to expand the ferry terminal, the Polynesia issued two-for-one coupons in appreciation of its loyal clientele. The restaurant closed in May 1975, but owner Dave Cohn had the building lifted onto a barge in hopes of finding a new home. It didn't work out, and eventually, the structure was burned by the fire department for practice.

Beef with Chinese Greens and Mushrooms
As prepared by the Polynesia Restaurant

1 ½ pounds thin sliced beef
Peanut oil
Salt
Pepper
1 clove garlic, chopped
2 pounds Chinese greens (bok choy)
½ pound fresh mushrooms
½ cup chicken broth
Soy sauce
Steamed rice for four

Fry beef in oil; season with salt, pepper and chopped garlic. Add greens, mushrooms and chicken stock. Simmer until vegetables are almost cooked. Add soy sauce and finish cooking. Serve with steamed rice. Serves four.

Back uptown was the Kalua Room in the Windsor Hotel, the creation of designer Ed Lawrence, who toured the South Seas for three months in search of appropriate tropical artifacts. It took three months to build at a cost of $100,000 (a lot of money in 1953), seated 150 and promised a "true tropical setting, unusual and exotic tropical foods and beverages." Patrons enjoyed authentic Hawaiian and Polynesian recipes such as flaming prawns Samoa served en casserole with mango chutney in the Kalua's three dining areas: the Bird Room, the Slide Room and the Orchid Waterfall, where bunched bananas hung from the thatched canopies over individual tables. The Polynesian dream lasted until 1969, when it became the Has-Been.

The Kau Kau Restaurant, at 1115½ Second Avenue, took up the Polynesian theme in 1959 with tropical cocktails and authentic Cantonese dinners until 2:00 a.m. Owner Wai C. Eng thoroughly remodeled the place in 1965 with new seating arrangements, wall paneling and booth lighting in the main dining room. Thirteen years later, Eng started up a branch location in Chinatown called the Kau Kau Barbecue Market; it was principally a lunch place and, contrary to the name, had not much barbecue on the menu—mostly mein and sweet-and-sour dishes. The downtown Kau Kau disappeared; the barbecue evolved into the still-existing Kau Kau Restaurant on King Street.

Behind the plain exterior of the Kalua Room was a tiki paradise of orchids and a real waterfall. *Seattle Municipal Archives, 26696.*

Also downtown was the Trade Winds, 2501 First Avenue. It opened around 1964 and persisted into the '70s with a complete menu of steaks and seafood, as well as Polynesian specialties, served in an informal South Seas atmosphere. North on Aurora Avenue, the Lapu Lapu opened in what had been Ida & Gene's Restaurant. Its specialty was Philippine cuisine "reminiscent of the romantic South Pacific Isles...Delicious Chicken Adobo for a taste thrill. Real Mango ice cream will be an enjoyable finish to your 'adventure' in dining Philippine style." Chef Luiggi's Restaurant had moved in by 1976; three years later, it was the Bamboo Tree Restaurant. On Broadway, the Luau Barbecue took over the former location of Carl Broome's hamburger shop and later Bon's Cafe. Operated by Albert Bon, it lasted for about four years before becoming DeCaro's Barbecue in 1964.

KOSHER

וַאראָטסער רעשאָק

Harry's Bohemian Restaurant claimed to be Seattle's original Kosher restaurant. Harry Ilwitz was owner and chef; his place was the type of delicatessen "where the ham and beef is sliced with a lavish hand"—common back east but rare on the West Coast. (Harry's motto was "If you think one sandwich can't make a meal, you haven't eaten at Harry's Bohemian.") The restaurant was at 1422 Sixth Avenue and was open by 1930. After Harry left the business in the late 1940s, Mary and Max Rosenberg leased the Bohemian with plans to reopen, but it apparently never happened.

A place with a similar name—the Bohemian Cafe—opened at Seventh and Bell in 1946. It, too, had a motto: "It's fun to be hungry at the Bohemian Cafe." On the menu: chopped chicken liver, pickled herring, matzo ball soup and specialties such as sauerbraten (spiced pot roast of beef), potato pancakes and Viennese cream chicken on short bread along with the usual steaks, chops and seafood. A full breakfast service was offered. The interior was comfortable green leather and walnut booths with murals depicting the Bohemian way of life. On the outside of the building was the Bohemian's big violin trademark. At some point in time, Ralph Grossman, one of the operators of the Igloo on Denny Way, was involved in the Bohemian Cafe. The building later became home to Bob Murray's Dog House.

Contrary to Harry's claim of being first, Ben Yeager operated a Kosher restaurant at Fourth Avenue and Cherry Street in 1910, and a few years later the National Kosher Restaurant made its appearance at 217 James Street. In the mid-1950s, Clara's Kosher Restaurant, 1426 E Madison Street, served lunches (corned beef and pastrami sandwiches), appetizers (gefilte fish, chopped liver, pickled or chopped herring and chicken soup with matzo balls) and dinners of roast beef, chicken and steak. Clara also had a delicatessen and a catering service.

VEGETARIAN

You Are What You Eat

While steaks and chops dominated the menus of most early Seattle restaurants, there were a few healthy-eating alternatives. As early as 1901, the Good Health Restaurant, a branch of the Battle Creek Sanitarium, was advertising "nuts, grains, fruits, vegetables served in an appetizing manner." It was located at 616 Third Avenue and lasted until about 1908. A contemporary was the Vegetarian Cafe, 214 Union Street. Owned by M.T. Madsen, it promised delicious meals made from healthful and wholesome foods. It was a long time before the next exclusively vegetarian restaurant opened in Seattle, a place with the ungainly name of Mother Morgan's Gumbo Factory and Live-In Restaurant Honey, on Capitol Hill. Its limited menu featured quiche, pasta, broccoli pie, dirty rice and chili; grilled cheese sandwiches plain or with mushrooms, onions, avocado or tomato; peanut butter, banana and raisin sandwiches; and smoothies. It was one of the first restaurants in Seattle to ban smoking. Owners Stephany and Ken Malecki later opened a branch in Kent; by 1980, both Mothers had closed.

7

Recent Departures and a Few Survivors

Restaurants continue to come and go at an alarming pace in Seattle. Recent closures include Cucina Cucina, a chain of Italian-themed restaurants founded in 1988 by Bill and John Schwartz. Their first location was at the south end of Lake Union. Eventually, there were six Cucina Cucinas in Seattle and two more elsewhere. The entire chain was purchased by Wolfgang Puck in 2002 and resold to a Canadian investment group. Some of the restaurants survive today under different names.

Victoria Station, a nationwide chain created in the 1970s, had over one hundred locations at its peak. Its Seattle outlet was at 1880 Fairview E, not far from Cucina Cucina. Like Andy's Diner in South Seattle, Victoria Station was constructed from repurposed railway cars. The firm ran into financial problems in the late 1980s and began shuttering its restaurants; only one remains in operation today.

The late, lamented Poor Italian Café, at 2002 Second Avenue, opened circa 1982 and closed in 2002. It was transformed into the Buenos Aires Grill, which survives in a different location on First Avenue. The building at 2002 Second is now home to Shaker + Spear, a seafood eatery featuring local ingredients.

Out on Lake City Way, the Italian Spaghetti House opened around 1954 just as pizza was becoming popular in Seattle. It was owned and operated by Vince Giuffre. The pizza makers threw the dough authentically, much to the delight of customers. It closed in 2012, and the building is now occupied by a liquor store.

In Pioneer Square, the J&M closed in 2009, and its contents were auctioned off. In business since pioneer days, it claimed to be Seattle's oldest bar. It somehow survived in modified form for a few more years, but recently the building was sold and may be turned into a hotel and offices.

Bruno's Mexican and Italian restaurant was downtown at 1417 Third Avenue. It boasted "the best place downtown for lunch or dinner, serving good Mexican food and fresh pizza daily at reasonable prices." Bruno's closed in 2014 after forty years when owner Bruno Mazzarella retired.

Louie's Cuisine of China, on Fifteenth Avenue NW a quarter mile north of the Ballard Bridge, was another of the many Chinese restaurants owned by the Louie family. It closed in 2014 after thirty-seven years in business. Mama's Mexican Kitchen, a Belltown favorite since 1974, was a victim of urban renewal and closed in 2016, though plans to reopen—modified and more upscale, as Mama's Cantina—are being floated. Whether the new place will retain the statue of Elvis at the front door hasn't been announced.

The Shanty, a fixture on Elliott Avenue, was shuttered in December 2016 after over one hundred years of business. It was originally known as Violet's Shanty Hamburger Tavern under owner Violet Haubrock and was famous for breakfast, especially chicken fried steak. It is sorely missed.

A FEW SURVIVORS

Not all is lost as far as vintage restaurants go in Seattle. A couple of true oldies still thrive in the Pioneer Square district. The Merchant's Café, on Yesler across from the pergola, lays claim to being Seattle's oldest restaurant. Opened as the Merchant's Exchange and Saloon in 1892, it occupies an 1890 brick building that took the place of a wooden structure destroyed in the great fire. The Central, on First Avenue, dates from the same period. It was originally the Watson Brothers Restaurant (1892) and sank into skid road mediocrity until new owners rescued it and renamed it the Central in 1970.

Beth's Cafe, 7311 Aurora, is legendary for its twelve-egg omelets. Beth's was opened in 1954 by Harold and Beth Eisenstadt. Mike's Chili Parlor, just off Fifteenth Avenue NW in Ballard, has been around since 1922. Chili dominates the menu: chili burgers, chili dogs and just plain chili—available in various sizes from a cup to the Big Ass Bowl (thirty-two ounces). Their fries are pretty good, too.

The 5 Points Café celebrated eighty-five years in business in 2014. It is the longest-run family-owned eatery in Seattle and is open twenty-four hours a day, seven days a week—one of a handful of Seattle restaurants (not including franchises) to still be round-the-clock operations. Two classic cafés—the Luna Park and the Chelan—are along (or just off) Spokane Street on the way to West Seattle. The Luna Park, named after the amusement park that used to be at Duwamish Head, is a relative newcomer—it opened in place of an old tavern in 1989, though from its authentic 1950s diner atmosphere one would think it much older. The Chelan Café is going on eighty years old, evolving over that time from a five-stool lunch counter to a one-hundred-seat restaurant.

Canlis maintains its sixty-five-plus-year reputation as one of—if not the—most iconic, exclusive and expensive places to dine in Seattle. Peter Canlis ushered in a new dimension of restaurant refinement in 1950 with outstanding service, excellent cuisine and an outstanding view. Canlis's charcoal broiler—one of the first in the city—was placed in the dining room where it could easily be seen. The restaurant is now run by grandsons Mark and Brian. Dressing up for dinner is expected.

Vito's continues to be a popular, well-reviewed Italian restaurant located at 927 Ninth Avenue, just east of the central business district. It is said that Vito Santaro, a one-time speakeasy operator, hocked his Cadillac to open a hole-in-the-wall restaurant in 1953; it quickly became a success due to a good location and popularity with "the sports crowd" and priests from nearby Seattle University. His brother Jimmy had been a bartender at Rosellini's 610. Vito's specialized in Tuscany cooking. In 2010, after falling into neglect, Vito's was purchased, refurbished and reopened.

In the International District, Maneki celebrated its one-hundred-year anniversary in 2007, by far the oldest Japanese restaurant in the city. Bush Garden, 614 Maynard Avenue, is well known for its elaborate Oriental garden–style entrance, though its future as a restaurant seems to be in some doubt. A few blocks away on King Street, the venerable Tai Tung seems little changed since it opened in 1935, though the menu has been updated, as Seattleites have become used to spicier Chinese foods than Cantonese, the old standby. Tai Tung's menu once warned customers that the house was not responsible for food spilled onto their clothing by the waiters.

A couple 1950s chains flourish in the Greater Seattle area. Burgermaster came along in 1952 with its first location on NE Forty-Fifth Street near University Village. Under Phil Jensen, the family-owned business has grown to six locations and is the only place with genuine carhops.

Dick's was named for co-founder Dick Spady, who died in 2016. The original Dick's, on Forty-Fifth in Wallingford, opened in 1954 with nineteen-cent hamburgers topping the menu. In the 1990s, it wasn't unusual to see Bill Gates in line patiently waiting for a burger just like everyone else. Dick's now has seven locations, the latest opening in 2011 in Edmonds after 112,000 people voted on where the new location should be.

Spud Fish and Chips started out as a takeaway stand along Alki Avenue in 1935. Brothers Jack and Frank Alger upgraded to a sit-down restaurant a few years later and added locations at Green Lake and several other spots in the Greater Seattle area.

Speaking of fish and chips, it is fitting to close with Ivar Haglund, one of Seattle's most colorful personalities. Ivar opened an aquarium on the waterfront in 1938; noticing that the crowds willing to pay to see local sea life also seemed to be hungry, he soon added a seafood bar serving fish and chips and clam chowder. Well known for his corny jokes and humorous songs, Ivar was a born showman and a larger-than-life part of the city. For many years, he sponsored the Fourth of July fireworks show over Elliott Bay. When he owned the Smith Tower (for many years Seattle's tallest building), he flew a salmon flag atop the highest point; the city council, irked that he was flaunting some obscure regulation, demanded that it be taken down, which of course he did not do, and the publicity surrounding the resulting "battle" only increased Ivar's name recognition. The council finally gave

Ivar's Fish Bar and Acres of Clams, as they looked in the early 1950s. *Author's collection.*

in; the salmon flag stayed, and Ivar added to it another pennant bearing his slogan: "Keep Clam."

In 1946, Ivar's Acres of Clams, a full-service restaurant, opened along the waterfront next to the old fish and chips stand. They are both still there today. Ivar's on Broadway came and went in the 1960s. In 1956, Don's Seafood on Fifth Avenue became Ivar's Captain's Table, which it remained until relocating to the edge of Elliott Bay in 1965. (It closed in 1991.) Ivar's Salmon House opened on the north shore of Lake Union in 1969. Later years saw Ivar's at Mukilteo Landing as well as two dozen Ivar's Seafood Bars scattered around Greater Seattle. Ivar Haglund passed away in 1985, but his legacy lives on—not only in his namesake restaurants but also for his persona as Seattle's unofficial goodwill ambassador.

Bibliography

Books and Directories

"Abstract of the Report on Japanese and Other Immigrant Races in the Pacific Coast and Rocky Mountain States." Washington, D.C.: Government Printing Office, 1911.

Bagley, Clarence B. *History of Seattle from the Earliest Settlement to the Present Time.* Chicago: S.J. Clarke Publishing Company, 1916.

Choir, M. *Choir's Pioneer Directory of the City of Seattle and King County, History, Business Directory, and Immigrant's Guide to and Throughout Washington Territory and Vicinity.* N.p.: Miners' Journal Book and Job Rooms, 1878.

De Broca, P. "On the Oyster Industries of the United States." United States Commission of Fish and Fisheries, Report of the Commissioner, 1873–1875; Washington, D.C.: Government Printing Office, 1876. Translated from DeBroca's original paper *"Étude sur l'Industrie huîtrière des États-Unis,"* 1865.

Denny, Emily Inez. *Blazing the Way, or True Stories, Songs and Sketches of Puget Sound and Other Pioneers.* Seattle, WA: Rainier Printing Company, 1909.

Elliott, Ralph Nelson. *Tea Room and Cafeteria Management.* Boston: Little, Brown & Company, 1927.

Grant, Frederic James. *History of Seattle, Washington, with Illustrations and Biographical Sketches of Some of Its Prominent Men and Pioneers.* New York: American Publishing and Engraving, 1891.

Herrick, Elisabeth Webb. *Native Northwest Novelties.* Seattle, WA: Carl W. Art, 1937.

Hines, Duncan. *Adventures in Good Eating*. Bowling Green, KY: Adventures in Good Eating, 1949.

Horrocks, Hattie Graham. "Restaurants of Seattle 1853–1960." Unpublished manuscript, 1960.

McIsaac, C.H. *C.H. McIsaac & Co.'s Seattle City and King County Directory 1885–86, Comprising an Alphabetically Arranged List of Business Firms, Farmers and Private Citizens—A Classified List of All Trades, Professions, and Pursuits—A Miscellaneous Directory, City and County Officers, Terms of Court, Public and Private Schools, Churches, Banks, Incorporated Institutions, Secret and Benevolent Societies, Etc., Etc.* Vol. 1. Portland, OR: C.H. McIsaac & Company, 1885.

Polk, R.L. *Polk's Seattle City Directory 1901. Comprising an Alphabetically Arranged List of Business Firms and Private Citizens, Miscellaneous Directory, City, County, State and Federal Officers, Public and Private Schools, Banks, Churches, Railroads, Secret and Benevolent Societies, Etc.* Seattle, WA: Seattle Directory Company, 1901.

———. *Polk's Seattle (Washington) City Directory.* Seattle, WA: R.L. Polk & Company, various years 1918–1966 (title varies slightly).

———. *Seattle City Directory 1888–89, Comprising an Alphabetically Arranged List of Business Firms, Farmers and Private Citizens—A Classified List of All Trades, Professions, and Pursuits—A Miscellaneous Directory, City and County Officers, Terms of Court, Public and Private Schools, Churches, Banks, Incorporated Institutions, Secret and Benevolent Societies, Etc.* Seattle, WA: Seattle Directory Company, 1888.

———. *Seattle City Directory for 1890. Comprising an Alphabetically Arranged List of Business Firms and Private Citizens—A Classified List of All Trades, Professions and Pursuits—A Miscellaneous Directory, City and County Officers, Public and Private Schools, Churches, Incorporated Institutions, Secret and Benevolent Societies Etc., Etc.* Seattle, WA: Seattle Directory Company, 1890.

(Sanborn) Seattle, Wash. Ter. 1888; New York: Sanborn Map & Publishing, 1888.

———. Insurance Maps of Seattle. New York: Sanborn Map Company, 1905 (revised 1949, 1950, 1951).

Seattle and Vicinity Telephone Directory; Pacific Bell, various years 1927–1963 (title varies slightly).

Speidel, William C., Jr. *You Can't Eat Mount Rainier!* Portland, OR: Binfords and Mort, Publishers, 1955.

———. *You Still Can't Eat Mount Rainier!* Vashon, WA: Nettle Creek Publishing, 1961.

Tibbetts, P.E. *Mr. Restaurant: A Biography of Restaurateur Walter F. Clark.* Seattle, WA: Murray Publishing, 1990.

United States Department of the Interior, National Park Service. National Register of Historic Places Registration Form, Columbia City Historic District, King County, WA; 2004.

Newspapers

Daily Intelligencer (Seattle, WA), 1871–81.
Puget Sound Dispatch, 1871–80.
Puget Sound Semi-Weekly, 1866.
Puget Sound Weekly, 1866–67.
Puget Sound Weekly Gazette, 1867.
Seattle Daily Post-Intelligencer, 1881–88.
Seattle Daily Times, 1885–2016 (title varies slightly).
Seattle Gazette, 1863–64.
Seattle Post-Intelligencer, 1889–2009 (title varies slightly).
Seattle Weekly Gazette, 1864–66.
Washington Gazette, 1863.

Websites

City of Seattle, www.seattle.gov.
Greeks in Washington, greeksinwashington.org.
historylink, www.historylink.org.
Pacific Coast Architecture Database, pcad.lib.washington.edu.
Wikipedia, www.wikipedia.org.

Index

G

Gabler, Arthur 94
Galletti's Italian Restaurant 239
Garden Spot 214
Gardner's Cafe & Lounge 181
Garski's Scarlet Tree 159
Garvey-Buchanan Tea Room 90
Gasperetti, Bill 235
Gasperetti, John 235
Gates Coffee Shop 170
Gatewood Grill 238
Gatewood Lunch 186
Gem Saloon 30
George Louie's 151
George Olsen's Seven Nations 126
George's Cafe 58
Georgetown Sandwich Shop 172
Gerald, Clarence 40
Gerald's Cafe 40
GG's Restaurant 142
Gilbert's Restaurant 85
Gil's Hamburgers 116, 185
Gim Ling 232
Gino's 185
Glendale Cafe 170
Glendale Card & Lunch Room 172
Godden, Jean 194
G.O. Guy Lunch Counters 76
Golden Anchors 132
Golden Gate Cafe 45, 103
Golden Gate Oyster House 62
Golden Goose Cafe 46
Golden Lion 85
Golden Pheasant Cafe 230
Golden Tub 214
Goldie's Airport Way Cafe 171
Goldie's Cafe 158
Good Health Restaurant 257

Gowman, Harry 81
Graham's Restaurant & Fountain 156
Greek Village 242
Green Cupboard Tea Room 96
Green Gate Tea Room 94
Green Hat Cafe, The 198
Green Lantern Cafe 160
Green Parrot Inn 192
Greenwood Cafe 137
Greenwood Mandarin Restaurant 137
Grose, William 26
Guadalajara 160, 241
Gunnar's Cafe 147
Guppy's Fish & Chips 162
Gus's Steak House 160
Gustino, Jack 235
Gust's Cafe 182
Gypsy Tea Room 96

H

Had's 212
Haglund, Ivar 62, 101, 124, 165
Hallberg, Peter 37
Hallberg's Bakery & Restaurant 37
Hamburger Round-Up 158
Hamilton, Fred 55
Hamilton, Seaver 55
Hang Chow Cafe 231
Hankow Cafe 230
Hansen's Cafe 143
Happy Hour Cafe 181
Harbin 137
Harbor Inn Cafe 176
Harbor Island Inn 174
Harmon, L.C. 23
Harold Frye's Charcoal Broiler 152

T

About the Author

When Chuck Flood retired from a thirty-plus-year career as an information technologies project manager, he had no trouble deciding how to spend his newly found free time. A longtime interest in historic highways, roadside Americana, ghost towns, pioneer trails and archaeology—set aside during his professional career—provided the answer. He delved into research and writing about places and things that are disappearing from the landscape. Vacations were planned around visiting abandoned sites; back roads over rough terrain were trekked to visit sites where only a few collapsed log cabins and rusty tin cans remained. Miles of legendary highways such as Route 66 and the Lincoln Highway were toured in search of reminders of the grand old days of travel, and urban streets were examined for hints of places that had come and gone.

The challenge, as he sees it, is to portray a place as if it were a person, to bring it to life as one would write a biography of an individual. A member of the Lincoln Highway Association, the Archaeological Conservancy, the Oregon-California Trails Association and the Montana Ghost Town Preservation Society (among others), he has authored several books in Arcadia Press's Images of America series—*Washington's Highway 99*, *Washington's Sunset Highway* and *Oregon's Highway 99*—along with numerous articles for magazines and periodicals, with several more in various stages of completion.